CHILDHOOD

CHILDHOOD

MAKSIM GORKY

Translated from the Russian,
with an Introduction and Notes, by Graham Hettlinger

IVAN R. DEE CHICAGO 2010

www.ivanrdee.com

Library of Congress Cataloging-in-Publication Data:
Gorky, Maksim, 1868–1936.
[Detstvo. English]
Childhood / Maksim Gorky ; translated from the Russian, with an introduction and notes, by Graham Hettlinger.
p. cm.
Includes bibliographical references.
ISBN 978-1-56663-840-1 (cloth : alk. paper)—ISBN 978-1-56663-906-4 (electronic)
1. Gorky, Maksim, 1868–1936—Childhood and youth. 2. Gorky, Maksim, 1868–1936—Family. 3. Authors, Russian—20th century—Biography. 4. Boys—Russia—Biography. 5. Russia—Social life and customs—19th century. 6. Child abuse—Russia—History—19th century. 7. Grandparent and child—Russia—History—19th century. I. Hettlinger, Graham. II. Title.
PG3465.A32H47 2010
891.78'309—dc22
[B]   2010035223

INTRODUCTION

When his father died of cholera in 1871, three-year-old Aleksey Peshkov went with his mother to live in the home of his maternal grandfather, Vasily Vasilevich Kashirin, a successful artisan and owner of a dye shop in Nizhny Novgorod. The new household was large, comprised of two grandparents, two profoundly odious uncles and their families, a nursemaid, a master craftsman, and an ebullient apprentice known as the Gypsy. The young Aleksey struggled to adapt to the strangers around him, sustained by the tender love of his grandmother and harrowed by the violent outbursts of his grandfather. Although once relatively prosperous, the family had begun a sharp and irreversible descent into poverty, doomed by the disastrous business decisions of its patriarch, the collateral damage of industrialization, and the age-old Russian custom of dividing a father's holdings among his sons. Aleksey's mother soon left the household, only to return several years later and eventually remarry an impoverished member of the nobility who abused her and further sapped the family's finances.

As their struggle to survive grew more and more acute, Aleksey moved with his grandparents to a series of smaller and smaller apartments until, at the age of eleven, he was turned out of the home and told to make do on his own. Thirteen years later, after wandering all the way to the Black Sea and working as a galley hand, a baker, a night watchman, a grape picker, an apprentice in an icon shop, a stevedore, and a barge hauler, he would publish his first works, adopt the pen name Maksim Gorky (meaning "bitter" in Russian), and eventually become one of the most famous authors of the twentieth century, producing more than fifteen volumes of stories, novels, and dramas, and playing an almost mythic role in the Russian Revolution and the rise of the Soviet Union. In 1914, at the age of forty-six, he published *Childhood*, a vibrant account of those trying years in his grandfather's household and the remarkable old woman who enabled him to survive them. The first part of an autobiographical trilogy collectively known as *My Universities*, it is widely considered one of Gorky's greatest works and remains a classic of Russian literature.

Gorky's sudden rise to fame began with the publication of his first stories, "Makar Chudra" (1892) and "Chelkash" (1895), and a two-volume collection of works that appeared in 1898. Depicting free-spirited vagabonds, wanderers, and social outcasts in a brash, unpolished style, these early works appealed enormously to a public hungry for "simpler, coarser nourishment" than the subtleties of Chekhov and the religious philosophy of Tolstoy.[1] Gorky's popularity grew further with the publication of several short, highly romantic works, including "The Song of the Falcon" and "The Stormy Petrel," which resembled prose poems more than traditional stories. With their allegorical portrayals of bold human aspirations and valiant struggles waged against impossible odds, they became favorites of Russia's social activists and revolutionaries, and soon were established as a kind of anthem for the left.[2] In 1902 the Moscow Art Theater produced *The Lower Depths*, Gorky's groundbreaking play depicting the bleak lives of Russia's underclass, which created a sensation on its first staging and became popular throughout Russia and Europe despite the government's efforts to prevent its production at home. One of Gorky's greatest literary successes, the play continues to be staged throughout the world today.

Gorky quickly grew into a kind of larger-than-life phenomenon. While he continued to write prodigiously, his persona as much as his writing seemed to grip the public's attention. Postcards with his image were sold in kiosks and shops; journalists hounded him in public; passersby gawked at him in the streets.[3] For many, he represented the true revolutionary, an authentic member of the underclass who spoke passionately, and sometimes roughly, about the coming storm of social change. Gorky acted as boldly as he wrote, joining student protests, signing his name to antigovernment screeds, and denouncing the oppression of the poor in public forums. Such activities led to several brief arrests, and in 1901 he was forcibly relocated to the provincial town of Arzamas, near Nizhny Novgorod.[4] But the government hesitated to take more drastic steps against the immensely popular writer and activist until the events of Bloody Sunday. After the massacre of more than eight hundred men, women, and children peacefully seeking to deliver a petition to the tsar in St.

1. Georgy V. Adamovich, "Maxim Gorky," in Donald Fanger, *Gorky's Tolstoy and Other Reminiscences* (New Haven: Yale University Press, 2008), 282.
2. Henry Troyat, *Gorky*, trans. Lowell Bair (New York: Crown, 1989), 67.
3. Boris Eikhenbaum, "Gorky as a Russian Writer," in Fanger, 276.
4. Troyat, 75.

Petersburg, Gorky was arrested for having led a delegation to the Ministry of Interior a day earlier to appeal for the removal of government forces before the bloodshed occurred.[5] He was imprisoned for three months in Peter and Paul Fortress until a campaign by Western European governments, supported by such prominent figures as Auguste Rodin, Anatole France, and Marie Curie, gained his release.[6] With unrest spreading across Russia, Gorky actively supported Lenin and the Bolsheviks as they organized street fighting against the tsarist government in 1905 in Moscow and St. Petersburg; when these uprisings were put down, he was forced to flee the country.[7]

Gorky went first to France, where he tried unsuccessfully to prevent the country's major banks from making loans to the tsarist government, and then to the United States to raise money for the Bolsheviks. He was at first warmly received in New York City, where he was the guest of honor at a banquet attended by Mark Twain. But when it became known that he was traveling with a woman who was not his wife (information released by the Russian embassy), the visit erupted in scandal, and Gorky and his companion, a Moscow actress named Maria Andreeva, were forced to take refuge in a cabin in the Adirondack Mountains.[8] There he wrote several polemical works about the United States and a doctrinaire novel called *Mother* depicting a simple peasant woman who adopts the Marxist cause. From the United States he went to Capri in Italy, where he spent eight years in exile, maintaining a substantial correspondence with friends and admirers, writing extensively, and actively supporting the Bolsheviks.

He was able to return to Russia in 1913 when Nicholas II declared a partial political amnesty. But as social unrest grew increasingly severe, Gorky's attitude toward the Bolsheviks and the coming revolution seemed to alter sharply. The bloodshed and the rage he saw spreading through Russia shook his faith in the masses, and he began to fear that the revolution would become a cause of uncontrollable destruction rather than a source of liberation and freedom. Writing a regular column in his newspaper, *New Life* (*Novaya Zhizn'*), Gorky became the chief critic of the new Bolshevik government after the 1917 Revolution, ardently denouncing its abuses of power, its reliance on mob justice, and its naked appeal to the class hatred of its supporters.[9] As civil war erupted and the Russian economy collapsed altogether, Gorky turned much of his energy to aiding writers and scholars who were either dying from hunger and cold or facing arrest and execution under the new

---

5. Troyat, 93, 94.
6. Orlando Figes, *A People's Tragedy* (New York: Penguin Books, 1998), 181.
7. Troyat, 99.
8. Troyat, 104.
9. Figes, 502.

state. He is widely believed to have saved thousands of people, including past critics and enemies as well as strangers and friends, many of whom were among the country's most important authors and thinkers.[10] "It is customary these days to curse Gorky," the poet Anna Akhmatova said many years later. "But without his help at that time, we would have all died of hunger."[11] In 1921, with his own health deteriorating and his relations with Lenin nearing a breaking point, Gorky chose to leave the country once more.

He spent three years in Germany and then made his way to Sorrento in Italy, where he remained in exile until 1928. Deeply homesick, desperate for news from Russia, and increasingly at odds with the Russian émigré community in Europe, he soon began to move closer to the Bolsheviks. Despite his angry dissent after the Revolution, he had not broken with the party entirely. He was grief-stricken by Lenin's death in 1924, which added to his anxiety over Russia's future and prompted him to write a series of canonizing reminiscences about the revolutionary leader. Lenin's death also alienated Gorky conclusively from his fellow émigrés, whose taunting reaction to the news of their enemy's demise left the author sickened and enraged.[12] For several years he concentrated on writing *The Life of Klim Samgin*, a massive novel depicting the failure of liberal intellectuals to defend the working classes; but this project alone was not enough to sustain him abroad, where he felt increasingly isolated as Italy descended into fascism and he continued to quarrel bitterly with the Russians around him. Meanwhile he enjoyed regular visits from Soviet authors who spoke optimistically about the country's progress since the end of the civil war; he received admiring letters from Soviet intellectuals, writers, and readers urging him to return; and his first wife, a committed party activist who remained close to Gorky despite their separate lives, traveled to Sorrento to assure him that the new government would welcome him home.[13]

In 1928 Gorky began a series of extended trips to the Soviet Union, culminating in his permanent return in May 1933. His homecoming was widely celebrated in the Soviet press; huge crowds and a detachment of the Red Guard greeted him when he arrived; politicians and workers made earnest speeches in his honor. Gorky soon embarked on a demanding schedule of tours, receptions, conferences, and public speeches, during which he trumpeted the progress of socialism and the bright future ahead. He traveled to the South Caucasus and dozens of provincial Soviet cities, all the while publishing a stream of upbeat articles about the new schools and

---

10. Figes, 607.
11. Quoted in Fanger, 5.
12. Troyat, 157.
13. Troyat, 163.

factories he had seen.[14] As one of the government's most prominent and important advocates, he was provided two houses, including the famous Ryabushinsky mansion in downtown Moscow, a personal physician, a secretary, and a car and driver. The main thoroughfare in Moscow, the Moscow Art Theater, and the city of Nizhny Novgorod were all renamed in his honor despite Gorky's professed discomfort with such grandiose gestures. He appeared periodically with Stalin, who declared one of his poems "better than Goethe's *Faust*" and occasionally visited him at home. Genrikh Yagoda, the head of the Soviet secret police, was a more regular guest.[15]

Gorky played the role of Soviet "literary archpriest," as he once ironically referred to himself,[16] with unflagging commitment from the day of his return to the Soviet Union until his death. He served as a mentor for young Soviet writers and sought to nurture those with genuine talent; he founded new magazines and journals and established a publishing series known as *The Lives of Remarkable People*,[17] which continues to print fresh new biographies of important historical and cultural figures for Russian readers today; and he publicly attacked the growing number of party hacks posing as writers and literary critics in Soviet Russia. At the same time Gorky's conviction that writers should concentrate on the uplifting truth of what-will-be rather than the more depressing facts of the present eventually gave rise to the concept of Socialist Realism, which would stifle Soviet art and literature for decades to come.[18] His criticism of Western, bourgeois culture grew increasingly shrill and came to include the condemnation of modernist authors such as Joyce and Proust. Furthermore, in his role as icon and advocate of Soviet culture, Gorky never hesitated in his unstinting public praise of the government and its actions, despite the enormous crimes of Stalin's regime. Wittingly or unwittingly, he sometimes even served as an apologist for such abuses, as in 1929 when he visited the Solovetsky Prison as part of a so-called fact-finding mission and later wrote in glowing terms about the therapeutic effects of the camp's conditions on wayward opponents of socialism.[19] Several years later Gorky edited and organized the production of a notorious volume of articles and stories celebrating the construction of the White Sea Canal, a disastrous feat of Stalinist engineering carried out by inmate labor under horrific conditions.[20]

---

14. Troyat, 167, 169.
15. Troyat, 174, 186.
16. Evgeny Zamiatin, "M. Gorky," in Fanger, 269.
17. Troyat, 178.
18. Fanger, 9.
19. Troyat, 172.
20. Richard Hare, *Maxim Gorky* (New York: Oxford, 1962), 128.

Actions such as these are difficult to square with Gorky's often valiant defense of human rights immediately after the revolution and the genuine concern for the welfare of others that often seemed an inherent part of his life. While it is unclear whether he could have understood the full scope of the government's abuses, it seems unlikely he was unaware of them altogether, and there is evidence that he had grave misgivings about Stalin. Some historians have suggested that Gorky may have actually been preparing to oppose the Soviet leader in some overt fashion—either by denouncing him in print or by working with other highly placed officials to bring about his overthrow—at the time of the author's death.[21] Others believe that Gorky was tormented by his awareness of Stalin's atrocities but felt powerless to combat them, because he feared for his safety and that of his family or because he simply felt he had no alternative to the now complicitous life he'd chosen by returning to Russia. It is well known that agents of the secret police, including his personal secretary, closely observed Gorky's movements and sought to control his contact with the public. And Gorky left several indications that, despite his eternally optimistic public statements, he was privately distressed by at least some of what he'd seen.[22] "I am like a dog," he wrote in his notes on the Solovetsky visit. "I understand everything, yet am silent."[23] The French writer Romain Rolland, with whom Gorky had been friends for decades, visited him in Moscow in the summer of 1935 and found the father of Soviet literature deeply troubled despite his professed enthusiasm for his new role in the socialist motherland. "It seems to me that if we could have been alone together," Rolland later wrote, "[He] might have hugged me and sobbed for a long time, without speaking."[24]

The aftermath of Gorky's death in 1936 only added to the many questions already surrounding him. More than a year after his elaborate state funeral, Gorky's "medical assassination" was included among the charges cited in the show trials of 1938, whose famous twenty-one defendants included Yagoda as well as Gorky's secretary and his personal physicians. After months of interrogation, all the defendants confessed to their alleged crimes and were shot. Speculation soon developed that Stalin had in fact ordered Gorky's assassination, perhaps after learning of the writer's plans to somehow act against him.[25] But KGB archives opened since the fall of the Soviet Union have not revealed evidence of

21. See Figes, 822.
22. Figes, 822.
23. Quoted in Cynthia Ruder, *Making History for Stalin: The Story of the Belomor Canal* (Gainesville: University Press of Florida, 1998), 39.
24. Quoted in Troyat, 190.
25. Figes, 822.

an assassination, and there is strong reason to believe that Gorky died of natural causes.[26]

Despite the mythic dimensions of his persona, the profound controversy surrounding his later years, and the many more ambitious works that he published in his lifetime, it is as the author of *Childhood* that Gorky is perhaps best remembered by the Russian reading public. With its vibrant descriptions of the strange and often funny characters who passed through his early life, its unflinching account of the brutalities of nineteenth century Russia, and its tender portrayal of the author's remarkable grandmother, the book is considered one of Gorky's most powerful and moving works. It enjoyed immediate, widespread appeal when it first appeared in 1914 in serial form in the newspaper *The Russian Word*,[27] and it has remained a cherished part of the Russian literary canon ever since.

Gorky's *Childhood* is often favorably compared to Tolstoy's autobiographical novel of the same name, which first appeared in 1852. But Gorky's early life was nothing like the young count's. Whereas Tolstoy's *Childhood* recreates idyllic days on the family estate, Gorky's memoir places us squarely in the squalid, violent, desperate world that was reality for the majority of Russians in the late nineteenth century. This vantage point was a unique accomplishment: no other author of the period ever revealed the lives of the poor with such intimacy and authority. While many great writers, including Tolstoy, frequently touched on the plight of Russia's lower classes, their narratives by and large left the struggling masses outside the main frame, somewhere in a landscape that their protagonists—usually wealthy and educated—could visit but never inhabit or fully understand. The poor were studied, regretted, admired, mourned, and feared, but they were generally seen from a distance. In Gorky's *Childhood*, by contrast, we quite inescapably enter the world of the underclass while the rich become distant ciphers. Here it is commonplace for people to die of hunger and disease, to abuse one another in drunken rages, to go blind and beg in the streets, to search in the garbage for rags and metal scraps that can be sold for a few kopeks. For Gorky, this world is as familiar as the manor house was for Tolstoy, and he depicts it in powerful, disturbing detail.

In many ways *Childhood* is atypical of its author. Gorky believed that the chief purpose of literature was to educate its readership, and a tendency to preach often marred his works. In *Childhood*, however, there's very little moralizing. Instead the author seems intent on capturing the experiences of his early life and letting them stand in sharp relief before

---

26. Dmitrii Bykov, *Byl li Gor'kii?* (Moscow: AST, Astrel', 2008), 111.
27. Viktor Petelin, *Zhizn' Maksima Gor'kogo* (Moscow: Tsentrpoligraf, 2007), 355.

the reader with minimal commentary. It may be for this reason that some reviewers noted a certain reticence, an absence of "rousing words"[28] in *Childhood*, and others felt that his latest work heralded the appearance of "a new, unexpected Gorky."[29] The audacious, sometimes fiery, forever forward-looking revolutionary was suddenly replaced by a troubled, often bewildered young boy with little understanding of the future and no reason to hope for a better life.

Gorky was famously guarded about his personal life, and despite the fact that *Childhood* is an autobiographical work, it seems—on the surface, at least—to contain surprisingly little information about the author. Reading *Childhood*, we do not see Aleksey Peshkov so much as we look at the world through his eyes. The work's narrative lens is not focused on him; instead it is aimed outward from his vantage point toward the objects and the people surrounding him. Consequently it provides far more direct, immediate information about secondary characters than it does about Aleksey himself. To a large degree, for example, we can only infer his physical appearance, his size, even his age (he is three when the book begins, eleven when it ends) from the comments of others, his actions, and his minimally revealed emotions. Furthermore, as Aleksey has the limited understanding of a child, the narrative often explains very little about the events he witnesses. Instead we struggle at times, with the boy, to fully grasp what's taking place. Gorky establishes this limited perspective in the book's first sentences, when, rather than explaining the facts of his father's death, he places us abruptly in a room with the man's body. Together with Aleksey, we slowly make sense of the scene before us: "My father lies on the floor under a window in the cramped and half-dark room. . . ." This narrative style comes at a certain cost. The work's subject remains a somewhat ephemeral presence, a figure we piece together by reading between the lines, and much is simply left unknown. Indeed, some early readers and critics felt that Gorky had neglected his protagonist too much when writing *Childhood* and the other two volumes of *My Universities*. It is "one of the strangest autobiographies ever written," the literary historian D. S. Mirsky complained. "[It is] . . . about everybody but himself."[30] "It is a very good book" the author M. M. Prishvin wrote to Gorky after reading *Childhood* in 1915. "But only half of what is needed—there isn't enough of the boy . . . Peshkov."[31]

28. E. Koltonovskaya, quoted in Maksim Gor'kii, *Sobranie sochinenii v 16 tomakh* (Moscow: Pravda, 1979) vol. 8, 416.

29. K. I. Chukovskii, quoted in Gor'kii, *Sobranie*, vol. 8, 417.

30. Quoted in Fanger, 7.

31. Quoted in Gor'kii, *Sobranie*, vol. 8, 414.

Yet Gorky manages to recreate young Aleksey's perspective with such freshness and authenticity that we seem, in some slight way, to actually share in his experiences as we read the text. For this reason it might be argued that, despite its lack of explication and analysis, *Childhood* provides a deeper understanding of its protagonist than more linear, conventional biographies can offer. Much has been written about Gorky's phenomenal memory—he was said to hold in his head a daunting number of details, figures, memories, and literary passages—and here he seems able to restore the exact thoughts and emotions he experienced some forty years earlier. When Aleksey looks at the liquid face of the one-eyed watchmaker or the features of the "green grandmother," for example, his thoughts are both hilariously funny and, in some elusive way, *exactly* the thoughts of a child confronted by such grotesqueries. In a similar vein there is something unforgettably real about those moments in which the three-year-old Aleksey watches his father's coffin being buried and thinks only of the frogs that have fallen into the grave. Gorky never exploits this perspective for cheap effect; he continually surprises his reader with the originality and the honesty of Aleksey's thoughts and reactions. Even at the story's most wrenching moments, he avoids all mawkishness. When Aleksey's distress is most severe, the narrative becomes terse, almost steely, like the voice of a child who, overwhelmed by grief, grows taciturn and withdrawn.

Despite the many hardships that *Childhood* depicts, a buoyant fascination with life runs through it like a kind of subterranean stream. As the narrative's impressionistic, outward focus illustrates so perfectly, Aleksey Peshkov never stops studying the people around him, noting their odd habits and their manner of speech, remembering their stories, watching as they go about their lives. Often these observations stem from a deeply felt compassion for others: Aleksey is haunted by a particular look that flits across the face of A Fine Business when he speaks of his loneliness; he notices the wave of wrinkles that passes across Grigory's bald pate and disappears at the back of his head when he is hurt. At other times, however, they are simply the result of paying close attention to the world around him. He observes, for instance, that the priest at school tends to pick up ordinary objects as if they are delicate artifacts that one must take care to preserve, that a gate creaks in a particular way depending on Uncle Pyotr's mood as he opens it, that his infant brother's fingers smell like violets. He turns the same careful attention to the natural world, finding great beauty in an orchard with a few apple trees, crows circling a church at dusk, a quiet garden under snow. To be sure, not all of Aleksey's observations are by any means happy and uplifting, but collectively they indicate a dynamic engagement with the world that sustains him through his many tribulations. Despite the violence and deprivations he encounters, he never stops registering the world's presence. On some fundamental level, he loves life.

The wellspring of this love is Aleksey's grandmother, Akulina Ivanovna. Fat, loquacious, illiterate, prone to drink, and boundless in her energy, she sustains Aleksey through years of abuse by his grandfather and neglect by his mother. She teaches him tenderness when he is surrounded by cruelty. With her endless repertoire of poetry and folktales, she instills in him a deep love of literature when the grind of poverty threatens to extinguish his imagination. And in sharp contrast to Aleksey's grandfather, who worships a wrathful, omnipotent God, Akulina Ivanovna presents to the child a deity of profound compassion and limited power who becomes a source of comfort and faith in his increasingly harsh life. Again and again the old woman turns her grandson away from anger and despair when they threaten to consume him. Again and again she tells him, "No, no, just look how good it is," and eventually, almost unconsciously, the boy is converted. It is perhaps the survival of this love for life's goodness amid the terror and depravity of human folly that is *Childhood*'s most promising message.

Any work of literature is inherently bound to its original language, but those bonds seem particularly deep and strong in *Childhood*. In part this is because poetry is extremely important to the text: the moments that Aleksey Peshkov spends listening to his grandmother recite stories in verse are clearly among the happiest in his life, and Gorky carefully, lovingly preserves several of these works for posterity in the course of his narrative. If the qualities of these poems are lost entirely in translation, it seems the overall effect of the book is badly weakened, for the reader is left to wonder what exactly the young listener was so excited about in the original. Further, several scenes are centered on Aleksey's efforts to memorize prayers, to recite poems, and to learn the names of the letters of the Russian Church Slavonic alphabet. In all these moments the link between sound and meaning—a link that virtually never coincides between two languages—takes on absolute importance. Finally, Gorky had a wonderful ear for dialogue; *Childhood* is filled with a wide variety of remarkably authentic voices, idiomatic speech, and rhymed aphorisms. These qualities too are deeply resistant to translation.

My goal in addressing these challenges has been to retain in English both the essential meaning and the effect of the Russian. That is, if Uncle

Pyotr utters a rhymed aphorism about life's vagaries that relies on fishing imagery, I have sought to create a similar aphorism in English, allowing myself, as necessary, to depart from an exact word-for-word rendering of the Russian in order to create an English equivalent that sounds reasonably natural and retains some of the irony of the original. In most instances these departures are relatively minor. But certain passages of *Childhood* are simply impossible to translate in the traditional sense. When, for example, he tries to memorize the words of "Our Heavenly Father," Aleksey becomes distracted by the Russian Church Slavonic phrase "*yako zhe*" which literally means simply "as" (coupled with an emphatic particle) but which he begins to turn into such phrases as *Yakov zhe* (the proper name plus an emphatic article, which might be rendered as "Yakov!") and "*Ya v kozhe*" (which could be translated literally as, "I am in skin" or "I am in leather"). It is of course impossible to repeat this linguistic play in English; therefore I have tried to create an equivalent moment with a different phrase from the prayer. It is a rough and unsatisfactory process, but hopefully it allows the English-language reader to experience some simulacrum of the original scene's light humor and energy.

CHILDHOOD

I dedicate this to my son

I

My father lies on the floor under a window in the cramped and half-dark room. All in white, he seems unusually long. His feet are bare and his toes are strangely spread apart. His gentle hands lie passively on his chest, their fingers also bent and splayed. His playful eyes are tightly covered up with copper coins that look like little black disks. His kind face has turned dark. I'm frightened by the ugly way his teeth are bared.

Half naked, my mother kneels in a red skirt and combs my father's long, soft hair back from his forehead. She uses a black comb with which I like to saw watermelon rinds in half. She keeps saying something in a deep, wheezing voice. Her grey eyes are swollen. They seem to melt, dissolving into the large teardrops that well from them.

My grandmother holds me by the hand. Round, with a big head, huge eyes, and a funny, bulging nose, she's all in black, all soft and fascinating. She too is crying. She accompanies my mother, echoes her voice in a way that seems especially good. She trembles all over and tugs at me, pushes me toward my father. Frightened and embarrassed, I refuse to move, try to hide behind her.

I've never seen big people cry, and I don't understand the words my grandmother keeps repeating:

"Say goodbye to your father—say farewell to my sweet soul. You won't see him anymore. He's died. Before his time was over. . . . Before his hour. . . ."

I've been seriously ill until now and only recently left my sickbed. During my illness—I remember this—my father busied himself happily with me. Then he disappeared, was suddenly replaced by my grandmother, a stranger.

"Where did you come from?"

"I was up in Nizhny. I came down from there."

"Why didn't you come down before?"

5

"Well, it's not so simple—people don't just walk on water, after all. . . . Be quiet now, you—shush!"

This was all very peculiar and funny. In the top of the house lived Persians with beards and dyed hair, and in the basement an old, yellow *Kalmyk* sold sheepskins. You could come down from the top by riding the banister, or, if you fell, tumble head-over-heels down the stairs—this I knew well. But what did water have to do with anything? None of it quite fit together. It was all so tangled up it made me want to laugh.

"Why am I a shush?"

"Because of all your chattering," she said, laughing too.

Her speech was tender, happy, and soothing, and we became friends from the first day of our meeting. Now all I want is for her to leave the room with me.

My mother crushes me. Her wailing and her tears ignite in me a feeling of alarm I've never known before. I've never seen her this way. She's always been strict and taciturn, clean and sleek, and large as a horse. She has a hard, tough body and terribly powerful arms. But now she's disturbingly swollen and disheveled; everything about her seems broken, torn. The hair that once lay neatly arranged like a large, light hat on her head now spills across her bare shoulder, falls over her face, half of it still woven in a braid that dangles loose, grazes my sleeping father's face. I've been standing in the room for a long time already, and she hasn't looked at me once. All she does is comb my father's hair and snarl, choking on her tears.

Some bedraggled peasants and a policeman look in through the door.

"Get it out of here now!" the policeman shouts angrily.

A black shawl is draped across the window. It swells like a sail. My father took me for a ride in a sailboat once. There was a sudden clap of thunder, and he laughed, pressed me between his knees.

"It's nothing, Lyosha," he shouted. "Don't be afraid."

Suddenly my mother lurches to her feet, then drops back down, collapses on her back, her hair spreading out on the floor. Her pale, blind face turns blue, and she bares her teeth like my father.

"Shut the door," she says in a terrible voice. "Get Lyosha out!"

My grandmother pushes me aside, throws herself at the door.

"Please don't be alarmed, my dears," she calls out. "And please don't interfere—just let us be a little while, may God be pleased. It isn't the cholera—her baby's coming. Excuse us, please. . . ."

I hide in a dark corner behind a trunk and watch from there as my mother writhes on the floor, groaning and grinding her teeth so hard they squeak while my grandmother crawls around her, says tender, joyful words:

"In the name of the Father and the Son! Be patient, Varyusha, hang on! Holy Mother, protector and defender . . ."

It's terrifying. Something occupies them on the floor near my father; they brush against him, moan and shout—and he stays motionless. He seems to be laughing at them. For a long time it continues—the small commotion on the floor, my mother trying to stand and falling back down, my grandmother racing in and out of the room like a large, soft, black ball. Then a baby starts to cry in the darkness.

"Thank you, God almighty," says my grandmother. "A boy."

She lights a candle.

I must have fallen asleep in the corner—I don't remember anything more.

The second imprint on my memory: a rainy day in an empty corner of a graveyard. I'm standing on a mound of slick and sticky mud, looking into the pit where my father's coffin has been lowered. The bottom of the pit is filled with water, and there are frogs down there. Two have already climbed onto the yellow lid of the casket.

Beside the grave with me are my grandmother, two ill-tempered peasants with shovels, and a soaking wet policeman. Beads of warm rain pour over us all.

"Fill it in," the policeman says, and steps aside.

My grandmother starts to cry, covering her face with the end of her headscarf. The peasants bend down and start to shovel dirt hurriedly into the grave; it plops into the water. The frogs jump from the casket lid and throw themselves at the walls of the pit. The clumps of dirt knock them down into the bottom.

"Come away now, Lyonya," grandmother says, taking me by the shoulder. I duck out from under her hand. I don't want to leave.

"Oh, you—dear God," my grandmother says, complaining either about me or about God. She stands silently at the grave for a long time, her head lowered. The grave's filled in—made level with the ground—and she's still standing there.

The peasants dully slap the earth with the flat sides of their shovels. A wind blows in and drives the rain away, carries it off. My grandmother takes me by the hand and leads me to a distant church surrounded by dark crosses.

"Why aren't you crying?" she asks once we're past the graveyard fence. "You probably need to cry a little."

"I don't feel like it."

"Well, if you don't want to, then you shouldn't," she says softly.

All of this is a surprise to me. I cried rarely, and only from outrage, never from pain. My father always laughed at my tears, while my mother would shout:

"Don't you dare start crying!"

Then we're riding in a *drozhky* past dark red houses on a wide and filthy street.

"Will the frogs get out?" I ask my grandmother.

"No, there's no way out for them," she answers. "God be with them!"

Neither my mother nor my father pronounced the name of God with such frequency and familiarity.

A few days later my mother, my grandmother, and I are traveling in a small cabin on a steamship. My newborn brother Maksim has died. He's lying on a table in the corner, wrapped in white and swaddled with a red ribbon.

Perched on bundles and trunks, I look out the window, which is round and bulging, like a horse's eye. Outside the wet glass flows an endless stream of turgid, foamy water. Occasionally it jumps up to lick the glass, which sends me leaping to the floor.

"Don't be afraid," my grandmother says, as she lifts me easily with her soft hands and positions me back on top of the bundles.

A wet grey fog hangs above the water; somewhere far away dark land appears, then vanishes again in the water and the mist. Everything around us trembles. Only my mother is motionless, unshakable as she leans against the wall with her hands clasped behind her head. Her face is dark and blank, like iron. Her eyes are pressed firmly shut. She is silent all the time; she is different, somehow new, all the time now. Even her dress is unfamiliar.

More than once grandmother's said to her: "Varya, eat a little, eh?"

And she stays silent, motionless.

My grandmother whispers when she talks to me. She speaks a little more loudly to my mother, but her voice is always cautious, timid, and her words are always sparse. It seems to me that my grandmother is afraid of my mother. I understand this—it draws me even closer to my grandmother.

"Saratov," my mother says in an unexpectedly loud and angry voice. "Where's that sailor?"

Even her words are strange and alien. Saratov. Sailor.

Dressed in dark blue, a wide-set man with grey hair comes into the cabin carrying a small box. My grandmother takes the box and begins to lay my brother's body inside it. She lays him down in there and starts toward

8

the door, carrying the coffin in her outstretched arms. But she is fat; she has to turn sideways to pass through the door, and she stumbles comically at its threshold.

"Oh, mother!" my mother shouts. She takes the coffin from her, and they both disappear. I remain in the cabin, studying the man in dark blue.

"Your little brother's gone away now, has he?" he says, leaning over me.

"Who are you?"

"A sailor."

"Who's Saratov?"

"Saratov is a town. Look out the window—there's Saratov!"

Land is passing outside the window. It's dark and steep. Wisps of fog curl around it like smoke. It makes me think of a large piece of bread just sliced from the loaf.

"Where did my grandmother go?"

"She went to bury her grandson."

"Will they cover him up in the ground?"

"Well, yes, of course. What else would they do?"

I tell him about the frogs they buried alive with my father's coffin. He picks me up and presses me firmly to him, kisses me.

"Oh, little brother, you don't understand a thing just yet," he says. "You shouldn't worry about the frogs, may God be with them. Worry about your mother—she's been all but swallowed up by grief!"

A horn begins to drone and howl overhead. I'm not afraid—I already know it's just the ship, but the sailor hurriedly puts me back on the floor and rushes to the door. "Have to run . . . ," he says.

I want to run away too. I step through the threshold of the cabin door. The dark and narrow passageway is empty. Not far from the door shine the copper steps of a ladder. I look up and see people with knapsacks and bundles in their arms. It's clear that everyone is leaving—which means that I should leave as well.

But when I wind up among a crowd of peasants gathered at the gangplank, everyone begins to shout at me:

"Whose is this? Whose are you?"

"I don't know."

For a long time they shake me, squeeze and push me. Finally the grey sailor appears and seizes me in his hands.

"Cabin passenger. From Astrakhan," he explains.

The sailor runs back to the cabin with me in his arms, sticks me in among the bundles, and shakes his finger at me:

"I'll give you one!"

The noise above my head subsides. The steamer doesn't pound the water, doesn't tremble. Some kind of wet wall blocks the window. It grows dark and stuffy. The bundles seem to swell, begin to crowd me. Everything is wrong. Could they have left me here for good? Alone like this, on an empty steamer?

I approach the door. It won't open—the copper handle doesn't turn. I pick up a bottle of milk and strike it against the handle as hard as I can. The bottle shatters; milk spills on my pants, runs into my boots.

Dismayed by this failure, I lie down on the bundles and begin crying quietly, fall asleep in tears.

But when I wake up the steamer is trembling and pounding on the water again. The window burns like the sun. My grandmother sits near me and combs her hair, wincing and whispering something. It's strange that she has so much hair. It lies thickly over her shoulders, breasts, and knees, spills onto the floor—a deep black with tints of dark blue. She lifts it from the floor and struggles to work a wooden, wide-toothed comb through the thick locks that dangle from her hand, her lips curling and her dark eyes flashing angrily, her face seeming small and comical now in the great mass of hair surrounding it.

She seems annoyed today, but when I ask why she has such long hair, she answers in the warm, soft voice of yesterday.

"It seems God gave it to me as a punishment—just combing it's a kind of retribution! In my girlhood I showed off with this mane and now, in my old age, I curse it. But you go back to sleep. It's still early. The sun's just barely gotten up from night."

"But I don't want to sleep."

"All right then, don't," she immediately agrees, starting to braid her hair and glancing at the couch where my mother sleeps with her face up-turned, her body stretched like a string pulled taut. "How did you manage to smash a bottle of milk yesterday? Speak quietly. . . ."

She seemed somehow to sing her words when she spoke, and they easily took root in my memory, for they were bright and lush and tender as flowers. Her pupils were like dark cherries, and when she smiled they widened and flashed, filled with a light lovelier than words. Her smile revealed strong white teeth, and all her face looked young and bright despite the many wrinkles in the dark skin of her cheeks. Only that bulging, porous nose, with its red tip and wide nostrils, kept her face from being beautiful— she snorted tobacco, which she kept in a black snuffbox with a silver decoration. All her features were dark, but a light burned from inside her—it shone through her eyes, warm and happy, inextinguishable. She was stooped, almost hunchbacked, and very plump, but she moved lightly and gracefully, like a large cat. She was gentle as a loving cat as well.

It was as if I'd been asleep, hidden in darkness before she came. But she appeared and woke me, led me into the light, bound everything around me with a single, constant thread, wove it all together into a lace of many colors, and immediately became my friend for life, became the person closest to my heart—the one I understood before all others, cherished above all else. It was her selfless love for the world that enriched me, infused me with the stubborn strength that a hard life demands.

Forty years ago steamships moved slowly; we traveled a long time to Nizhny, and I remember well the sating beauty of those first few days.

Good weather settles in. From morning until evening, grandmother and I stay on deck, under the clear sky, between the silks that fall has spun with golden thread along the Volga's banks. The blades of its paddle wheel beat the grey-blue water with a lazy rumbling as the light red steamer makes its way unhurriedly upriver, a barge in tow on a long line, like a grey wood louse in the distance. The sun floats imperceptibly above the Volga. Every hour everything is new around us; everything changes. Green hills spread out before us like luxuriant folds in some rich garment that cloaks the earth. Villages and towns rise along the shore, their far-off walls made of ginger-bread. A golden leaf floats in the water.

"Just look how lovely it is," my grandmother says every minute, crossing from one side of the ship to the other, her eyes wide with joy, all of her glowing. Often she forgets about me as she looks at the shore. Standing at the ship's side with her arms folded across her chest, she smiles and doesn't speak, tears filling her eyes. I tug on her dark floral skirt.

"Hmm?" she says, rousing herself. "It's like I fell asleep and started dreaming. . . ."

"What are you crying about?"

"From joy, my dear. Joy and old age," she says, smiling. "I'm old, after all. My summers and my springs have cantered out beyond six decades now."

She takes a pinch of snuff, then starts to tell me wondrous tales about holy people and good-hearted thieves, animals of every kind, the Evil One. She tells her stories in a quiet, secretive voice, bending down toward my face, looking into my eyes with her widened pupils. It's as if she's pouring strength into my heart, lifting me up. She speaks as if singing, and the longer she talks the more melodic her speech becomes. Hearing her is pleasant beyond words. I listen and I plead:

"More!"

"Well, here's a little more. Eating noodles at the stove, the house spirit got a splinter in his toe. 'Oh my little mice,' he cried with woe. 'Oh my dears, it hurts me so!'"

She lifts her leg and grasps it, shakes it comically, and creases her face as if in pain. Sailors stand around us. Bearded, good-hearted peasants, they listen and laugh, praise her stories. And like me, they implore her to continue:

"Please, grandmother, tell us just one more!"

And then they say, "Come and dine with us, come on!"

At dinner they share their vodka with her, give me cantaloupe and melon. All this is done in secret because there's a man on board who forbids everyone from eating fruit—takes it away and throws it right into the river. He's dressed like a policeman with copper buttons on his coat, and he's always drunk. People hide from him.

My mother rarely comes on deck. She keeps to herself, stays silent all the time, my mother. Her large and graceful figure, her dark iron face, her heavy crown of braided, light brown hair—everything about her, all her strength and her immovability—all of it comes back to me in a fog, some kind of transparent cloud from which peer two severe, remote, and unwelcoming grey eyes—eyes as big as my grandmother's.

Once she said reprovingly: "People are laughing at you, *mamasha*."

"May God be with them, then," my grandmother answered lightheartedly. "Let them laugh. It's good for them!"

I remember grandmother's childlike joy when Nizhny came into view. She pushed and pulled me by the hand to the ship's side, shouting:

"Look, look—there it is, there's mighty Nizhny! A true city of God! The churches—see? It's like they're flying!"

And she asked my mother, almost in tears: "Varyusha, look at it, eh? You've forgotten, probably. Rejoice a little!"

My mother smiled gloomily.

The ship stopped directly across from that beautiful city, in the middle of the river, which was tightly crowded with vessels, bristling with hundreds of sharp masts. A large boat filled with people came along the ship's side. It hooked onto the ship's ladder, and one after another people came streaming onto the deck. Before them all came a small, wizened old man in long black garments. He had a beard of reddish gold, a beaklike nose, and little green eyes.

"*Papasha!*" my mother shouted in a loud, deep voice, toppling into his arms. He clasped her head and quickly stroked her cheeks with his small red hands, screeching:

"Akh, you little fool. . . . You little fool. . . . Akh, you . . ."

Grandmother somehow seemed to kiss and embrace everyone at once, turning like a screw. She pushed me toward the new people, saying hurriedly:

"Well, come on now, quickly. . . . This is Uncle Mikhail, and this is Uncle Yakov . . . Aunt Natalya. . . . Your cousins—both the boys are Sasha, and the girl is Katerina. . . . This is all our clan! Just look how many!"

"Are you well, mother?" my grandfather said to her. They kissed three times. Grandfather pulled me from the crowd.

"And whose are you?" he asked, clutching my head with his hand.

"Cabin passenger. From Astrakhan."

"What's he saying?" He turned to my mother and without waiting for an answer moved me aside, saying, "Those cheekbones are his father's. . . . Everyone down to the boat!"

We came ashore and set off as a crowd, walking up a steep slope that was paved with large cobblestones and rose between two high hills covered in withered grass. Grandfather led the way with my mother. He only reached her shoulder, and he walked with quick, short steps while she, looking down at him, seemed to float through the air. They were followed silently by the uncles: Yakov, who was light and curly-headed and Mikhail, who had straight black hair and like my grandfather seemed to be just skin and bone. Along with them came a collection of fat women in bright dresses and some six children—all of them older than I, and all of them quiet. I walked with grandmother and Aunt Natalya. Small, with blue eyes and a huge stomach, she stopped often, whispering, "Oh, I can't keep going. . . ."

"Why did they trouble you?" my grandmother muttered angrily. "This is a dim-witted clan!"

I liked neither the children nor the adults and felt completely alien among them. Even my grandmother had somehow grown darker and more distant.

I felt a particular dislike for my grandfather. From the very first he seemed to be an enemy, and this produced in me a keen attention toward him, a constant, wary curiosity.

We reached the top of the incline. At the very summit, marking the start of the road and leaning into the hillside to its right, stood a squat, one-story house painted a dirty pink, with bulging windows and a low, sagging roof. The house looked quite large to me from the street, but once inside I found the rooms were small, dark, and crowded. Everywhere it reminded me of the docked steamer, with its constant commotion of angry adults, its flocks of children flitting past like furtive sparrows, and an unfamiliar, acrid smell filling every passageway.

I wound up outside in the yard. It was unpleasant there as well, crowded with vats of thick, colored water—rags soaking in them all. Huge sheets of wet cloth hung everywhere, and in the corner, under a half-collapsed lean-to, a woodstove burned hotly. Something boiled and gurgled there, and a man I couldn't see was calling out strange words:

"Fuchsia . . . vitriol . . . sandalwood . . ."

II

Then began a life that was turbid, mottled, strange beyond all words—with terrifying speed it started on its course. And now it returns to my memory like a harsh fairly tale well told by a genius who's kind but brutally devoted to the truth. Reviving the past, I myself must struggle now, at times, to believe that everything was truly as it was, and there are many things I'd like to question and deny, for the dark life of that "dim-witted clan" was far too rich in cruelty.

But truth is higher than pity, and, after all, I'm not speaking of myself but of that cramped, stifling circle of terrifying impressions that the ordinary Russian once inhabited—and to the present day inhabits still.

A thick, hot fog of universal enmity filled my grandfather's house. It poisoned all the adults, and even the children took an active part in it. As I later learned from my grandmother's stories, my mother had arrived on those very days when her brothers began demanding that the family property be divided up and each son allotted his legal share. The unexpected return of my mother had made their demands even more urgent and insistent, for they feared that she would claim the dowry that my grandfather had set aside for her but then refused to grant when she eloped and married against his will. The uncles believed this dowry should now be split between them. At the same time they were engaged in a long-standing, bitter dispute about who should open a dye shop in town and who should open one on the other side of the Oka River, in the Kunavino district.

We had still only recently arrived when a fight broke out in the kitchen during lunch. Both uncles suddenly jumped to their feet and, leaning across the table, began to snarl and wail at my grandfather, trembling and baring their teeth pathetically, like dogs, while grandfather pounded on the table with a spoon and turned completely red, shouting in a voice that rang out like a rooster's cry:

"I'll put you both in the street!"

"Give them what they want, father," said my grandmother, her face painfully contorted. "It will be less trouble for you. Just give them what they want."

"Quiet! You panderer!" shouted my grandfather, his eyes flashing. It was surprising that someone so small could shout so deafeningly.

My mother rose from the table and turned her back on them as she moved unhurriedly toward the window.

Suddenly Uncle Mikhail struck his brother with the back of his hand. Howling, Yakov seized him in his arms and the two brothers began rolling on the floor, wheezing, groaning, cursing each other.

The children began to cry, and pregnant Aunt Natalya began shouting despairingly until my mother bundled her up in her arms and carried her off somewhere. The nursemaid, a happy, pockmarked woman named Evgeniya, drove the children from the kitchen. Chairs toppled over. A young, broad-shouldered apprentice from the dye shop called the Gypsy straddled Mikhail's back, and the master craftsman, Grigory Ivanovich, a balding, bearded man in dark glasses, calmly bound my uncle's hands with a towel.

Mikhail craned his neck and rubbed his sparse black beard on the floor, wheezing terribly, while grandfather ran in circles around the table, shouting in a doleful voice:

"Brothers! Your own blood! Akh, you-u . . ."

Alarmed at the very start of the fight, I'd jumped up onto the stove. From there I watched in terrified confusion as my grandmother took water from the copper washstand to wipe blood from Yakov's beaten face while he wept and stamped his feet.

"You're cursed, you savages! Come to your senses!" she said gravely.

Grandfather railed at her as he pulled his torn shirt back over his shoulders: "Well, you witch! See what beasts you bore me!"

When Uncle Yakov left, grandmother thrust herself into the corner, crying in a voice that stunned me:

"Holy Mother of God, bring reason to my children!"

Grandfather stood with his side to her, surveying the table where everything had been spilled and overturned. "You keep an eye on them, mother," he said quietly. "God knows what they could do to Varvara. . . ."

"Enough, already. Enough of that. Take off your shirt so I can sew it up."

She held his head between her palms and kissed him on the forehead. He pressed his face lightly against her shoulder, seeming even smaller as he stood before her.

"I'll have to split things up with them, mother."

"You have to, father. You have no choice. . . ."

They spoke for a long time. The conversation was friendly at first, but then grandfather began to shuffle his feet along the floor like a rooster before a fight.

"I know you love them more than me," he said, shaking his finger at grandmother and whispering loudly. "That Mishka's a Jesuit! And Yashka's a damn Freemason! They'll drink up everything I own. They'll squander it!"

I turned awkwardly and knocked the iron from the top of the stove. It clattered down the ladder steps and plopped into a wooden tub filled with dishwater. My grandfather leaped onto the ladder and pulled me down.

"Who put you up there? Your mother?" he said, looking me in the face as if it were the first time he'd seen me.

"I did."

"You lie."

"No, I climbed up by myself. I was frightened."

He struck me lightly with his palm on my forehead and pushed me away. "Just like his father. . . . Get out of here."

I was glad to flee the kitchen.

I knew very well that my grandfather was watching me with his keen and cunning green eyes, and I was afraid of him. I remember how I always wanted to hide from those burning eyes. He seemed evil to me. He addressed everyone in a mocking voice, teasing and insulting them, egging them on toward a fight or a fit of anger.

"Akh, you-u," he would often exclaim, and the sound of that elongated "ou-u" never failed to stir in me a feeling of cold gloom.

During the rest hour—that time at evening tea when grandfather, my uncles, and the workers came from the dye shop to the kitchen, all of them tired, their hands stained with sandalwood and burned with vitriol, a band tied around each of their heads to keep the hair from their eyes, and all their faces resembling those of the dark icons in the corner—at that dangerous hour grandfather would sit across from me and talk, often stirring the jealousy of the other children, to whom he spoke much less. Everything about him was neatly proportioned, sharp, precise. His thick satin waistcoat was old and threadbare, his cotton shirt was wrinkled, and his pants displayed large patches at the knees, but despite all this he seemed cleaner, neater, more finely dressed than either of his sons, who wore jackets with shirtfronts and silk kerchiefs around their necks.

A few days after our arrival he told me to begin learning prayers. All the other children were older than I and already studied reading and writing with the deacon from the Church of the Assumption, whose golden cupolas we could see through our windows.

I was instructed by Aunt Natalya, a quiet, timorous woman with a child's face and such transparent eyes it seemed I could see through them all the way to the back of her head.

I liked to stare into them for long stretches without blinking or looking away. She would narrow her eyes and turn her head, saying in a voice so quiet it was almost a whisper:

"Well, repeat after me, please: 'Our Father who art in Heaven' . . ."

And if I asked the meaning of a phrase like "Hallowed be Thy name," she would look around nervously before saying, "Don't ask—that's worse. Just say it after me: 'Our Father' . . . Well?"

But this bothered me. Why was asking worse? The words "Hallowed be" took on a hidden significance, and I deliberately distorted them.

"Hollow tree's thy name." "How old be thy name."

My aunt seemed to melt away as she hurriedly corrected me, her face pale, her voice all broken.

"No, just say it. 'Hallowed be.' It's simple."

But there was nothing simple about her demeanor or her words. This irritated me, distracted me from learning the prayer.

One day my grandfather asked:

"Well, Olyosha. What'd you do today? Just fooled around! I can tell from that bump on your head. Getting a bump on your head's no great wisdom. Well, have you learned 'Our Father?'"

"He has a bad memory," said my aunt softly.

Grandfather smirked and raised his ginger colored eyebrows playfully.

"Well, if that's so, then he needs a beating."

He turned to me again. "Did your father switch you?"

I didn't understand what he was talking about and stayed silent. My mother spoke:

"No, Maksim didn't beat him. And he forbade me to as well."

"How's that?"

"He said you can't teach by beating."

"He was a fool in every way, that Maksim, may he rest in peace, and God forgive me," grandfather said. He spoke angrily, his words distinct and clear. They rankled me, and he immediately saw my reaction.

"What are you puffing out your lips about? Eh? What's that supposed to be?"

He smoothed back his silvery red hair and added:

"I'm going to tan Sashka on Saturday for the thimble."

"What do you mean, 'tan him'?" I asked.

Everyone laughed.

"Wait. You'll see," said my grandfather.

I hid away and tried to make sense of what I'd heard. "To tan" meant to make an animal hide soft, while "to switch" and "to beat" evidently meant the same thing. They beat horses, dogs, cats. In Astrakhan the police beat Persians—I'd seen that. But I had never seen little children being beaten, and although my uncles would sometimes rap the children on their heads, they seemed indifferent to these blows, merely scratching the place where they'd been struck. More than once I'd asked if it hurt, and every time I'd heard the same stoic answer, "Nah—didn't even feel it."

I knew about the uproar caused by the thimble. In the evenings, between tea and supper time, Grigory and my uncles would sew small pieces of dyed material into larger sheets and attach cardboard labels to them. Wanting to play a joke on Grigory, who was half blind, Uncle Mikhail told his nine-year-old nephew to heat the master craftsman's thimble over a candle flame. Sasha gripped the thimble with a pair of pincers used for trimming snuff, held it over the candle until it was red hot, then placed it unnoticed near Grigory and hid behind the stove. But at that moment grandfather sat down to work and stuck his own finger into the searing thimble.

I remember how I ran toward the commotion in the kitchen and saw my grandfather jumping comically around the room, grasping his earlobe with his singed fingers as he shouted:

"Infidels! Whose work is this?"

Uncle Mikhail was hunched over, blowing on the thimble as he tapped it with his fingers and it rolled along the tabletop. The master craftsman continued sewing imperturbably, shadows jumping across the huge bald spot on his head. Uncle Yakov ran into the room and ducked behind the stove, where he began laughing quietly to himself while grandmother grated potatoes.

"Yakov's Sasha did it," Uncle Mikhail said suddenly.

"You lie!" shouted Yakov, jumping out from behind the stove. But somewhere in the corner his son was crying and shouting:

"Don't believe him, papa. He told me to himself. . . ."

The uncles began to shout at each other. Grandfather immediately calmed down, pressed some potato gratings to his finger, and left the room silently, taking me in tow.

Everyone said that Uncle Mikhail was to blame for the incident. It therefore seemed quite natural for me to ask at tea whether he would be tanned and switched.

"He should be," muttered my grandfather, glancing at me from the corner of his eye.

Uncle Mikhail slammed his hand on the table.

"Varvara, you better teach this mutt to behave, or I'm going to wring its neck!"

"Just try it," my mother said. "Touch him."

No one spoke.

She could utter a few, concise words in such a way that they seemed to repel people, knock them back. She would throw out words and people seemed to shrink before her.

It was clear to me that everyone feared my mother. Even my grandfather spoke to her differently than he did to the others—more quietly. This pleased me, and I boasted proudly to my cousins:

"My mother's strongest of all."

They didn't argue.

But Saturday's events would begin to unravel my relationship with my mother.

I too had time to go astray by Saturday.

I was fascinated by the way adults could so quickly change a fabric's color. They take something yellow, soak it in black water, and the material turns a dense, dark blue—"indigo." They rinse something grey in rust-colored water and it comes out all reddish—"claret." It's very simple, really—but impossible to understand.

I wanted to color something myself, and I talked about this with Uncle Yakov's Sasha, a serious boy who always behaved well in the presence of adults and treated everyone with polite deference, ready to serve everyone in every way. The adults praised him for his good behavior and his intelligence, but grandfather always looked askance at Sasha, growling "Ekh—fawning toad. . . ."

Skinny, dark, with the bulging eyes of a crawfish, Sasha spoke hurriedly, quietly, swallowing his words and always glancing furtively around, as if he planned to run away and hide somewhere. He had chestnut-brown pupils that stayed motionless unless he became excited—then they would tremble together with the whites of his eyes.

I found him unpleasant. Uncle Mikhail's Sasha, a quiet, clumsy, inconspicuous boy with sad eyes and a good smile, who resembled very much his

20

timid mother, was more appealing to me. He had ugly teeth; they protruded from his mouth and grew in two rows on his upper jaw. This preoccupied him greatly, and he constantly had his fingers in his mouth, wiggling his teeth, trying to pluck them out from the back row. He would calmly open his mouth for anyone else who wanted to try pulling on his teeth as well. Other than this I found nothing remarkable in him. In a house packed tightly with people, he kept a solitary life, preferring most of all to sit in a dark corner or, in the evening, by a window. It was good to sit with him and not speak—sit by the window, pressed up close to him, and not speak for an entire hour while watching jackdaws wheel in circles around the golden domes of the Church of the Assumption, shooting up and plunging back down in the red evening sky until they'd covered the dusk with a black net, and suddenly disappeared, leaving only emptiness behind. When you watch this you don't feel like talking about anything, and a pleasant sorrow fills your chest.

But Uncle Yakov's Sasha could speak long and confidently about any-thing at all, just like an adult. Having learned that I wanted to practice the dyer's craft, he advised me to take from the cupboard the white tablecloth that was always used for special occasions and dye it dark blue.

"It's always easier to dye white material—I know!" he said very seriously.

I pulled out the heavy tablecloth and ran with it into the yard. But as I put one end into the "indigo" vat, the Gypsy came flying at me from out of nowhere. He tore the tablecloth away and started wringing it out with his big hands.

"Get your grandmother, right away," he shouted at my cousin, who'd been standing in the doorway to observe my handiwork.

"You're going to catch it for this," he said, ominously shaking his head of black, shaggy hair.

My grandmother came running, gasped, and then began to weep as she upbraided me with funny phrases:

"*Permyak!* Pickles for brains! I should slap the nonsense out of you!"

Then she began to implore the Gypsy.

"You won't tell grandfather, now will you, Vanya? I can cover this up for now, and maybe it will pass us by somehow."

Wiping his hands on his mottled apron, Vanka said anxiously:

"Why would I? I won't say anything. But watch that Sashka doesn't go off yammering about it."

"I'll give him a kopek," grandmother said, leading me away to the house.

On Saturday, before the evening church service, someone led me to the kitchen. It was dark and quiet. I remember the tightly closed doors to the vestibule and the bedrooms, the grey murk of an autumn evening that hung outside the windows, the rustling of the rain. The Gypsy was sitting on a wide bench near the black belly of the stove. He looked angry, not at all like himself. Grandfather stood in the corner by the washtub, taking long switches from a bucket of water, measuring them, laying them side by side, slicing them through the air with a whistling sound. Somewhere in the darkness stood my grandmother. She loudly snorted a pinch of tobacco and muttered:

"He's glad, the torturer. . . ."

Sitting on a chair in the middle of the room, Uncle Yakov's Sasha rubbed his fists in his eyes and moaned:

"Forgive me, please. For the love of Jesus."

It was not his voice. It was the voice of an old beggar.

Uncle Mikhail's children, brother and sister, stood shoulder to shoulder behind the chair, like statues carved from wood.

"A beating first—and then forgiveness," my grandfather said, drawing a long, wet switch through his open fist. "Come on then, drop your pants."

He spoke calmly, and neither the sound of his voice, nor the squirming of the boy in that squeaking chair, nor the shuffling of my grandmother's feet could disturb the silence I remember in the gloom of that kitchen, under its low, smoke-stained ceiling.

Sasha got up, unbuttoned his pants, and lowered them to his knees. Holding them with both hands, he moved toward the bench, hunched over and stumbling. My legs were trembling like his; watching him move, I felt sick.

But it got even worse when he obediently lay face down on the bench, and Vanka tied him there with a wide towel that he wound around Sasha's neck and under his armpits, and then, bending over him, grasped the boy by the ankles with his black hands.

"Leksey," my grandfather shouted. "Come closer! Well—who am I talking to? Look, look here. This is what it means to give someone a tanning. . . . One!"

He raised his arm slightly and lashed the naked body with his switch. Sasha shrieked.

"You're lying!" grandfather said. "That doesn't hurt. Here's one that hurts!"

He hit him so sharply that a red stripe immediately welled up and began to burn on Sasha's body while he let out a prolonged wail.

"Not so sweet?" asked grandfather, raising and lowering his arm in even strokes. "Don't like it? That's for the thimble!"

Everything in my chest seemed to rise as he lifted his arm, and when he lowered it, everything within me fell.

Sasha's scream was thin and sickening.

"I wooon't. . . . I told about the tablecloth. . . . I tooold!"

Calmly, as if reading from his Psalter, grandfather said:

"Denunciation does not bring absolution! The first whip is for the denouncer! Here's one for the tablecloth!"

My grandmother rushed to me, seized me in her arms, and started shouting:

"I won't give you Leksey! I won't let you have him, you monster!"

She kicked at the door, imploring:

"Varvara, Varvara!"

Grandfather leaped at her and knocked her down, snatched me away, and started toward the bench. I struggled to break free, twisted, pulled at his beard, bit his finger. He roared and squeezed me harder in his grip. My face hit the bench as he threw me onto it. I remember his savage cry:

"Tie him down! I'm going to kill him!"

I remember my mother's white face. She ran toward the bench, wheezing:

"*Papasha*, no! Give him to me!"

My grandfather beat me until I lost consciousness. I was ill for several days afterward, lying face down on a wide, hot bed in a small room with one window and a red lamp that glowed before a case of many icons in the corner, its flame kept constantly alight.

Those days of illness were a large part of my life. I must have grown up quickly then, for I began to feel something new, distinct. A kind of restless attention to other people arose in me during those days, and it remained with me from that point on, as if the skin had been torn from my heart, leaving it unbearably sensitive to the slightest insult or injury inflicted upon me or those around me.

More than anything, I was shocked by an argument between my grandmother and my mother. Dark and looming large in that cramped room, my grandmother bore down on my mother, forced her into the corner where the icons hung.

"Why didn't you get him away?" she hissed.

"I was afraid."

"But you're strong as an ox! Shame, Varvara! I'm an old woman and I'm not afraid. You should be ashamed!"

"Leave me alone, mama. I'm sick to my stomach."

"No, you don't love him. You have no sorrow for that poor little orphan."

"I'm an orphan now myself—for the rest of my life," my mother said, her voice heavy and loud.

They both wept for a long time, sitting in the corner on a trunk.

Then my mother said: "If it weren't for Aleksey, I'd leave. I'd go away. I can't live in this hell, *mamasha*. I don't have the strength."

"You are my blood," my grandmother said. "You are my heart."

I remembered this: my mother was not strong after all. Like everyone else, she was afraid of my grandfather. I was forcing her to stay in this house, where she couldn't live. It was very sad. And soon she really did disappear from the house. Went away to stay somewhere else.

One day, as if he'd dropped from the ceiling, my grandfather suddenly appeared. He sat down on the edge of the bed and touched my head with his ice-cold hand:

"Hello, young sir. . . . Well, now, you answer back. Don't be angry. Well? Come on now. . . ."

I wanted to kick him but it was very painful to move. His hair seemed even redder than before. His head rocked uneasily, and his bright eyes searched for something on the wall.

He took from his pocket two carob pods, a little gingerbread goat, an apple, and a twig of dark blue raisins.

"I brought you some presents, see—just look at that," he said, placing them on the pillow near my nose.

He bent down to kiss my forehead and began to talk while quietly stroking my head. The yellow stains that covered his small, tough hand were particularly noticeable on his nails—they made his fingers look like a bird's claw.

"I overdid it with you, brother. Got overheated. You bit me, scratched me—and, well, I got angry too. Still, it's no great tragedy you went through a little extra. I'll count the balance later. But you should know: when your own people beat you that's not an insult, it's a lesson. Don't ever give in to strangers, but if it's your own people, well, that's fine. Do you think I never had a beating? They beat me in ways, Olyosha, that you'd never even see in your nightmares. They hurt me so that God Himself was probably crying when He saw it. And what came of it? An orphan, the son of a mother with nothing, and here I went and found my place. The head of my guild. The boss of people."

He rested his lean, worn body alongside mine and began to tell stories about his childhood. He used solid, heavy words, stacking them together with lightness and grace.

His green eyes flashed brightly, and the reddish gold strands of his hair seemed to bristle as he lowered his voice and bellowed his words straight into my face.

"You came here on a steamer—steam brought you up the river. But when I was young I used to pull barges up the Volga with just my own strength. The barge would be on the water and I'd be on the riverbank, barefoot, going over sharp stones and scree—just like that from sunrise until night. The sun heats the back of your head like a cast-iron pot, and everything inside it boils. And you're all bent double, your bones squeak. You push on and on and you can't even see the path because your eyes are all filled with sweat and even your soul weeps while the tears roll down. Akh, Olyosha, don't you talk about how bad you've got it. On the Volga you'd go on and on until you fall out of the strap and your face goes right into the dirt—and you're glad then, because it means that all your strength's been given up clean and you can rest at last, can keel over now in peace. That's how we lived before God's eyes, under the watch of merciful Jesus! ... Three times I measured out the Volga that way—from Simbirsk to Rybinsk, from Saratov to here, and from Astrakhan to Makarev, to the trade fairs there. That's thousands of *versts*—many thousands. And in the fourth year I became head of the barge crew. I showed the owners I had brains."

As he spoke he grew before my eyes, quickly, like a cloud, changing from a small, dried-up old man to a person of mythic strength—alone he pulled a huge grey barge against the Volga's current.

Sometimes he would jump up from the bed and, waving his arms, show me how the bargemen walked in their harnesses, how they pumped water from the boats. He sang the bargemen's song in a deep voice and then, as if young again, he jumped back onto the bed, his words growing ever stronger and richer as he spoke. Everything about him was astounding.

"But still, Olyosha," he said. "All the same, sometimes, when you're at a stopping place, when you're resting somewhere like Zhiguli, a summer evening in the green hills, and someone makes a fire to cook a little *kasha*—sometimes then one of those wretched bargemen starts to sing with all his heart, and the whole group joins in, and it's like the frost is pulling your skin tight. It's like the Volga starts to run faster—like it wants to rear up the way a horse does on its hind legs, rise right up to the clouds! And any bitterness, any pain you had—it's dust scattered in the wind. Sometimes the people would get so caught up in their singing that all the *kasha* would go boiling over the pot! That's when you've got to give the cook a ladle right between the eyes! Fine, sing all you want—but remember what you're doing!"

Several times someone looked in from the door and called him away, but I pleaded:

"Don't leave!"

He let out a little laugh and waved the people off.

"Wait out there for me."

25

He told me stories right up to the evening, and when he left after tenderly saying goodbye, I knew that my grandfather was neither terrible nor evil. It was painful to the point of tears to remember that it was he who had beaten me so cruelly. But I could not forget this.

Grandfather's visit opened the door wide for everyone else, and soon someone would be sitting from morning until night beside the bed, trying to amuse and entertain me, which sometimes, I remember, was neither entertaining nor amusing. My grandmother was with me more than anyone, and she slept in the same bed as me. But it was the Gypsy who made the strongest impression on me during those days. Squarely built and broad shouldered, with a huge head of curly hair, he appeared toward evening, dressed up as if for a special occasion in a gold silk shirt, velveteen pants, and squeaky boots with accordion tops. His hair glistened, his cheerful, narrow eyes flashed under his thick eyebrows, and his white teeth glinted below the black strip of his youthful mustache. Even his shirt seemed to burn, softly reflecting the red glow of the ever-burning icon lamp.

"Take a look at this," he said, rolling up his sleeve to show me his arm, covered in red welts up to the elbow. "Just look how it's all swollen up. And it was worse before! It's already started healing now."

"See what a frenzy your grandfather was in? I can tell he's going to beat you to death, so I start sticking out my arm, thinking the switch will break, and when he goes to get another one your grandma or your mother will haul you away. But the switch—it never breaks! It's a tough one—all green and wet. Still, it landed on you a little less—see how much it missed you by? I'm a tricky one, brother!"

He let out a silky, tender laugh, looked at his swollen arm once more, and, laughing again, said:

"It was like someone grabbed me around the throat I felt so bad for you. Misery! And he just keeps lashing away."

He snorted like a horse and, shaking his head, started to say something about my grandfather—and right away he was close to me, simple as a child.

I told him that I loved him very much, and he answered directly, with no joking:

"I love you too. That's why I took on that pain—for love! Do you think I'd do the same for just anybody? I'd just as soon spit on them."

Then he quietly began to coach me, often glancing at the door:

"When you're getting your next beating, remember, don't clench up, don't tighten up your body—see? When you clench up it's twice as bad. So you relax it, let it go all loose, so it's soft. You lie there like a big pudding!

And don't puff up your chest and hold your breath. You breathe as full as you can. And shout at the top of your lungs. Remember that—it's good!"

"Will I really get another beating?" I asked.

"Well, how else could it be?" said the Gypsy calmly. "Of course you will. I'd say you'll be torn up pretty often."

"What for?"

"Your grandfather's bound to find reasons."

He began again to coach me carefully:

"If he's hitting you with high strokes, just hitting you on the surface with his switch, then you just lie there nice and soft, all calm. But if he's drawing it out, dragging the switch so he tears off some skin, then you move your body toward him right along with the switch—understand? It's better that way!"

He winked at me with one of his dark, narrow eyes.

"I'm smarter than the chief detective when it comes to this! They've tanned my hide so many times you could use it for a pair of gloves!"

Looking at his cheerful face I remembered the stories my grandmother had told me of Ivan the prince, and Ivan the happy fool.

III

When I'd recovered, it became clear to me that the Gypsy occupied a unique place in the household. Grandfather yelled at him far less often than he did at his sons, and always with less rancor. In the Gypsy's absence he'd squeeze his eyes shut and shake his head, saying, "Ivan has hands of gold! Pure gold! Mark my words—he'll be no small man in this world!"

The uncles also addressed the Gypsy with affection and never "played a joke" on him the way they did the master craftsman, Grigory, for whom they devised some cruel and painful trick almost every evening: one day they would heat the scissors handles over the fire, the next they would put a nail point-side up on his chair or mix materials of different colors into his pile for sewing so that he, being half-blind, would work them into a single sheet—and be berated once again by grandfather.

Once while he slept on the stove bench after lunch in the kitchen, they painted his face with fuchsin, and he walked around that way for a long time, both funny and frightening. The round lenses of his glasses were like turbid spots above his grey beard, and his long nose, stained crimson as a tongue, seemed to droop dejectedly.

They never tired of these little tricks, and the master endured them all silently, only wheezing softly and wetting the tips of his fingers with saliva before touching the iron, the scissors, the thimble, or the pliers. This became a habit for him, and even at lunch he would lick his fingertips before picking up his fork or knife, stirring laughter among the children. When he was in pain, a wave of wrinkles passed over his large face, lifting his eyebrows and spreading strangely over his forehead until it disappeared somewhere on his bald pate.

I don't remember how my grandfather felt about the amusements that his sons devised, but grandmother would threaten them with her fist and shout:

"Shameless thugs! Miscreants!"

But when he wasn't nearby, the uncles spoke angrily even about the Gypsy, mocking him and deriding his work, attacking him for laziness and theft.

I asked my grandmother why they spoke this way. As always, she answered readily and clearly:

"You see, they both want Vanyushka for themselves, when each has his own dye shop. So they say he's a bad worker, run him down in front of each other. They're lying, just trying to trick each other. All the while they're afraid that Vanyushka won't go to work with either of them—that he'll just stay with grandfather. Your grandfather has his own set of rules, and he just might open up a third shop with the Gypsy—and that would be no good for your uncles—follow?"

She began to laugh quietly:

"They scheme and scheme, and God just laughs! And your grandfather sees all this scheming—he teases Yasha and Misha on purpose, says, 'I'll buy Ivan a recruiter's pass so they don't put him in the army—I need him here with me!' Then they start fuming—they don't want Ivan staying on with grandfather, but at the same time they don't want to spend the money themselves on getting him out of the army. Those passes are expensive!"

Grandmother and I were living in one room at that time, as we had on the steamer, and every evening before I went to sleep she told me a story or talked about her life, which itself resembled a children's tale. She spoke too about family affairs—the uncles' plans to split up all the household, grandfather's hopes of buying a new house for himself—and then her voice grew both amused and removed, as if she were speaking from somewhere far away—more like a neighbor than the second elder of the house.

I learned from her that the Gypsy was a foundling. On a rainy night in early spring they'd come across him on a bench near the gate to the house.

"He's lying there in a workman's apron," grandmother said, secretive, absorbed in her memories. "So frozen he barely peeps."

"Why do they throw children out?"

"The mother has no milk—no way to feed the child, so she finds out where a baby was born and died not long ago, then tries to slip her own in there. . . ."

She scratched her head without speaking for a little while and then went on, sighing as she stared at the ceiling.

"Being poor is all it is, Olyosha. Sometimes people are so poor there's nothing anyone can say. And they consider it shameful for an unwed girl to have a baby! Grandfather wanted to give Vanyushka to the police, but I talked him out of it. We'll take him for ourselves, I said. God's sent us this one in place of those who died. I'd given birth eighteen times, after all, and if they all had lived there'd be another whole street of people—eighteen houses! They gave me away to marry when I was thirteen, you see, and before my fifteenth year I'd already had my first baby. But then God took a liking to my blood—He loved my blood so much He kept taking and taking my little children to be angels. I didn't want to give them away, but I was glad for them to go to Him."

She sat on the edge of the bed in just a nightshirt with her long black hair falling all around her, huge and shaggy as the mother bear that a bearded man from the forest in Sergach had led into our courtyard a few days earlier. Making the sign of the cross over her breast, which was white and clean as snow, she shook with quiet laughter:

"He took the best for Himself and left the worst for me. Ivanka brought me so much joy! I love you little ones so much it hurts. And so we made him part of the family, christened him—and here he is, alive, good. I called him Bug at first because he buzzed all the time—he'd crawl around the room just buzzing like a bug. You should love him. He has a simple soul."

I did love him. And he often left me speechless with amazement.

After flogging the children for the various sins they'd committed during the week, grandfather would leave the house on Saturday for evening services—and then began a life of games in the kitchen, a life of levity that exceeds description. From behind the stove the Gypsy would catch black cockroaches. He'd quickly make a harness out of thread, and then four black horses would go cantering across the newly planed yellow surface of the kitchen table, drawing behind them a little sled he'd cut from paper while the Gypsy guided them with a thin piece of kindling, screeching with excitement:

"They've gone to get the bishop!"

Sometimes he'd stick a little piece of paper to the back of another cockroach and send it scurrying after the sled:

"They forgot a bag! Here comes a monk—he's running after them with it!"

Or he'd tie another roach's legs, and as it used its head to go tottering along the table's surface, the Gypsy would clap his hands and shout:

"The deacon's coming from the tavern to his evening services!"

He would show us young mice that stood and walked on their hind legs at his command, dragging their long tails behind them and blinking hilariously, their animated eyes shining like polished black beads. He was always very careful with the mice—he carried them in his breast pocket and even fed them sugar from his mouth. He would kiss them and declare, "It's good to share your house with mice. They're smart and tenderhearted, and the house spirit loves them. Whoever feeds a mouse will have the house spirit's favor."

He knew tricks with cards and money, and he shouted more than the other children, from whom he was virtually indistinguishable. Once the other children "made him the fool" several times in a row while playing cards. Deeply dejected, he quit the game and began to pout. "I know they were cheating," he complained, sniffling. "They were winking at each other, passing cards under the table! What kind of game is that! I can cheat as good as them. . . ."

He was nineteen years old, and he was bigger than the four of us put together.

But I remember him most on holiday evenings when grandfather and Uncle Mikhail went visiting. Then Uncle Yakov would appear in the kitchen with his disheveled curly hair and his guitar. Grandmother would serve tea with many different treats and vodka from the green *shtoff* bottle with red flowers formed in the glass on the bottom. The Gypsy wore his best clothes and spun like a top, and the master would slip quietly into the room, his dark spectacles glinting. The nursemaid Evgeniya would appear as well with her cunning eyes, her red, pockmarked face, her voice like a trumpet, and her body like a fat clay pot. Sometimes we were also joined by the local long-haired sexton or some other series of dark and slippery people who resembled eel pouts and pikes.

Everyone ate and drank a great deal, breathing heavily from the effort. The children were given special delicacies and sweet liquor. Gradually a powerful and strange exuberance would begin to warm us all.

Uncle Yakov would lovingly tune his guitar, then say the same words every time:

"Well, I'll start."

He shook his curly head and bent low over his instrument, stretching out his neck like a goose. His round, carefree face grew sleepy; an oily cloud dulled his lively, furtive eyes. Lightly plucking the strings, he'd begin to play a song so rousing it would force you to your feet.

His music demanded a tense silence. It flowed in hurried streams from some distant place, seeping through the floor and walls to agitate the heart and coax from it a restlessness, a sorrow that you couldn't understand. Under its influence you felt sorry for everyone—and for yourself as well. Even the grown-ups seemed small. Everyone sat motionless, walled off in pensive silence.

Uncle Mikhail's Sasha listened with particular intensity. His entire body seemed to stretch toward Yakov as he looked at the guitar, his mouth hanging open, a thread of saliva dangling from his lips. Sometimes he forgot himself so completely that he fell from his chair, his hands striking the floor. When this happened he would stay wherever he'd landed, his eyes wide and fixed.

Everyone sits motionless, enthralled. Only the samovar sings softly, distracting no one from the plaintive notes of the guitar. Two small, square windows peer out into the gloom of the autumn night. Someone softly taps on them from time to time. Sharp as spearheads, the yellow flames of two tallow candles sway on the table's surface.

Uncle Yakov seems more and more transfixed, holding his jaw firmly shut like a man deep in sleep. His hands alone lead a separate life, the bent fingers of the right trembling like an injured bird, fluttering and writhing over the sound hole while those of the left run along the guitar's frets in a blur.

Once he'd drunk a little, he would almost always start an endless song, his voice whistling unpleasantly as it passed through his clenched teeth:

If Yakov was a dog
He'd howl from dawn to dusk,
O, how dull it's all become!
O, what sorrow clings to me!
A nun comes down the street,
A crow sits on the fence,
    O, how dull it's all become!
A cricket sings behind the stove
And makes the roaches stir,
    O, how dull it's all become!
A beggar hangs his rags to dry
Another steals them from the line—
    O, how dull it's all become!
    O, what sorrow clings to me!

I couldn't bear this song. Whenever Yakov started singing about the beggars, my sorrow would overwhelm me, and I'd wind up sobbing uncontrollably.

· The Gypsy listened as raptly as the rest of us, staring into a corner of the room and breathing heavily, his fingers thrust deep into his mane of curly black hair. Sometimes he would suddenly exclaim in a mournful voice:

"If I just had a voice—God, how I'd sing!"

33

Grandmother would sigh and say, "Enough now, Yasha. You're tearing my heart apart. Why don't you dance a little, Vanyatka?"

They didn't always carry out her request right away, but sometimes the musician would still his guitar strings with the palm of his hand, then make a fist and fling away something soundless and invisible as he shouted in a blustery voice:

"Sadness and sorrow—enough! Vanka, let's go!"

The Gypsy would pull down his yellow shirt and straighten his clothes, then move to the center of the kitchen, stepping carefully, as if walking on nails while his dark cheeks blushed and he said,

"Only good and fast, Yakov Vasilich."

The guitar burst out at a furious pace, boot heels beat the floor in a staccato rhythm, dishes rattled in the cupboard and on the table, and in the center of the room the Gypsy shone like a flame, spread his arms wide apart like wings, and soared like a kite, his legs moving imperceptibly beneath him as he whooped, then crouched to the floor and shot like a golden swift around the room, lighting everything before him with the glow of his silk shirt, which seemed to burn and melt in shuddering streams.

The Gypsy danced tirelessly, losing himself so completely in the music that it seemed he might start off down the street if you opened the door for him—go dancing through the town to God knows where. . . .

Uncle Yakov would stamp his feet and cry, "He'll start a fire with those heels!" then whistle piercingly and shout out little rhymes in a grating voice:

If my shoes weren't worn so thin
I'd ditch my woman and her kin!

This brought people at the table to their feet; they too would begin to shout and shriek as if burned, while the bearded master slapped his palm against his bald head and rumbled something. Once he bent down to me, covering my shoulder with his soft beard, and spoke into my ear as if addressing an adult:

"If your father was here, Leksey Maksimych—he'd light a different fire! He was full of joy—a comfort to be near. Do you remember him?"

"No."

"Well, sometimes he danced with grandmother and—wait, hold on . . ."

He rose to his feet, tall and gaunt like a figure from an icon painting, and bowed toward grandmother, then began imploring her in an unusually husky voice:

"Akulina Ivanovna, do us a kindness! Make one pass for us! The way you used to do with Maksim Savvateich. Give us that comfort. . . ."

"Oh no, no—my dear Grigory Ivanych, my light. What dancing could there be for me now? It would only make people laugh," she said, laughing herself and shrinking away.

But everyone began to implore her, and suddenly she rose to her feet like a young girl. She smoothed out her skirt and pulled her shoulders back, raised high her heavy head and began to move around the kitchen as she shouted:

"But then—go ahead and laugh, it's good for you! Come on, Yasha, play it right for me!"

My uncle drew himself up and began to play more slowly than before, his eyes half closed, his shoulders raised. The Gypsy stopped for a moment, leaped once, then squatted and began to dance around grandmother as she floated noiselessly across the floor, spreading out her arms, her eyebrows raised, her dark eyes looking somewhere far into the distance. She looked silly to me, and I chortled; the master shook his finger sternly, and all the other adults looked reprovingly in my direction.

"Don't stamp, Ivan," the master said, smiling. The Gypsy jumped aside amenably and sat down on the threshold while the nursemaid Evgeniya began to sing in a low and pleasant voice, her Adam's apple bulging as she raised her chin:

All week long she makes her lace,
Right to Saturday without a break,
Until she's so worn out from weaving
As the bobbins click she's all but sleeping. . . .

Grandmother didn't dance so much as she told a story. At first her movements are slight; she's lost in thought, rocking a little as she moves, glancing all around from beneath her upraised arm. More and more she wavers, rocks with indecision, all of her great body seeming to sway as her feet feel their way cautiously along the floor. She stops and suddenly takes fright; her face begins to quaver and turn dark—but then, just as suddenly, it begins to shine with a kind and friendly smile. She reels to the side, as if to let a person pass, then guides someone away with her hand. She lowers her head and goes still, listening, her smile growing more and more radiant—and then she breaks from the place of her pausing, begins to reel and spin as if caught in a whirlwind, her figure growing taller and ever more graceful until she becomes so tender, so wildly beautiful that you cannot look away, and for a few minutes she returns, miraculously, to her youth.

And the nursemaid Evgeniya keeps on droning like a trumpet:

But Sunday after church she starts to dance,
All night long she whirls and prances,

35

Until the very last have left she stays—
How sad we have so little time to play!

Her dancing finished, grandmother returned to her seat near the samovar. Everyone praised her performance.

"Oh, enough already," she said, fixing her hair. "You just haven't seen real dancing. There was a girl in Balakhna—I can't remember her name or whose she was—but sometimes people wept with joy from watching her dance. Just look at her and there's a holiday for you—nothing more to ask for, nothing more to want. I envied her, sinner that I am."

"Singers and dancers are first among people," Evgeniya said sternly, and began singing something about King David while Uncle Yakov threw his arms around the Gypsy and said to him:

"You should dance at the inns! People would go out of their minds watching you!"

"I want a voice," the Gypsy complained. "I'd do anything if God would just let me sing for a good ten years—I'd even join the monastery after that!"

Everyone drank vodka—especially Grigory. Pouring him glass after glass, my grandmother would warn him:

"Careful, Grisha—you'll drink yourself blind."

He answered unwaveringly:

"Good. I don't need my eyes anymore. I've seen everything."

He drank and drank, but instead of getting drunk he grew only more loquacious. He almost always spoke to me of my father:

"Maksim Savvateich was a man of great heart—a dear friend. . . ."

Grandmother would sigh in agreement. "A true child of God. . . ."

All of this fascinated me, held me in a state of strained excitement, steeped my heart in a kind of quiet, inexhaustible sadness. Sadness and joy lived side by side in people, almost inseparably, replacing each other faster than anyone could understand or comprehend.

Once, while not yet very drunk, Uncle Yakov began to tear his shirt and pull violently at his curly hair, his thin blond mustache, his nose, and his drooping lower lip.

"What is this? What is it?" he howled, his tears pouring out. "Why this?"

Sobbing, he began to beat at his forehead, his cheeks and his chest.

"Villain! Swine! Poisoned soul!"

"Yes," Grigory snarled. "Yes—that's right!"

Far from sober herself, my grandmother began to talk him out of it, catching his hands as she spoke.

"That's enough, Yasha. . . . God knows best how to teach us."

She became even lovelier when she'd had a little to drink. The warm light of her soul seemed to pour from her dark, smiling eyes as she fanned her flushed cheeks with a handkerchief and said in her songlike voice, "Lord, dear Lord—how good it all is! No, just look how good it is!"

This was her heart's cry, her life's refrain.

I was shocked by the tears and shouts of my uncle, who before had seemed so carefree. I asked my grandmother why he cried and cursed and beat himself.

"You always have to know everything!" she said. Her unwillingness to answer me was out of keeping with her usual reaction to my questions. "Wait a little," she said. "It's still early for you to be poking around in that."

This stirred my curiosity even more. I went to the dye shop and latched onto Ivan, but he didn't want to answer me either. Looking at the master from the corner of his eye, he laughed quietly and pushed me out of the workspace, shouting:

"Go on—get out of here or I'll dye you—drop you right in the pot!"

The master was standing before three cauldrons cemented into the surface of a wide, low stove, stirring each pot and pausing to study the colored drops that slid from the end of the long, black mixing stick as he lifted it. The fire burned hotly, and in its variegated light the hem of his leather apron resembled a priest's vestments. The colored water hissed in the pots, and a cloud of acrid steam stretched to the door. In the courtyard snow was swirling along the ground in a fierce wind.

The master glanced at me from under his glasses. His eyes were red and cloudy.

"Firewood—can't you see!" he said gruffly to Ivan.

When the Gypsy ran out to the courtyard, Grigory sat down on a bag of sandalwood and motioned me toward him.

"Come here!"

He held me on his knees and began to talk, his warm, soft beard brushing my cheek. His words stayed with me.

"Your uncle beat his wife to death. Tortured her until there was nothing left. And now his conscience yanks at him—understand? You have to understand all of this. Pay attention—you won't make it otherwise."

Everything was simple with Grigory, the way it was with grandmother, but it was also frightening—he seemed to see through everything from behind his glasses.

"How did he do it?" he says unhurriedly. "Well, like this: he goes to bed with her and covers her with a blanket—puts it over her head. Squeezes her inside the blanket, beats her. What for? He himself doesn't know, I'd bet."

Ivan comes back with an armload of firewood and squats before the stove to warm his hands, but the master pays him no attention, doesn't pause in his staggering speech:

"Maybe he beat her because she was better than him and that made him jealous. The Kashirins, brother, do not love goodness—they envy it, but they can't accept it. They tear it out by the roots. You just ask your grandmother how they drove your father to his grave. She'll tell you everything. Your grandmother doesn't like deceit, doesn't understand lying. She's like a saint, even if she does drink and snort a little tobacco. It's like she's blessed. You hold tight to her!"

He pushed me away. I went into the yard, dejected and alarmed. Vanyushka caught up to me in the entranceway to the house and put his hands on my head, whispered quietly:

"Don't be afraid of him. He's kind. Just look him straight in the eye—he likes that."

It was all very strange and troubling. Although I knew no other life, I vaguely remembered that my mother and father did not live this way. They had another way of speaking, a different happiness. They always walked and sat together, side by side, close. They would often laugh for a long time in the evening. They would sit by the window and sing loudly, and people would gather to look at them. The upturned faces of those people were always funny to me—they reminded me of dirty plates after dinner. The people here laughed very little, and the cause of their laughter was often unclear. They shouted often at one another, threatened one another with something, whispered secretively in the corners of rooms. The children were quiet and inconspicuous, pressed flat to the earth like dust under rain. I felt alien in that household, and as if pricking me with a dozen different pins, life there kept me constantly off balance, made me wary and suspicious—made me study everyone with strained attention.

My friendship with Ivan was growing all the time. Grandmother was busy with household chores from sunrise until late at night, and I spent almost every day lingering around him. He continued as before to stick his hand out when grandfather switched me, complaining the next day as he showed me his swollen fingers:

"No, this is all just pointless! It's no better for you, and for me—just look! I'm not doing this anymore for you—enough already!"

And then, once more, he'd take on that pain he could so easily avoid.

"You said you didn't want to do that anymore."

"I didn't. I just stuck my hand out, somehow, without noticing. . . ."

Soon I learned another fact about the Gypsy that deepened even further the love and fascination I felt for him. Every Friday he put on a heavy hat and a knee-length sheepskin coat that he belted tightly with a green sash, harnessed my grandmother's favorite horse—a bay gelding named Sharap, who loved sweets and often acted like a mischievous child—and drove to the market in a wide sled to buy provisions.

Sometimes he'd be gone for a long time. Everyone in the house would begin to worry, walking up to the windows and breathing on the ice to melt away a little patch and look out at the street.

"Is he coming?"

"No."

My grandmother worried the most of all.

"You're going to kill a good man—and a good horse!" she told her husband and her sons. "Why aren't you ashamed of yourselves? Unrepentant thugs! Isn't what you have enough? Oh, what a dim-witted clan! Hoarders and misers . . . God will punish you."

"All right, all right," grandfather said gloomily. "It'll be the last time."

Sometimes the Gypsy would return only toward midday. My grandfather and uncles would hurry into the yard, followed by my grandmother, who was always out of sorts at that hour, moving ponderously as a bear and snorting her tobacco with sharp, bitter inhalations.

The children ran into the yard as well, and everyone began happily unloading the sled, which was packed with suckling pigs, poultry, fish, and meat of all sorts.

"Did you buy everything like I told you to?" grandfather asked, measuring the load with a quick, sidelong glance.

"Just like I was supposed to," the Gypsy called back happily. He began to warm himself by jumping around the courtyard and loudly clapping his mittens together.

"Don't bang your gloves around—they cost money!" grandfather said sternly. "Any change?"

"None."

Grandfather slowly walked around the cart and said quietly:

"You brought a lot again. But listen—you didn't get it without paying, did you? I don't want any of that going on!"

He walked off quickly, frowning.

The uncles rushed toward the mound of provisions and began whis-tling and exclaiming loudly as they weighed in their hands the poultry and fish, goose giblets, legs of veal, huge cuts of meat.

"You picked well!"

Uncle Mikhail was particularly excited, springing lightly around the pile of goods, smacking his lips elatedly and putting his nose to everything, like a woodpecker with its beak, his restless eyes narrowing in relish. He resembled his father with his wizened features, but he was taller, and black as burnt wood. Hiding his frozen hands in his sleeves, he began to question the Gypsy:

"How much did my father give you?"

"Five rubles."

"And all this is worth fifteen. How much did you pay?"

"Four and ten kopeks."

"Then you have ninety kopeks in your pocket. See, Yakov, how money grows around here?"

Wearing just a shirt in the bitter cold, Yakov chuckled softly as he squinted into the freezing blue sky.

"You share a little of that with us now, Vanya," he said lazily. "At least enough for a half-bottle."

Grandmother was unharnessing the horse. Shaking his thick mane, the huge Sharap nipped gently at her shoulder and then, glancing at her face with his playful eyes, pulled the silk headscarf from her hair.

"What is it, little one? Hmm, little kitten? You want to play? Go ahead, go ahead—God's glad for you."

Sharap shook the frost from his eyelashes and neighed softly.

"What are you after? A piece of bread?"

She slipped a large, well-salted crust between his teeth, then held her apron like a feed bag under his mouth, watching pensively as he ate.

The Gypsy bounded toward her, himself like a playful young horse.

"He's such a good horse, *babanya*—so smart!"

Grandmother stamped her foot. "Don't come wagging your tail around here," she shouted. "You know I don't like you on this day."

She explained to me that the Gypsy didn't buy so much as he stole at the market.

"Grandfather gives him five rubles and the Gypsy uses three to actually buy something, then steals another ten rubles' worth," she said unhappily. "He likes to steal, the little fool! He tried it once and it worked—fine. But they laughed about it and praised him for pulling it off, and he went and made stealing a habit. Your grandfather had his fill of poverty's bitter taste when he was young. Now he's grown greedy in his old age, and money's dearer to him than his own children. He's thrilled to get something for nothing. And Mikhail and Yakov . . ."

She waved her hand and fell silent for a moment. "This here, it's all a piece of lace, Lyonya," she added resentfully, looking at her open snuffbox. "A piece of lace sewn by a blind woman. How are we supposed to find a pattern in it all? They'll beat Ivan to death if they catch him stealing."

She fell silent again, then said quietly: "We have so many rules. So many rules and no reasons."

The next day I began to plead with the Gypsy to stop stealing.

"They'll beat you to death otherwise!"

"They can't get hold of me—I just keep slipping away. I'm tricky, and I've got a fast horse!" he said, smiling. But then he frowned sadly. "I know that stealing's bad—and dangerous. I just do it out of boredom. I don't even save the money—your uncles get it out of me before the week's over. It doesn't matter to me—go ahead and take the money! I've got what I need."

He suddenly picked me up and shook me gently in his arms.

"You're light and thin, but your bones are solid. You're going to be strong! You know what? You should learn to play guitar. Ask Uncle Yakov— really, you should! You're still small, that's the only problem. You're small but you're fierce. You don't like your grandfather much, do you?"

"I don't know."

"I don't like any of the Kashirins, other than *babanya*. Let a demon care for them!"

"And me?"

"You're not a Kashirin, you're a Peshkov. Different blood. Different clan."

Suddenly he hugged me tightly and all but moaned: "If I could just sing! If I had a voice—oh, what I'd do! I'd set people on fire! . . . But it's time for you to go now, brother. I have work to do."

He set me back on the floor, put a handful of little nails in his mouth, and began to spread a large, wet sheet of black material across a square board, nailing it down as he pulled it taut.

Soon he was dead.

It happened like this: A large oak cross with a thick, gnarled base lay leaning against the fence near the entrance to the courtyard. It had been lying there for a long time. I noticed it during my first days in the house—it was still yellow and new then, but during the fall it had turned black from the rain, and it reeked with the acrid scent of fumed oak. It was the last thing that anyone needed in that dirty, crowded yard.

41

Uncle Yakov had bought it for his wife's grave, and he vowed to carry the cross on his shoulder to the cemetery on the anniversary of her death.

That date fell on a Saturday in the early winter. It was cold and windy; snow scattered from the roofs. Everyone went out into the courtyard. Grandmother and grandfather had already left with three of the children for requiem at the graveyard, but I had been left behind as punishment for some sin or other.

Dressed in identical black sheepskin coats, the uncles raised the front end of the cross and stood under its arms while Grigory and someone I didn't know struggled to lift the base and set it on the Gypsy's broad shoulder. He stumbled, then set his feet apart.

"Too much?" Grigory asked.

"I don't know. Seems heavy."

"Open the gate, you blind devil!" Uncle Mikhail shouted angrily.

"Vanka, you should be ashamed," said Uncle Yakov. "We're both skinnier than you!"

As he opened the gate, Grigory warned the Gypsy sternly:

"Be careful—don't push yourself too far. Go with God."

"Balding old woman!" Uncle Mikhail shouted from the street.

Everyone in the courtyard laughed and talked loudly, seemingly glad that the cross was being taken away.

Leading me by the hand to the dye shop, Grigory Ivanovich said, "Maybe your grandfather won't switch you today. It looks like he's in a good mood."

In the shop he sat me on a pile of wool that had been brought for dying and carefully covered me up to my shoulders with it. He sniffed the steam rising from the cauldrons, then started speaking pensively.

"I've known your grandfather for thirty-seven years, my little friend. I saw him when the business started, and now I'm here watching him as it ends. We were friends before—we thought this business up together, started it together. He's a smart man, your grandfather. He went ahead and made himself boss while I just wasn't sharp enough. But the Lord is wiser than us all. He just smiles, and in an instant the very smartest man among us takes his place among fools. You don't understand just yet why certain things are being said or done, but you need to understand it all. An orphan has a hard life. Your father, Maksim Savvateich, was an ace—always ahead of the game. That's why your grandfather didn't like him, never took to him. . . ."

It was pleasant to listen to those kind words while watching the red and golden fire playing in the stove, a milky cloud of steam rising from the pots, coating with dove-grey rime the ceiling's slanted rafters, between

42

which blue ribbons of sky showed through rough cracks. The wind settles down, and somewhere the sun shines. The entire yard looks as if it's been dusted with ground glass. Sled runners squeal in the street. Blue smoke twists from the chimneys. Light shadows slip across the snow, tell a story of their own.

Tall and bony, bearded, big-eared, hatless—Grigory stirs the boiling dye like some benevolent wizard and never stops instructing me:

"Look everyone straight in the eye. . . . If a dog starts to rush at you, you do just the same to him—he'll back down. . . ."

His heavy glasses pinch the bridge of his nose; its tip is filled with dark blue blood, resembling my grandmother's.

"Wait, what's that?" he said suddenly. He listened to something outside, then kicked the stove door shut and ran leaping across the courtyard. I raced after him.

The Gypsy was lying on his back on the floor in the middle of the kitchen. Wide strips of light fell on him from the windows—one on his head and chest, another on his legs. His forehead shone strangely, and his narrow eyes stared fixedly at the black ceiling, his brows raised high. Pink bubbles slid from his quivering dark lips while blood ran from the corners of his mouth, flowed down his cheeks and neck onto the floor. It was running in thick streams from under his back as well. His legs were awkwardly splayed, and you could see that his wide pants were wet—they stuck heavily to the floorboards. The floor had been recently scrubbed with gravel, and now it shone like the sun. The streams of blood crossed the strips of light from the windows and stretched toward the room's threshold. They were very bright.

The Gypsy didn't move. His arms were stretched along his sides and only his fingers twitched, grabbing at the floor, his dye-discolored fingernails flashing in the sun.

The nursemaid Evgeniya squatted beside Ivan and placed a thin candle in his hand. Ivan held it for a moment, but then the candle fell over. Its flame went out in the blood. The nursemaid picked it up and dried it off with the end of her apron, tried again to make it stay in his restless fingers. A powerful whispering rose like a strong wind in the kitchen. It felt like it would sweep me from the threshold of the room, but I clung tightly to the door latch.

"He stumbled," Uncle Yakov was saying in a kind of expressionless voice, twitching and turning his head as he spoke. He was completely grey and haggard. His eyes looked faded; they blinked all the time.

"He fell and it crushed him—hit him in the back. It would have smashed us too, but we threw it off in time."

43

"You crushed him," Grigory said blankly.

"What? How?"

"You did it!"

The blood was still flowing. At the threshold it had already gathered in a puddle, turned dark, and seemingly begun to rise. The Gypsy mumbled as if asleep, and pink froth came from between his lips. He was melting, growing flatter and flatter, sticking to the floor, disappearing into it.

"Mikhail went by horseback to get father from church," whispered Yakov. "I piled him in a cab and came here as fast as I could. It's good I didn't take the base, or that'd be . . ."

The nursemaid was trying to make the candle stay in Ivan's hand again, dripping wax and tears on his palm.

"Stick it on the floor near his head, you fool!" Grigory said in a loud, harsh voice.

"Oh . . ."

"And take his hat off!"

The nursemaid removed Ivan's hat and his head knocked dully against the floor, then rolled to the side. The blood began to flow more thickly then, but from just one side of his mouth. It went on for a terribly long time. At first I kept waiting for the Gypsy to finish resting, sit up and spit, say:

"Ugh, it's hot in here!"

This is what he usually did on Sunday afternoons, waking up from a nap after lunch. But now he didn't get up. He just kept melting. The sun had already left him; the light strips had grown short and now lay only on the windowsills. He was turning completely dark. His fingers no longer twitched. The foam was gone from his lips. Three candles had been placed on the floor around his head—one at each ear and one at the top of the arc that they formed. Waving their small gold wicks in the dark, they shone on his shaggy blue-black hair, cast little pools of trembling light on his dark cheeks, caught the tip of his sharp nose and his pink lips in their glow.

The nursemaid knelt and wept, whispering:

"My tender little hawk. My heart . . ."

It was frightening and cold. I crawled under the table to hide. And then a crowd burst into the room—grandfather in a coat of raccoon fur, grandmother in a cloak with fox tails hanging from the collar, Uncle Mikhail, the children, many strangers. . . .

Grandfather threw his coat on the floor and began to shout:

"Swine! What a man you've ruined for nothing! He'd have no equal in five year's time!"

The coats strewn on the floor blocked my view of Ivan, so I climbed out from under the table and wound up at grandfather's feet. He threw me out of his way and began threatening the uncles with his small red fist:

"Wolves!"

Then he sat down on the bench, bracing himself with both hands, and started to sob dryly.

"I know," he said in a rasping voice. "He caught in your throats, I know. Akh, Vanyushechka. . . . Little fool! . . . What can you do? What can anyone do? . . . We're left with rotting reins and a stranger's horse. . . . God's had no love for us these last years, has He mother? Mother?"

Grandmother had collapsed onto the floor. She pressed her hands to Ivan's face, his head and chest. She breathed into his eyes, grabbed his hands and kneaded them, knocked over all the candles. Then she rose heavily to her feet, all black in a shiny black dress. She held her eyes terrifyingly wide open. She spoke in a soft voice:

"Out, all of you. Accursed."

Everyone but grandfather left.

They buried the Gypsy with little fuss, forgettably.

IV

I'm lying in a wide bed, wrapped four times in a heavy blanket, listening to grandmother pray. Kneeling, she presses one hand to her chest and occasionally crosses herself, unhurriedly, with the other.

The frost crackles sharply outside. The moon's greenish light peers through the ice-patterned panes of the window, illuminates her kind face and her generous nose, glows like phosphorescence in her dark eyes. The silk headscarf covering her hair glints like thinly hammered tin. Her dark dress rustles when she moves, streaming from her shoulders, pooling on the floor.

Her prayers finished, she undresses silently, places her clothes carefully on top of the trunk in the corner, and comes to bed, where I pretend to be sound asleep.

"You're just fooling now, aren't you, my little thief?" she says softly. "You aren't sleeping now, are you, my soul? Well, come on—let's have a little of that blanket!"

Anticipating what's to come, I can't suppress a smile.

"Aha," she growls. "You've set out to trick your poor old grand-mother!"

She takes hold of the blanket's edge and yanks it with such skill and strength that I'm sent spinning into the air, then land with a plop on the soft feather bed.

"Oh, you son of a radish!" she laughs loudly. "What happened? Swallow a mosquito?"

But sometimes she prays for such a long time that I really do fall asleep and don't hear her come to bed.

Long prayers always cap days of disappointment, arguments, and fights. It's always interesting to listen to them, because grandmother tells God in detail about everything that's happened in the house. Her kneeling figure like a great mound in the dark, she whispers quickly and indistinctly at first, but then her voice grows into a steady rumbling:

"You know Yourself, Lord, how each wants the best for himself. Mikhail is older, after all, and so it should be him who stays in town. It's hurtful for him to be the one that moves across the river, and it's a new place there—untested. No one knows what will come of it. But father, well, he loves Yakov more. Is it really right to love your children differently? The old man's stubborn. You'd do right, Lord, to make him see a little reason."

She raises her large, shining eyes to the dark icons and gives her God advice:

"You send him a good dream, Lord, so he sees how to divide things up fairly for his children."

She crosses herself and bows, beats her large forehead against the floor, then straightens herself once again, begins to speak imposingly:

"You might smile with a little joy on Varvara, too! What's she done to make You so angry? Why are her sins so much worse than others'? What's that—a young woman, healthy—and she lives her life in sorrow! And remember Grigory, Lord—his eyes just get worse and worse. He'll go blind and be left to wander as a beggar through the world—that's no good at all. He's spent all his strength for grandfather—and will grandfather really help him in the end? O Lord, Lord . . ."

She falls silent for a long time, her head and arms lowered submissively, as if she's frozen or asleep.

"What else?" she wonders out loud, knitting her brow as she tries to remember. "Save all the Russian Orthodox, please. And forgive me, accursed fool that I am. You know I don't sin from evil but from stupid thinking."

She lets out a deep sigh, then speaks with tender satisfaction:

"You know everything, my darling one. You see everything, dear Father."

I found grandmother's God, who seemed so close to her, extremely appealing, and I would often ask her:

"Tell a story about God."

She had a particular way of talking about him—invariably sitting, her voice very quiet, her eyes half closed, her words strangely drawn out. She rises up, sits down, covers her hair with a headscarf, then starts to tell a long, long story—one that lasts until you fall asleep:

"God sits on a hill in a meadow in heaven, on a throne of blue sapphires under silver limes, and the lime trees bloom year round: heaven has no fall or winter, and the flowers never fade, never tire of blossoming and giving joy to all the saints. Like snow, like bees in a swarm, the angels fly in multitudes around Him—like white pigeons they fly down from heaven to the earth and then back again to heaven to tell God about us, about people. There's one for you and me and grandfather—every person has an angel, for God sees everyone the same. Here your angel comes to God and says, 'Leksey stuck his tongue out at grandfather.' And God commands: 'Let the old man flog him then.' So it is with everything and everyone—every day He delivers us our due. For some it's joy, for others grief. And everything's so good with God that the angels play and entertain themselves. They flutter their wings and never stop singing to Him, 'Glory to Thee, God, glory to Thee!' and He, the dear, just smiles, as if to say, 'Enough already.'"

She smiles herself, shaking her head.

"Did you see that?"

"I didn't see it, but I know," she answers pensively.

Speaking about God, heaven, and angels, she became small and meek; her face grew young, and a particularly warm light seemed to stream from her damp eyes. I would take her heavy satin braids in my hands, wrap them around my neck, and lie motionless, listening carefully to those endless stories, never growing tired of them.

"It's not given to a person to see God—you'd be blinded. Only saints can look at Him direct. But I have seen angels. They show themselves when the soul is clean. I was standing in church at early service and here come two just like a mist at the altar—you can see right through them and they're light, light, light, with wings right down to the floor, all lace and muslin. They walk around the communion table and help Father Ilya, the old priest. He lifts his old, worn-out arms to pray to God and they prop up his elbows. He was awfully old—all blind and always bumping into things; he died a little while after that. I almost fainted with joy when I saw them there. My heart ached, and I was all in tears—oh, how wonderful it was, Lyonka, my soul! How good are all God's works, both in heaven and on earth—how good it is!"

"Is it really good here?"

Grandmother made the sign of the cross over herself and said:

"Yes, it is. Praise the Holy Mother—it is good!"

This confused me. It was hard to accept that everything was good in our home. To me it seemed that life there was growing worse and worse. Once while passing Uncle Mikhail's open door, I'd seen Aunt Natalya rushing around the room dressed all in white, her arms pressed to her chest.

"Gather me in, dear God," she cried out. Her voice wasn't loud, but it was terrible. . . . "Take me to You."

I understood that prayer, just as I understood Grigory when he'd say:

"I'll go blind and wander the world, live on what I'm given. That'll be better than this."

49

I wanted him to go blind as soon as possible, for I planned to convince him to take me as his guide—we would wander through the world together. I even mentioned this to him.

"Well, all right then—let's go," the master said, smiling into his beard. "I'll tell them in town that you're the grandson of Vasily Kashirin, head of the dyers' guild. That should go down well."

More than once I'd seen Aunt Natalya's yellow face with puffy lips, a dark blue swelling under her empty eyes.

"Does my uncle beat her?" I asked my grandmother.

"He beats her, secretly, the wretch," she answered, sighing. "Grandfather forbids him to do it, so he beats her at night. He's vicious, and she's mild as milk pudding."

She grows animated as she talks about it:

"Still, they don't beat us like they used to! Maybe they hit you in the mouth or on the ear, pull your braid a bit. But before they'd torture you for hours! Once grandfather beat me from morning service until evening on the first day of Easter. He'd beat me a little, get tired, take a rest—then start again. With reins—whatever else he found. . . ."

"What for?"

"Oh, I don't remember. Another time he beat me half to death and didn't let me eat for five days straight. I barely came through that. And another time. . . ."

This astounded me. Grandmother was twice the size of grandfather. It was impossible to believe that he could overcome her.

"Is he really stronger than you?"

"Not stronger—older. And my husband. God will make him answer for the things he does to me, but I'm commanded to submit."

It was pleasant and interesting to watch her wipe the dust from the icons, clean the metal casings molded over the figures. They were opulent icons, with halos made of pearls and colored stones and silver. She'd take one down with her quick hands and look at it smiling, say tenderly:

"What a darling face."

She kisses it and crosses herself.

"So much dust. And all stained with smoke—ah you, Mother and helper of all, unfading joy! Look, Lyonya dear, how delicate the lines are drawn. The figures are all tiny, but every one of them's made separate. This one's called 'The Twelve Great Feasts.' That one in the center is the 'Fyodorovskaya Holy Mother,' and this one's called, 'Weep Not for Me, O Mother.'"

Sometimes it seemed to me that she played with her icons as earnestly as my invalid cousin Katerina played with her dolls.

She saw devils quite often—both in groups and out alone.

"I'm going past the Rudolfs' house one night during Lent. It's a clear night and the moonlight's strong. All of a sudden I see one sitting there, on top of the house, straddling the roof near the chimney. He leans his head with its horns over the chimney and sniffs, snorts—a big one, all black and hairy. He's sniffing and running his tail back and forth, dragging it over the roof. I made the sign of the cross before him. 'Let God arise and let His enemies be scattered!' I say, and all of a sudden he lets out a little yelp, goes tumbling head over heels down from the roof into the courtyard. Scattered! The Rudolfs must have been cooking meat during the Fast—he was so excited, sniffing it. . . ."

I laugh, picturing the devil falling head over heels from the roof into the courtyard, and she laughs as well, saying:

"They love to get into trouble—they're just like little children. Once I was doing the wash in the bathhouse, and the time got to midnight. All of a sudden the stove doors come flying open! And they start pouring out of there—one smaller than the next. Little red ones, green ones, some black as cockroaches. I try for the door, but there's no getting past. I'm surrounded by demons! They pack the entire bathhouse—you can't even turn around there's so many. They get underfoot, yank on me, crowd me so tight I can't even cross myself. They're all furry and soft, hot—like little kittens only they all walk on their hind legs. They whirl around, raise havoc everywhere, bare their little mouse-teeth. They have green eyes, and their horns are just starting to poke through, like little bumps on their heads—and they have the tails of pigs! O Father! I must have blacked out then. And when I come back to myself, the candle's barely burning, the water in the washtub's cold, and all the washing's scattered on the floor. 'Akh,' I think. 'May you all be blown off the mountain!'"

I close my eyes and see a thick stream of those brightly colored, furry creatures spilling from the mouth of the stove. They stream over its grey cobblestones to fill the little bathhouse. They blow at the candle flame, stick out their pink tongues like unruly children. This too is funny, but also frightening. Grandmother shakes her head without speaking for a minute, then suddenly grows bright again, like a flame given fuel.

"I've seen the damned as well. That was at night too. In winter, during a snowstorm. I was going through Dyukov Gully where, remember, I said Yakov and Mikhail wanted to drown your father in an ice hole in the pond? Well, I was walking there—I'd just plunked down at the bottom of the trail—and oh, what whistling and shouting starts in the gully! I look and a black troika's flying right at me. A burly devil in a red cap's driving it. He's standing on the driver's box, sticking up like a post with his arms stretched out, reins made of chains in his hands. There's no room for a sled to get through that gully, and the troika all but disappears in the snow clouds as it goes flying toward the pond. It's all devils riding in the sled too—whistling and waving their caps. Seven sleds must have passed me, flying like a fire brigade. All of them were pulled by black horses—except these horses were people—people who'd been damned by their mothers and fathers. Devils use those people for amusement. They ride them and drive sleds with them at night during their holidays. It was probably a demon wedding that I saw. . . ."

It was impossible not to believe grandmother—she spoke so simply, so convincingly.

There was a poem about the Holy Mother that she recited particularly well. It told of the Holy Mother passing through the torments of this world and exhorting the Bandit Princess, Engalycheva, to cease her killing and her robbing of the Russian people. Grandmother could recite poems about the Holy Man Aleksey and Ivan the Warrior as well. She knew stories about Wise Vasilisa, about the priest who turned into a goat, about the peasant child who sat on God's throne. And she told terrible legends about Marfa of Novgorod; about Baba Usta, the ataman of a robber gang; about Maria, the sinner of Egypt; about the great sorrows suffered by the bandit's mother. There was no end to the stories and the legends and the poems she knew.

Undaunted by people, grandfather, devils, and other dark powers, she suffered a horror of black cockroaches, sensing their presence even at great distances. She would wake me at night, whispering:

"Olyosha, darling, there's a cockroach crawling around. Go and kill it in the name of Christ, huh?"

I would sleepily light a candle and crawl around the floor, searching for our enemy. Sometimes the search went on for a long time—sometimes it failed completely.

"There's nothing here," I'd say, and she, lying motionless, her head buried under the blanket, would beg almost inaudibly:

"Oh, he's there! Please, look again. I'm begging you—he's there, I know. . . ."

She was never wrong; eventually I'd find a cockroach somewhere far from the bed.

"Did you kill it? Well, glory to God! And thank you. . . ."

Then she'd pull the blanket from her head and sigh with relief, smile.

But if I didn't find the insect, she couldn't fall asleep. I could feel her body shuddering at the slightest rustling in the dead silence of the night, could hear her whisper with bated breath:

"Near the doorway. . . . He crawled under the trunk. . . ."

"Why are you afraid of cockroaches?"

Her answer was well reasoned:

"It doesn't make sense to me—what are they for? They're always crawling around, all black. God gave a purpose to every little flea. A wood louse means it's damp in the house. A bedbug means the walls are dirty. If a person gets lice you know he'll soon be ill—it all makes sense. But those— who knows what power lives in them, what they've been sent to do?"

Once as she knelt and talked intimately with God, grandfather threw open the door.

"Well, mother!" he said hoarsely. "God's paid a visit—we're on fire!"

"What are you saying!" shouted grandmother. She leaped to her feet and they both raced into the darkness of the big front room, their footsteps pounding heavily.

"Evgeniya, take down the icons! Natalya, dress the children!" grand-mother ordered in a stern voice while grandfather let out a thin howl:

"E-e-e-e-e-e . . ."

I ran into the kitchen. The window on the courtyard gleamed like gold. Yellow spots spilled onto the floor and slipped along its surface. Pulling on his boots, Uncle Yakov hopped barefoot among them, as if they were burning his soles.

"Mishka did it!" he shouted. "Set it on fire and left!"

"Not now, you hound!" grandmother said, pushing him toward the door so hard he almost fell.

Through the frost on the windows I could see the burning roof of the dye shop, and through its open door the whirling, twisting fire. Its red flow-ers were blooming with no smoke in the quiet night—only high above them did a dark cloud sway, and even it left clear the silver stream of the Milky Way. The snow shone purple while all the walls of the buildings trembled and heaved, as if straining to reach that hot corner of the courtyard where the fire played happily, flooding the wide cracks in the studio walls with red, or poking out from them like mangled, scalding nails. Red and golden ribbons quickly wrapped themselves around the roof, coiling along its dark, dry rafters while the studio's thin, tiled chimney still rose promi-nently amid the flames, smoking heavily. A quiet crackling, a rustling like silk seemed to beat against the windowpane as the fire grew thicker and thicker. Richly decorated with its flames, the dye shop now resembled the icon wall of a church. Invincible, it beckoned me.

I threw a heavy sheepskin coat over my head, stuck my feet in some-one's boots, went clomping through the vestibule and out onto the porch, where immediately I fell into a daze, blinded by the fire's brilliant revelry, deafened by its crash and the cries of my grandfather, Grigory, and my uncle—and terrified by the sight of my grandmother as she threw an empty sack over her head, wrapped a horse blanket around her shoulders, and plunged into the fire, shouting:

"The vitriol, you fools! The vitriol will explode!"

"Hold her back, Grigory," grandfather howled. "Oh God, she's lost!"

But then she reemerged, shaking her head, all her body stooped and smoking as she carried in her outstretched arms a small drum of vitriol.

"Father, get the horse out!" she shouted, coughing and wheezing. "Get this off me! Can't you see it's burning?"

Grigory pulled the smoldering blanket from her shoulders and, stooping low, began frantically shoveling large chunks of snow through the door of the dye shop. My uncle leaped around him with an axe in his hand while grandfather ran after my grandmother, dousing her with snow. She thrust the drum of vitriol into a snow bank, then ran to open the gate. Bowing to the people who rushed in, she said:

"Save the storehouse, neighbors. If it jumps over to the storehouse, to the hayloft, it'll burn us to the ground and then start on you. Tear the roof down! Throw the hay in the garden! Grigory, get the snow up higher—why are you aiming at the floor? Yakov, do something useful—get these people shovels and axes! Respected neighbors, all as one now—let us work together with God's help!"

She was as fascinating as the fire itself, illuminated by flames that seemed to grasp at her as she raced, all black, around the courtyard, appearing everywhere at once, giving everyone commands, seeing everything.

Sharap ran into the courtyard, rearing up on his hind legs and tossing grandfather to the side. The fire's light struck his eyes and made them flash red as the horse snorted and thrust his front legs straight out against the ground. Grandfather let go of the lead rope and jumped away, shouting:

"Hold him, mother!"

She rushed up to the horse as he reared once more and stood before him with her arms spread wide; he whinnied plaintively and stretched toward her, watching flames from the corner of his eye.

"Now, don't you be afraid!" grandmother said in a deep voice, patting his neck and taking the lead rope. "Would I leave you in all this trouble? My little mouse . . ."

Three times her size, the little mouse quietly followed her to the gate, snorting as he looked at her red face.

The nursemaid Evgeniya brought the children from the house. Wrapped up against the cold, they mumbled indistinctly.

"Vasily Vasilich!" Evgeniya shouted. "Leksey isn't here!"

"Come on, come on!" shouted grandfather, waving his hand while I hid behind the porch steps to keep from being led away.

The roof of the studio had already collapsed. The thin poles of its rafters jutted into the sky, smoking, glittering with golden embers. Whirling streams of red, dark blue, and green flames exploded with cracks and howls inside the building, the blaze billowing in sheaves onto the courtyard and the people crowded before the great fire, throwing snow on it with shovels. The cauldrons boiled furiously in the flames inside the studio, releasing thick clouds of smoke and steam. Strange smells enveloped the courtyard, filling our eyes with tears. I came out from under the porch and wound up right at grandmother's feet.

"Get out of here!" she shouted. "They'll trample you—get out of here!"

A rider wearing a copper helmet with a crest burst into the courtyard, his roan horse spraying foam as the rider raised high his whip and roared:

"Make way!"

Bells rang out hurriedly, lightheartedly, and everything took on a festive kind of beauty.

"Who am I talking to?" grandmother said, pushing me toward the porch. "Get out of here!"

It was impossible to disobey her at that moment. I went into the kitchen and again pressed myself against the window, but the fire was no longer visible beyond the dark mass of people—just copper helmets flashed among peaked caps and black winter hats.

They quickly pressed the fire down, poured water all over it, trampled it into the ground. The police drove off the people, and grandmother came into the kitchen.

"Who's there? You? You're not asleep? Too frightened? There's no need to be afraid now, everything's over."

She sat down next to me and fell silent, rocking slightly. It was good the quiet night and the darkness had come back, but I was sorry that the fire was gone.

Grandfather came inside and stood at the room's threshold.

"Mother?"

"Ahh?"

"You burnt?"

"Not much."

He struck a sulfur match, and its blue flame lit up his polecat face, covered in soot. He found a candle on the table and slowly sat down next to grandmother.

"You might wash," she said, herself covered in soot and reeking of bitter smoke.

Grandfather sighed. "God still grants you favor now and then—gives you wisdom," he said. He stroked her shoulder, then added through his bared teeth: "He gives it to you for a little while—an hour maybe."

Grandmother smiled too and wanted to say something, but grandfather began to frown.

"I should clear Grigory out!" he said. "This is his carelessness. He's no use anymore—worn out! . . . Yashka's sitting out there on the porch, sobbing, the idiot. You might go to him. . . ."

She rose and left, holding her hand in front of her mouth, blowing on it. Without looking at me, grandfather asked quietly:

"Did you see the whole fire—from the start? Your grandmother was something, eh? An old woman. All broken, beaten down. . . . Uh-uuh. . . . Just look at her. Just look. . . . Akh, yo-u . . ."

He bent over and sat without speaking for a long time, then rose to his feet.

"Were you afraid?" he asked, picking snuff from the candle with his fingers.

"No."

"That's right—there was nothing to be afraid of."

He angrily yanked off his shirt and walked toward the washbasin in the corner. There in the dark he stamped his foot and said loudly:

"A fire's just stupidity! You should take whoever suffers in a fire and beat him with a whip on the square! He's a fool—or else a thief! That's what you should do—there wouldn't be any more fires then! Go to bed. What are you sitting around for?"

I went to bed, but I never managed to sleep that night. As soon as I got under the covers, an inhuman howl sent me leaping to my feet. Again I rushed into the kitchen. Grandfather was standing in the middle of the room, shirtless, a candle trembling as he held it with both hands. He shuffled his feet along the floor without moving from his place and wheezed:

"Mother, Yakov—what is that?"

I jumped onto the stove and squeezed into a corner. A great commotion like that which had surrounded the fire began once more. The oppressive howling rose in waves, beat against the ceiling and the walls, steadily growing louder. Grandfather and my uncle seemed delirious as they ran around the kitchen while grandmother shouted and tried to drive them away. Grigory crammed firewood into the stove with a great crash, then filled cast iron pots with water, and walked around the kitchen, swinging his head back and forth like a camel from Astrakhan.

"Heat the stove up first," grandmother ordered.

Rushing to get the kindling from the top of the stove, Grigory grabbed my leg. "Who's that?" he shouted uneasily. "Akh, you startled me. You're everywhere you're not supposed to be."

"What's going on out there?"

"Aunt Natalya's giving birth," he said indifferently, jumping back down to the floor.

It occurred to me that my mother never shouted like that when she was in labor.

Grigory put the pots on to boil and climbed back up on the stove to sit next to me. He took a clay pipe from his pocket and showed it to me.

"I'm starting to smoke for my eyes. Grandmother told me to snort tobacco, but I think smoking will be better."

He sat with his legs dangling over the edge of the stove, looking down at the candles' poor light. His ear and cheek were smudged with soot. His shirt was torn at the side, and I could see his ribs, wide as the hoops of a barrel. One of his lenses was broken; half the glass had fallen from the frame, and his red, damp eye showed like a wound through the hole. Packing leaf tobacco into his pipe, he listened to the moans of the woman in labor and began to mutter incoherently, as if drunk:

"Grandmother got burned, though. . . . How's she supposed to deliver it? My, how she groans! We forgot about her. She was starting to twist up at the very start of the fire, they said, from all the fear. . . . Just think how hard it is to give birth to a person—and women aren't respected! You remember—always respect women, mothers I mean."

I dozed a little, then woke up once more to tumult, slamming doors, Uncle Mikhail's drunken shouts, and strange words entering my head:

"We have to get the altar doors opened. . . ."

"Give her oil from the icon lamp with rum and soot—half a glass of oil, half a glass of rum, and a tablespoon of soot. . . ."

Uncle Mikhail demanded with grating insistence:

"Let me take a look at her!"

He sat on the floor with his legs spread wide apart, spitting straight ahead and slapping his palms on the floor. It had grown unbearably hot on the stove, and I began to climb down. When I drew level with Uncle Mikhail, he grabbed my leg and pulled so that I fell and hit the back of my head on the floor.

"Idiot," I said to him.

He leaped to his feet, grabbed me again, and began to roar as he swung me around:

"I'll smash you on the stove! . . ."

I came to in the front room, in the corner under the icons, lying in grandfather's lap. Looking up at the ceiling, he rocked me and said softly:

"We'll see no forgiveness, not one of us. . . ."

The icon lamp glowed brightly above his head, and a candle burned on a table in the middle of the room; a dull winter morning already hung outside the window. Grandfather leaned over me and asked, "What hurts?"

Everything hurt. My head was damp and my body weighted down, but everything surrounding me was so strange that I didn't want to talk about it. On almost every chair sat an unfamiliar person—a priest in lilac robes, a grey old man in glasses and military dress, and many others, all of them sitting motionless, like something carved from wood, frozen in expectation, as they listened to the splash of water somewhere nearby. Uncle Yakov stood in the doorway, hiding his hands behind his back as he stretched.

"Well, take this one to bed," grandfather said to him.

Uncle Yakov motioned me toward him with his finger and started tiptoeing to grandmother's room. When I climbed into bed, he whispered:

"Your aunt died—Natalya."

It didn't surprise me. She'd lived invisibly for a long time already, never coming to the kitchen or the table.

"Where's grandmother?"

My uncle waved his hand. "There," he said, and tiptoed away in his bare feet.

I lay in bed looking around. Grey, blind faces full of hair were pressed against the window panes. Grandmother's dress was hanging in the corner over the trunk—I knew that—but now it seemed that someone alive was hiding there and waiting. I buried my head under the pillow and watched the room with just one eye. I wanted to leap up from the bed and run away. It was hot. A thick, heavy scent made it hard to breathe, made me think of how the Gypsy died and the little streams of blood ran across the floor. Something was swelling, growing larger and larger in my head or heart. Everything I saw in the house was moving through me in a chain, like sleds passing down the street in a line, crushing me, grinding me down to nothing. . . .

The door opened very slowly, and grandmother came into the room. She pushed the door shut with her shoulder and leaned her back against it. She stretched her hands toward the dark blue flame that always burned in the icon lamp. She said in a quiet, plaintive, childlike voice:

"My hands hurt. . . . My hands."

V

Toward spring the uncles made their division. Yakov stayed in town and Mikhail moved across the river. Grandfather bought himself a large, interesting house on Polevaya Street, with a tavern on the ground floor, which was made of stone; a pleasant little room in the attic; and a garden that descended into a densely overgrown ravine, bristling with the bare limbs of willow bushes.

"All these switches, eh?" grandfather said, winking happily at me when I went with him to look at the garden and walk along the soft paths of thawing earth. "I'll start to teach you reading soon, so they'll be useful."

The entire building was filled with lodgers. Grandfather kept one large room for himself and for receiving visitors on the top floor; grandmother and I settled in the attic. Its window opened onto the street, and if you bent out over the sill during evenings and holidays you could watch the drunks stumbling from the tavern, swaying along the street, shouting and toppling over. Sometimes they were flung into the street like sacks, only to rise and try to force their way back into the tavern, pounding on the door so hard it banged and rattled and its hinges squealed until a fight broke out. Watching all of this from up above was extremely entertaining.

In the morning grandfather drove out to his sons' studios to help them settle in. He would return in the evening, tired, depressed, and angry. Grandmother cooked, sewed, tended to the orchard and the garden, whirled around all day like a huge top driven by an invisible lash. She'd sniff a pinch of tobacco, sneeze vigorously, and, wiping the sweat from her face, call out:

"Hello, you lovely world! Hello! May you keep well for all of time! Well now, Olyosha, my soul—just look! We've begun a quiet life! Everything's worked out just wonderfully. Glory to You, Holy Mother!"

But it didn't seem to me that we were living quietly. From morning until late evening the lodgers' wives would scurry and fuss around the courtyard and the house. Neighbors constantly appeared at our door. Someone was always running somewhere, late and gasping; someone was always preparing for something and calling out:

"Akulina Ivanovna!"

Smiling at everyone with equal tenderness, extending to all the same gentle attention, Akulina Ivanovna would use her large finger to stick one more pinch of tobacco in each nostril, neatly wipe her hand and her nose with a red checkered handkerchief, and say:

"To treat lice, madam, you must wash more often in the bath and use mint in the steam. If the lice get under your skin, you should take a tablespoon of the best goose fat you can find, a teaspoon of corrosive powder, and three drops of mercury; mix it all together seven times in a saucer with a piece of glazed earthenware; then rub it on yourself. If you use a wooden spoon or bone, you'll lose the mercury. And avoid copper or silver—they're very harmful!"

Sometimes she would say pensively to someone seeking advice:

"I can't answer you, my dear. You'd better go to the monastery at Pechory, to Father Asaf, a *skhimnik* there. . . ."

She served as midwife, sorted out family arguments and quarrels, treated ailing children, and recited "The Virgin's Dream" from memory so that other women could learn it for their "good luck." She gave advice on managing a household too:

"The cucumber will tell you all by itself when it's ready to be pickled. When it smells only like a cucumber—not dirt or anything else—then you take it. . . . You have to insult *kvas*—make it good and angry so it grows hearty. *Kvas* hates sweet things, so you mix in some raisins or sugar—a few good pinches per pale. . . . There's different ways of fermenting milk. There's a Danube way that has its own taste; there's a Spanish way—and then there's a Caucus way as well. . . ."

All day I'd linger near her in the garden or the courtyard, go with her to the neighbors, where she'd drink tea for hours, telling endless stories. It was as if I'd become a part of her. Through that entire period of my life, all I remember seeing is an exuberant and inexhaustibly kind old woman.

Sometimes my mother would appear for short periods—proud, stern, she looked at everything with cold, grey eyes that resembled the winter sun, then quickly disappeared, leaving nothing for me to remember her.

Once I asked my grandmother:

"Are you a sorceress?"

60

"Oh, what comes into your head!" she said, smiling. But then she answered thoughtfully, "Where would I have the time? Sorcery's a difficult science. And I can't read or write—don't know a single letter. Now your grandfather—there's a reader with some bite. The Holy Mother didn't give such wisdom to me."

And then she revealed a new part of her life:

"I too grew up an orphan, after all. My mother was a cripple—all alone and homeless, didn't have a thing. When she was still a girl the owner frightened her. She threw herself from a window in the night out of fear and broke her side, hurt her shoulder too, and because of that her arm withered up—her right arm, the one she needed most. Many people knew my mother for the lace she made back then, but after that—well, the owners had no use for her. They gave her freedom to her—'Go live how you like!' But how are you to live with just one arm? So she went out into the world, seeking help from those she came across. The people lived richer then, and they were kinder. The carpenters in Balakhna were glorious! The lacemakers too—the kind of people you want everyone to see! She and I would walk around town in fall and winter, and then, as soon as Gabriel the Archangel waved his sword to drive the winter off, as soon as spring embraced the world, we'd go wherever our eyes led us. We'd be in Murom or Yurevets, on the upper Volga, along the banks of the peaceful Oka. In spring and summer it's good to be walking on this earth. The earth is gentle then. The grass is like velvet. The Holy Mother scatters flowers in the fields, and everything is filled with joy. Your heart has all the space it needs. Sometimes mother would close her deep blue eyes and start to sing in a pure, high note. Her voice wasn't strong, but it was clear as a bell, and everything around us seemed to drowse, hold still just listening to her. It was good to live on Christ's mercy. But when I turned nine my mother felt disgraced to be out wandering with me. She felt ashamed, and so she settled back in Balakhna, went begging there alone from house to house and at the churches during holidays. And I sat home and tried to teach myself lacemaking. I wanted to learn it quickly so I could help my mother right away, and when I failed, I'd wind up all in tears. But in a little more than two years—just think!—I'd learned the trade, and my name went all around the town. Soon anyone who wants good work comes straight to us, and it's 'Well now, Akulya, get those bobbins clicking!' And I'm so glad! It's like a holiday for me! Of course, it's not my skill so much as it's my mother showing me just right. Since she had only one arm, she couldn't work, but she could show me what to do. And one good teacher's worth at least ten workers. But here I got proud and said, 'You should stop your begging, *matushka*—I can feed you on my own.' And she says to me, 'Be quiet, now, and listen—all you make is going to your dowry.' And soon enough grandfather did come butting in—he was quite a figure then, only twenty-two and in charge of a barge-haulers' crew. His mother picked me out. She saw that I'm a hard worker, and a beggar's daughter—sure to listen and submit. . . . Uh huh. . . . She made bread—*kalach*—and her soul was cruel, may all that be forgotten. Why should we remember people who were cruel? God sees them Himself. . . . They're seen by God and loved by devils."

She chuckles happily. If you saw the way her nose trembles while she chortles, you yourself might break out laughing. But her eyes are pensive, full of light—and they caress me, speak to me of everything more lucidly than words.

I remember that it was a quiet evening. Grandmother and I were drinking tea in grandfather's room. He wasn't feeling well, sitting on the bedcovers without a shirt, a long towel covering his shoulders. He wiped a heavy sweat away every few minutes and breathed heavily, wheezing. His green eyes were cloudy and his face was swollen, purple—especially his sharp little ears. When he extended his hand for a cup of tea, it trembled pitifully. He was timid, not at all like himself.

"What—I don't get any sugar?" he asked grandmother like a spoiled child.

She answered tenderly, but firmly. "Drink it with honey—that's better for you."

Struggling for breath, wheezing, he quickly swallowed a mouthful of hot tea and said:

"Watch I don't die now."

"Don't worry, I'll keep an eye on you."

"Die now and it's like I never lived. Everything will just turn to dust."

"Don't talk anymore, now. You lie quiet."

He closed his eyes and didn't speak for a minute, noisily smacking his dark lips. Then he flinched as if he'd been pricked with a pin, and began thinking out loud:

"We need to get Yashka and Mishka married as soon as we can. Maybe wives and new children will hold them back a little—eh?"

He began to recollect what families in town had daughters who would make appropriate wives. Grandmother said nothing, drinking cup after cup of tea. I sat by the window, watching the evening sun glow above the town, its red light gleaming in the windowpanes. Grandfather had forbidden me to go into the garden or the courtyard as punishment for some offense or other.

In the garden, beetles were flying around the birch trees, buzzing. A cooper was repairing a barrel in the neighboring courtyard, and someone was sharpening knives somewhere nearby. In the ravine past the garden, boys were playing loudly, crashing in and out of the thick bushes, getting tangled in their limbs. An evening sadness filled my heart as I sat there, dreaming of going free.

Grandfather suddenly took a new-looking book from somewhere and slapped it noisily in his palm.

"Let's go then, you little *Permyak*, you boney-faced *Kalmyk*," he called to me boisterously. "Come here and sit down, Pickles-for-Brains. You see this letter, *A*? It's *Az*. Say it—*Az*! Now this one, *B*—it's called *Books*. This one, *V*, is called *Vessel*. What's this?"

"*Books*."

"Right. And this?"

"*Vessel.*"

"Wrong—it's *Az*! Now look at this one: *G* is called *Get*. This letter, *D*, is *Deliver*. This one here, *Ye* is called *Yes*. What's this?"

"*Deliver.*"

"Good. This one?"

"*Get.*"

"Right. This one?"

"*Az.*"

Grandmother intervened:

"You lie still now, father. Rest."

"Quiet! Go away! This is what I need just now. I'll think too much otherwise. Leksey, let's go!"

He put his hot, damp arm around my neck, holding the book under my nose and reaching around my shoulder to poke at the letters. He smelled hotly of vinegar, sweat, and baked onions and I could barely breathe as he entered a kind of frenzy, wheezing and shouting in my ear:

"S—*Soil*! L—*Life*!"

The words were familiar, but the Slavonic signs didn't match them. *Soil* looked like a worm, and *Get* reminded me of Grigory with his sloped back; *Yes* looked like grandmother standing next to me, and grandfather seemed to have something in common with all the letters of the alphabet. He drilled me for a long time on the letters, asking them in order and at random. He somehow infected me with his frenzied energy, and I too began to sweat and shout as loud as I could. This confounded him. Grabbing at his chest, coughing, he crumpled the book's pages and wheezed:

"Look at him, mother—he's raving! You little fit of insanity—what are you shouting for, eh?"

"You're who's shouting."

It was fun looking at him and grandmother just then. Sitting with her elbow on the table and her cheek resting on her fist, she stared at us, laughing softly, and said:

"You're both going to burst."

Grandfather explained to me in a friendly voice:

"I'm shouting because I'm unwell—but you?"

Shaking his damp head, he said to grandmother:

"May she rest in peace, Natalya had it wrong when she said he's got no memory. His memory works like a well-kept horse, may God be praised! Keep going, you little snub-nose!"

At last he playfully pushed me off the bed.

"That's enough. Hold on to the book. Tomorrow you'll recite the whole alphabet without a mistake, and I'll give you five kopeks."

When I reached out my hand for the book, he pulled me close and said gloomily:

"Your mother left you rootless on this earth, brother . . ."

Grandmother started.

"Oh, father, why would you say such a thing?"

"It would eat at me otherwise. Such a fine girl to get dragged down."

He pushed me away brusquely:

"Go play. But don't go in the street. Just the courtyard and the garden."

The garden was exactly where I needed to be. As soon as I reached its little hill, the boys in the ravine started throwing stones at me, and I was glad to answer them in kind.

"The Gobbler's here!" they shouted, quickly arming themselves. "Bust him open!"

I didn't know what "Gobbler" was supposed to mean and so took no offense at the name. But it was pleasant to fight alone against many, to see how a stone you'd aimed accurately could send your enemy scrambling for cover in the bushes. We carried out these small battles amicably and ended them with almost no offense on either side.

I learned to read and write fairly easily, and grandfather observed me with growing interest. He also switched me less and less, although it seemed to me he had more reason now to beat me than ever before. I grew steadily bolder with age and violated his rules and his commands with increasing frequency. But in response grandfather would only rail and raise his hand to me. It occurred to me that he had beaten me for no good reason earlier, and I once told him this.

With a light blow to my chin he tipped my head back.

"Whaaaat?" he said, drawing out the word, blinking as he looked at me.

He let out a sharp, staccato laugh. "Akh, you little heretic! How could you know how much you need to be beaten? Who could know that other than me? Now get out of my sight."

But just then he grabbed me by the shoulder and staring once more into my eyes, asked:

"What are you—simple-hearted or cunning? Eh?"

"I don't know."

"Don't know? Well then I'll tell you—be cunning. Simple-hearted's just the same as stupid—understand? A sheep's simple-hearted! Remember that. Now go outside!"

Soon I was able to sound out by syllable the words of the Psalter. We usually studied reading after evening tea. I had to read a psalm every time.

"*Books-Life-Yes-Soil-Soil-Yes-Deliver*," I read, moving the pointer along the letters. "Bles-sed is the man."

Out of boredom I asked: "The blessed man—is that Uncle Yakov?"

"I'll crack the back of your skull—then you'll know the blessed man," grandfather said with an angry snort. But I could tell that he was angry only out of habit, a sense of obligation.

I was almost never wrong about such things: a minute later he seemed to have forgotten me and began to mutter:

"Yes, of course, when it comes to playing music and singing he's another King David. But when it comes to work—to business—he's poisonous as Absalom! Wordsmith! Musicmaker! Cicero! . . . Akh, you-u. 'To skip and play with joyful feet.' But how far can you skip? How far can you get like that, eh?"

I stopped reading to listen to him, glancing at his sullen, preoccupied expression. His narrowed eyes looked through me to some far-off place, gleaming with both warmth and sadness. Seeing them, I knew that grandfather's usual severity was melting inside him. He drummed his fingers on the table, his dye-stained nails flashing, his golden eyebrows twitching.

"Grandfather?"

"Ahh?"

"Tell me a story."

"You get on with your reading, little shirker," he said, rubbing his eyes as if he'd just woken up. "You love stories, but you don't love the Psalter."

I had a feeling that he himself liked stories more than the Psalter, which he knew almost completely by heart, and from which, in keeping with a vow he'd taken long ago, he recited an entire kathisma each night before going to sleep, like a sexton reading the Book of Hours in a church.

I implored him still more earnestly for a story, and the old man, softening all along, finally gave in to me.

"Well, all right. The Psalter will be with you forever, but I'll soon go to God for judgment."

He settled into the ancient armchair, leaning flat against its cover of embroidered wool and tipping his head back to stare at the ceiling as he talked in a quiet, thoughtful voice about old times and about his father. Once a band of thieves rode into Balakhna to rob a merchant there named Zaev, and grandfather's father rushed to the bell tower to sound the alarm, but the robbers caught him, cut him with their swords, and threw him from the tower.

"I was just a little child then, so I didn't see any of that, and I don't remember it. I started remembering things with the French in 1812—it was my twelfth year too. They brought about thirty prisoners to Balakhna—all of them small and scrawny, shaking, some of them frostbitten and too weak to stand. They were all dressed in whatever they could find, worse than beggars. The local peasants wanted to kill them at first, but the escort wouldn't allow it. The garrison forced all the peasants back to their houses, and after that it was fine—everyone got used to it. The French—they're a smart people, quick-witted, lighthearted even—sometimes they'd sing songs. Landowners would come from Nizhny in their troikas to look at the prisoners. Sometimes they'd come and shout at the French, shake their fists at them, beat them even, while others would talk to them very nicely in their own language, give them money, whatever warm clothes they had. And one owner, an old man, he just covers his face with his hands and starts sobbing, says, 'Bonaparte's destroyed them—destroyed the French for good, that scourge!' Think of that—he was Russian, an owner even, but he was kind. He was sorry for those foreign people."

He stops talking for a minute, his eyes still closed. He smoothes his hair with his palms and then goes on, carefully stirring the past.

"Winter. A blizzard whirling in the streets. The cold clamping down on all the huts. . . . And the French, they come running to our window, to my mother—she baked and sold *kalach*. They knock on the window, shout, jump up and down, asking for hot *kalach*. My mother doesn't let them in—instead she sticks the loaves of *kalach* out the window and the French grab it right there, still steaming hot, and press it to their chests, right against their skin, against their hearts—I don't know how they could stand it! Many of them died from the cold—they're from warm parts, not at all used to snow and heavy frost. Two of them lived in our garden, in the bathhouse there—an officer and his servant—a soldier named Miron. The officer was tall and lean, just skin and bones. He went around in a woman's coat that only reached his knees. He was softhearted, and he was a drunk. My mother made beer and sold it on the quiet; he'd buy it, get drunk, and sing. He learned a little of our language too, and sometimes he'd jabber something like, 'Your side not white—he is black, evil.' He spoke badly, but you could understand what he meant. And he was right about that—our upper regions aren't at all kind. Lower down, along the Volga, it's warmer, and beyond the Caspian they say it never snows. You can believe that too, since there's no mention of winter, no mention of snow in the Gospel or the Book of the Apostles or the Psalms. And all the places where Christ lived, they're down there—in those warm places. Once we finish the Psalter you and I will start to read the Gospel. . . ."

He falls silent again, as if he's dozed off. Thinking about something, he stares out the window, squinting, all sharp and small.

"Tell more," I say quietly, trying to bring him back to the story.

"Well, so," he says, flinching, and starts again. "The French are people too—no worse than the rest of us sinners. Sometimes they'd shout to my mother, 'Madame, Madame'—that would be something like, 'My Lady' or 'Dear Gentlewoman'—and that gentlewoman, well, she could haul a sack of flour that weighed five *pood* on her back all the way from the warehouse. The strength she had was not a woman's. She could easily shake me by the hair right up to the time that I turned twenty, and at twenty I wasn't too bad myself. That officer's servant, Miron, he loved horses. He'd go around the courtyards and make signs with his hands, asking if he could groom any of the horses there. At first everyone was afraid—he's the enemy, he'll ruin the animal somehow! But afterward the peasants started calling him themselves— 'Hey Miron, Come here! Come on!' He smiles and lowers his head, goes charging off like a bull. He had red hair—bright red, a big nose and thick lips. He took very good care of horses, and he could treat them like a miracle worker when they were sick. After Balakhna he became a horse doctor in Nizhny, but he lost his mind, and a fire crew beat him to death. And toward spring the officer started getting weak. He died quietly on the day of St. Nikolai, sitting in the bathhouse under the open window, thinking about something, his head sticking out in the open air. I was sorry for him, even cried for him a little on the quiet when he died. He was very gentle. He'd take me by the ears and say something tenderly in his language. You couldn't understand it, but it was good! You won't buy a bit of gentleness like that at the market. He would have taught me a few of his words too, but my mother forbade it, even took me to the priest. He ordered her to whip me and made a complaint against the officer. We lived strictly back then, brother—something you'll never know! Others have already been through insults and pain for you—you remember that! One time, for example, I was . . ."

It had grown dark. In the gloom grandfather grew strangely larger. His eyes gleamed like a cat's. He speaks about everything with quiet circumspection—unless he himself is the subject, then his words grow heated, rushed, and boastful. I don't like it when he talks about himself. I don't like his constant command:

"Remember! You remember that!"

Much of what he told me I hoped to forget, but even without grandfather's insistence it often lodged itself in my memory like a painful splinter. He never told tales—only real life stories, and I noticed that he didn't like questions, so I made a point of asking as many as I could.

"Who's better—Russians or French?"

"Well, how can I say? I've never seen how a Frenchman lives at home," he grumbles, then adds: "Even the mole is happy in his hole."

"Are Russians good people?"

"They're mixed. They were better under the owners—they were hammered into shape back then. Now everybody's free and you can't get bread or salt. The owners weren't kind people, of course, but some sense had collected in their heads. You couldn't say it about all of them, but when an owner was good, he'd win your heart and soul. And then another owner, he'll turn out to be as stupid as a sack—whatever you stick inside, he'll keep and carry. We have a lot of empty shells. You look once and it seems like a person before you. But you get to know him and it turns out he's just a shell without a kernel, nothing inside—it's all been eaten up. We have to learn. We have to sharpen our minds. But you can't even find a good whetstone. . . ."

"Are Russians strong?"

"There are some strong ones. But it isn't strength that matters most—its sense and skill. No matter how strong you are, any horse will still be stronger."

"Why did the French go to war with us?"

"Well, war—that's the Tsar's business. That's not given to us to understand."

But when I asked him who Bonaparte was, his answer was memorable:

"He was an evil man. He wanted to conquer the whole world so that afterward we'd all live the same—no owners, no officials, just live without divisions, no higher-ups. Only names would be different while rights would be the same for everyone. And one faith for all. Of course that's all stupidity. Crawfish are the only things that you can't tell apart! Even fish are all different. A sturgeon's no companion for a sheatfish. And a sterlet isn't friends with a herring. We already had these Bonapartes around here—Stepan Timofeev Razin, Emelyan Ivanov Pugach. I'll tell you about them later one day. . . ."

Sometimes he would stare at me with rounded eyes for a long time, as if he'd never seen me before. It was unpleasant.

He never spoke to me about my father or my mother.

Grandmother would quite often come into the room during these discussions, quietly sit down in the corner, and stay there a long time, silent, hidden in the dark. And then she'd suddenly ask a question in a soft, enfolding voice:

"Remember, father, how good it was when we went on pilgrimage to Murom? What year was that?"

Grandfather would think a little, then answer precisely:

"I can't say for sure what year it was. But it was before the cholera. And they were still hunting for Olonchans in the woods."

"Oh, that's right—we were still afraid of them!"

"Right—see?"

I asked who the Olonchans were and why they were running around in the forests. Grandfather explained unwillingly:

"The Olonchans—they were just some peasants that ran away from their duties, ran away from the factories, from work."

"How did they catch them?"

"How? Well, the same way boys play. One group runs and hides and the others search for them, try to catch them. If they do catch them, they beat them with a whip and tear their nostrils out, put a brand on their foreheads to show they've been punished."

"What for?"

"For asking too many questions! . . . The whole business was murky. Who's in the wrong—the ones running or the ones trying to catch them?— it's not for us to know."

"Do you remember, father," grandmother spoke again, "how it was after the big fire?"

But grandfather wanted everything in exact detail. "Which big fire?" he'd ask sternly.

Departing for the past, they forgot about me. Their voices and their words grew soft, often falling into such harmony that it seemed they were singing a song—an unhappy song about diseases and fires, beatings, sudden deaths and cunning deceits, vicious owners, and holy fools who wandered through the land.

"To have lived through all of that, seen all that," grandfather muttered quietly.

"Has it really been such a bad life?" grandmother asked. "Remember how well the spring began after I gave birth to Varya?"

"That was in '48—the year of the Hungarian campaign. They pressed Tikhon the day after her christening—took her godfather off in the army."

"And he never came back," grandmother sighed.

"Never. And from that year on God's favor poured down on the house like water on a raft. Oh, Varvara."

"That's enough now, father."

He frowned, turned angry. "Enough of what? No matter how you look at it, our children are a failure. Where did our sap go, our strength? You and I thought we were pouring it into a basket, but instead God put a sieve full of holes in our hands!"

He shrieked and began to run around the room as if scalded, wheezing heavily, cursing his children, threatening grandmother with his small, shriveled fist.

"And you indulged those thieves every day! Indulger! Witch!"

His hysteria rose to a tearful howl as he barged into the corner where the icons hung, flailing his arms as he beat his withered chest, which resonated dully with the blows.

"Lord, are my sins really so much worse than those of all the others? Why?"

His entire body shook, and his damp eyes gleamed with tears of spite and pain.

Sitting in the dark, grandmother crossed herself, then rose and carefully approached him.

"Now, now, why such black misery?" she'd say, trying to talk him out of it. "The Lord knows what He is doing. Do so many people really have children better than ours? It's the same everywhere, father—arguments and quarrels and commotion. All mothers and fathers wash their sins with tears, not you alone. . . ."

Sometimes these words would calm him down and he'd collapse silently into bed, exhausted, and grandmother and I would withdraw to the attic.

But once when she approached him with these gentle words he suddenly turned, pulled his arm back, and struck her hard in the face with his fist, the crack of the blow resounding loudly across the room. Grandmother staggered back, rocking on her feet, then raised her hand to her lips and righted herself, said softly, calmly:

"Ekh, you fool."

She spit blood at grandfather's feet, and he let out two long howls, raising his arms above his head:

"Get out! I'll kill you!"

70

"Fool," grandmother said again as she left the room. He lunged at her but she stepped unhurriedly across the threshold and slammed the door in his face.

"Old hide!" grandfather hissed, his face as red as a hot coal. His finger-nails dug into the doorway as he clutched it.

I sat on the stove bench neither dead nor alive, unable to believe what I'd seen. This was the first time he'd ever struck grandmother in my pres-ence, and it was unbearably foul. It revealed something new in him, some-thing I could never come to terms with, something that crushed me like a weight. And he kept standing there, clutching at the doorway, shrinking, turning grey as if covered in ash. Suddenly he moved into the center of the room. Dropping to his knees, he pitched forward with one hand to the floor, then righted himself and beat his chest.

"Well, God? Well? . . ."

As if its heated tiles had turned to ice, I jumped down from the stove and bolted from the room. Upstairs grandmother was pacing around the attic, rinsing her mouth.

"Does it hurt?"

She moved away into the corner, spit some water into the slops bucket, and answered calmly:

"It's all right. My teeth are whole. Just broke my lip."

"Why?"

She looked out the window and said:

"He's angry. It's hard for him—nothing's worked out. You lie down now with God. Don't think about it anymore."

I asked her about something else, and she shouted with unusual severity:

"Who am I talking to? Get to bed! Don't you listen?"

She sat down by the window, sucking at her lip and spitting into a handkerchief. I looked at her as I undressed. Stars were shining in the dark blue square of glass that hung above her silhouette. It was quiet in the street, dark in the room. She came to me when I was lying down and softly stroked my head:

"Sleep peacefully now," she said. "I'll go back down to him. Don't you suffer too hard for me, my soul. I must be to blame as well. Sleep now. . . ."

She kissed me and left, and a terrible sadness settled on me. I got up from the wide, soft, hot bed and went to the window, looked down at the empty street, in sorrow turned to stone.

VI

Something like a nightmare started yet again. One evening after tea, as grandmother washed the dishes and grandfather studied the Psalter with me, Uncle Yakov burst into the room. Disheveled as always, he resembled a worn-out broom. He threw his hat in a corner without greeting anyone and started talking frantically, all his body shaking as he waved his arms.

"Papa, Mishka's gone completely out of control! He had lunch at my house, got drunk, and started showing us the most unbelievable insanity! He smashed our dishes, tore up a wool dress that we had ready for a customer, broke our windows, swore at Grigory and me. And now he's coming here. He was shouting, 'I'll kill father! I'll rip his beard out!' You watch out for him. . . ."

Grandfather slowly rose, bracing himself with both hands on the table. His face was pinched, its flesh all drawn toward his nose. In some awful way it looked like an axe.

"Hear that, mother?" he screeched. "How's that, eh? Coming to kill his own father! My son! . . . Well, it's time, then. It's time, friends. . . ."

He walked up and down the room, straightening his shoulders, then went up to the door and sharply threw the deadbolt in the lock.

"This is all about getting your hands on Varvara's dowry, isn't it?" he said, turning to Yakov. "Well, here it is—right here, take it!"

He shoved his fist under Yakov's nose, who jumped back in dismay.

"Papa—what's this got to do with me?"

"You? I know you!"

Grandmother remained silent, hurriedly putting cups in the cupboard.

"I came here to defend you!"

"Really?" grandfather shouted mockingly. "That's good! Thank you, my sweet little son! Mother, give this clever little fox something to hold in his hands—a fire poker or an iron at least. And you, Yakov Vasilev, when your brother comes crashing through that door, you be sure to make it seem you're taking a big swing at him, when all you're really aiming at is me!"

My uncle stuck his hands in his pockets and stalked off into the corner.

"If you really don't believe me . . ."

"Believe you?" shouted grandfather, stamping his foot. "No, I'll believe all kinds of beasts—a dog, a hedgehog. But with you I'll wait and see. I know you got him drunk and whipped him up! Well then—now it's time for you to beat him. It's your choice—beat him or me."

Grandmother whispered to me quietly:

"Run upstairs and look out the window. When you see Uncle Mikhail in the street, you run down and tell us. Hurry now, quick."

And so, slightly alarmed by the impending attack of my enraged uncle, but proud of the mission entrusted to me, I keep to the window and study the street. Wide, covered in a thick dust from which the large cobblestones protrude like swollen lumps, it stretches far away to the left, crossing a ravine and emptying onto Ostrozhnaya Square, where a grey building with a tower in each of its four corners stands firmly on the clayey earth—the old prison. There's something sadly beautiful about it, something striking. Sennaya Square lies three houses over to the right from ours, its wide expanse closed off by the yellow walls of the prison barracks and a lead-colored fire tower with a round turret that looks out over the town. The watchman follows its circumference like a dog pacing at the end of its chain. Ravines cut all across the square. At the bottom of one lies a greenish sludge; further to the right is the stagnant Dyukov Pond where, according to grandmother, the uncles threw my father through a hole in the ice one winter. Almost directly across from the window there's an alley; lined with florid little houses, it runs into the squat and stolid Church of Three Prelates. If you look straight ahead, you can see the roofs of more houses like the hulls of overturned boats among the green waves of the gardens.

The faded houses on our street are powdered with dust, their facades worn down by the blizzards of long winters, washed out by endless autumn rains. They huddle together like beggars on a church portico and with me wait for someone, their windows held wide open in suspicion. There are only a few people on the streets, moving slowly, like the cockroaches that linger at the edge of the hearth as if lost in thought. A wave of hot air rises toward me, smelling heavily of pastries baked with carrot and green onion—a smell I've never liked, one that always stirs despondency in me.

Tedium takes hold—a particular, almost unbearable kind of tedium. Thick warm lead fills my chest. It presses outward from within in me, swells my breast, spreads my ribs apart. I feel as if I'm inflating, like a bubble, and the room is crowding in on me, its ceiling like a coffin lid.

There's Uncle Mikhail. He emerges from the alley, from behind the corner of the grey house. He's pulled his hat down low on his head, pushing his ears out to the sides. He's wearing a reddish brown jacket and dusty, knee-high boots. He has one hand in the pocket of his checkered pants; the other grasps his beard. I can't see his face, but he stands as if he's ready to leap across the street and seize grandfather's house with his dark, hairy hands. I should run downstairs to tell them that he's come, but I can't tear myself away from the window. I see him cross the street, stepping carefully, as if afraid of dirtying his grey boots; then I hear him pull the tavern door open—hear the squeal of its hinges, the jingling of its glass panes.

I run downstairs and knock on the door to grandfather's room.

"Who's that?" he asks gruffly, not opening the door. "You? He's in the tavern? All right—go on!"

"I'm frightened up there."

"Put up with it."

Again I'm stuck at the window. It's turning dark. The dust in the street has swollen, grown deeper, blacker. The windows run with oily streaks of light from the yellow spots of candle flames. In the house across from ours, music begins to sing sadly, beautifully from many strings. There's singing in the tavern too. When the door opens, a tired, broken voice flows into the street. I know this is the voice of Nikitushka, a wandering, bearded, stooped old beggar. His left eye is always tightly shut, and the right one's missing altogether—there's just an empty socket in its place, like a piece of red coal. The door slams shut and cuts off his song like an axe.

Grandmother envies him. Listening to the beggar sing, she sighs:

"Oh, what grace God's shared with you! What poetry you know! Such a gift to have!"

Sometimes she presses him to come into the courtyard. He sits on the porch, leaning on his walking stick, and sings, recites. Grandmother stays right beside him, listening and asking questions:

"But wait, now, was the Holy Virgin in Ryazan as well?"

The beggar answers her in a deep, self-assured voice:

"She was everywhere—in all the provinces."

A drowsy weariness is flowing through the streets, invisible. It weighs me down, presses on my eyes and heart. If only grandmother would come now! Or at least grandfather. What kind of person was my father? Why didn't my uncles and my grandfather like him when my grandmother and Grigory and the nursemaid Evgeniya all speak so well of him? Where is my mother?

75

I think of her more and more, placing her at the center of all the tales and true stories my grandmother has told me. The fact that she doesn't want to live with her family only places her higher in my imaginings. I have the idea she is living at an inn near a big road, with a band of robbers who steal from rich travelers and share their loot with beggars. Or it could be that she's living in the forest, in a cave, with good-hearted robbers, of course, cooking for them and guarding their stolen gold. Or maybe she is wandering the earth, counting its treasure the way Engalycheva, the Bandit Princess, wandered with the Holy Virgin, and all the time the Holy Virgin implores my mother, just the way she did the Bandit Princess:

It's not for you, sad soul of greed
To gather all the riches of this earth,
To use its silver and its gold
To clothe your nakedness alone.

And my mother answers her with the same words the Bandit Princess spoke:

Forgive me please, most Holy One,
Take pity on my sinful soul,
It's not for me I fought and stole,
But for my one, my only son . . .

And the Holy Virgin's kind, like grandmother. She forgives my mother, saying:

Oh you, *Maryushka*, Tatar blood,
Spring of Christian fear and pain,
You must forgo your old ways now:
The path you take from here is yours alone,
And all the tears that fall will be your own.
You shall no longer harm the Russian clans,
But haunt instead the forests of Mordova,
And Kalmyks drive across the open lands.

Remembering these stories I seem to slip into a dream, from which I'm roused by shouts and stamping in the courtyard below, a commotion from the vestibule. Leaning out the window, I see grandfather, Uncle Yakov, and the tavern worker—a funny Cheremis named Melyan—pushing Uncle Mikhail through the gate into the street. He struggles against them and they beat at his arms, his back and neck, kick him until he finally flies headlong into the dust of the street. The gate slams shut; the deadbolt rattles in the catch; a crumpled hat goes sailing over the entrance. And then it's quiet.

After lying there a little, Uncle Mikhail gets up, his clothes all torn and disheveled. He picks up one of the paving stones and hurls it at the gate. The blow resounds dully, as if he'd dropped the stone into a barrel. Shadowy figures begin to emerge from the tavern, shouting and snorting, waving their arms. Human heads emerge from the windows of the houses. The street comes back to life, begins to shout, laugh. All this is like a story too— curious, but frightening and unpleasant.

And suddenly it all breaks off; everyone goes silent, vanishes.

Grandmother is sitting on the trunk at the room's threshold, bent over, motionless, not breathing. I stand before her, stroking her warm, soft, wet cheeks, but she doesn't seem to notice.

"Lord, darling, couldn't you have shared a little more reason with my children and me?" she mutters dejectedly. "Was there really not enough for us, dear God?"

I had the impression that my grandfather had lived on Polevaya Street for no more than a year—from just one spring to the next—and yet, even in that short time, the house took on a clamorous notoriety. Almost every Sunday boys came running to our gate, joyfully alerting the entire street:

"They're fighting again at Kashirins!"

Uncle Mikhail usually appeared in the evening and laid siege to the house all night, its occupants kept in quivering panic the entire time. Sometimes two or three of his thuggish peers from Kunavino came along to help. They'd climb from the ravine into the garden, where they assiduously carried out every whim of their drunken imaginations, tearing out entire bushes of raspberry cane and black currant. Once they demolished the bathhouse, breaking everything that could be broken, including the shelves, the benches, and the cauldrons for heating water. They scattered the stove in bits, tore it loose along with several floorboards, pulled off the door and its frame.

Grandfather stood dark and silent at the window, listening to the steady work of people diligently destroying his property. Grandmother was running around somewhere in the courtyard, invisible in the darkness, calling out, pleading:

"Misha, what are you doing? Misha!"

In answer she received a stream of foul and idiotic Russian cursing, the meaning of which must have lain beyond both the reason and the senses of those swine who uttered it.

There was no keeping up with grandmother during those hours, and it was terrifying without her. I'd go down to grandfather's room, but as soon as he saw me, he'd wheeze:

"Out, anathema!"

I climb back up to the attack and through the dormer window peer into the darkness of the garden and the courtyard, trying to keep grandmother from falling out of sight, fearing they'll kill her, shouting, calling out. She doesn't come, but my drunken uncle hears my voice, begins to curse my mother crudely, savagely.

During one such evening grandfather was unwell. He lay in bed, his head wrapped in a towel as he rolled it from side to side on the pillow, railing:

"Here it is—this is it, the thing we lived for, sinned for! The reason why we built up property! If it wasn't such a pure disgrace, I'd call the police and tomorrow go to the governor! . . . But what disgrace! What kind of parents hunt their children down with the police? So lie still, old man, and take it."

He suddenly lowered his feet from the bed and began to walk, swaying, toward the window. Grandmother caught him under the arms.

"Where are you going?"

"Light a candle!" he demanded, drawing air noisily as he struggled to breathe.

When grandmother had lit a candle, he took it in his hands, and holding it before him like a soldier with a rifle, he shouted loudly from the window in a mocking voice:

"Hey, Mishka, you thief in the night! You rabid, mangy dog!"

The upper pane of glass shattered instantly, and half a brick landed on the table near grandmother.

"You missed!" grandfather howled, and began either to laugh or sob.

Grandmother gathered him up in her arms just as she would me and carried him back to bed, repeating worriedly:

"Now, now, you don't mean that, Christ be with you! That would mean Siberia for him! What could he understand about Siberia in this frenzy!"

Grandfather flailed his legs and sobbed in a dry, hoarse voice:

"Let him kill . . ."

Beneath the window they were snarling and stamping their feet, scratching at the wall. I picked up the brick and ran toward the window, but grandmother managed to catch me. She hurled me into the corner, whispering:

"Akh, you, accursed . . ."

On another night my uncle had forced his way through the courtyard to the house's vestibule. Armed with a heavy stake, he stood on the steps of the back porch and worked at breaking down the door while behind it waited grandfather with a stick in his hands, two lodgers bearing staves of some sort, and the tavernkeeper's wife, a tall woman armed with a rolling pin. Behind them grandmother stamped her feet and pleaded:

"Let me go to him, let me say a word. . . ."

Grandfather stood with one foot planted forward, like the man with the bear spear in the painting *Bear Hunt*. Whenever grandmother ran up to him, he pushed her back wordlessly with his elbow and his leg. A lamp was hanging on the wall. Its unsteady light fell convulsively across their heads as the four of them stood there, dreadfully prepared. I was watching all of this from the steps to the attic. I wanted to take grandmother away.

My uncle's efforts to demolish our back door were both zealous and effective. The door now rocked and shuddered under his blows, ready to slip from its upper hinge—the bottom one had already blown apart and jangled unpleasantly. When he spoke to his comrades, my grandfather's voice seemed to jangle as well:

"Hit him on the arms and legs, but, please, not the head."

There was a small window next to the door—just big enough for someone to stick his head through. My uncle had already smashed out the glass and with a few splinters still sticking up, it had turned black, like a socket with its eye knocked out. Grandmother rushed up to it and thrust her arm into the courtyard.

"Misha, for the love of Christ, get away!" she began to shout, waving her arm at him. "They're going to maim you! Get away!"

He hit her on the arm with the stake. You could see something wide flash past the window and fall on her arm. Grandmother collapsed on the floor, toppled onto her back, having managed to shout once more:

"Mish-sha, run!"

"Ahh, mother!" grandfather howled terribly.

The door flew open and Uncle Mikhail leaped into its black space, only to be thrown from the porch like dirt flung from a shovel.

The tavernkeeper's wife led grandmother to grandfather's room. Soon grandfather appeared and sullenly approached her.

"Did the bone stay whole?"

"Akh, no—looks like it broke," grandmother said, not opening her eyes. "And him—what did you do with him?"

"Calm down!" shouted grandfather sternly. "What am I, a beast? We tied him up. He's lying in the barn. I dumped some water on him. . . . What rage! Where did he get such rage?"

Grandmother moaned.

"I sent for the bone-setter. You hang on a little," he said, sitting down on the bed next to her. "They'll kill us off, mother—kill us off before our time!"

"Give them everything."

"And Varvara?"

79

They talked for a long time—grandmother calmly, plaintively; grandfather with angry shouts.

Then came a small, hunchbacked old woman with a huge mouth that seemed to stretch from ear to ear. Her lower jaw trembled and her sharp nose bent over her upper lip as if to peer into her mouth, which hung open like a fish's. You couldn't see her eyes. She barely moved her feet as she dragged her walking stick along the floor, a rattling, knotted bundle in her hand.

I believed that grandmother's death had come. I ran up to the old woman and shouted with all my strength:

"Get out! Out! Go away!"

Grandfather snatched me up offhandedly, and without the slightest ceremony, hauled me to the attic.

VII

I understood from very early on that my grandfather had one God, my grandmother another.

Sometimes she'd wake up and sit on the side of the bed for a long time, dragging a comb through her remarkably long hair, her head jerking slightly and her teeth clenched as she pulled out full strands of that black silk, cursing in a whisper to keep from waking me:

"Damned Polish plait! I ought to cut you off! Take you out and shoot you!"

She untangles it all as best she can, weaves it into thick braids, and hurriedly washes, exhaling through her nose in sharp, angry little bursts. She hasn't washed away her annoyance, and her large face is still creased with sleep when she stands before the icons. But here the morning's true ablutions start, and immediately she's all refreshed.

Straightening her stooped back, lifting her head, she looks tenderly at the round face of the Holy Mother of Kazan. She crosses herself with a broad and diligent sweep of her hand. She whispers loudly, urgently:

"Holy Mother, may You grant the coming day Your grace."

She bows to the floor, then slowly rises, begins to whisper again, her voice ever more urgent and imploring:

"Dear spring of all joy, dear beauty in its purest sense, tender apple tree in bloom . . ."

Almost every morning she finds new words of praise, and this makes me listen to her prayers with close attention.

"My pure and sacred heart! My defender and protector, my golden sun! Mother of God, shield me from the delusions of evil, let me offend no one and let no one offend me without cause!"

She seemed to grow younger as she crossed herself again, slowly moving her heavy arm, a smile in her dark eyes.

"Jesus Christ, Son of God, in the name of Your Mother, grant to me, a sinner, Your mercy. . . ."

All her prayers were hymns of gratitude and simple, heartfelt praise.

She didn't pray for a long time in the mornings. She had to light the samovar for grandfather—he no longer kept a servant, and he'd berate her at length if she was late with tea.

Sometimes he would wake up earlier than grandmother and come up to the attic while she was still praying. Finding her before the icons, he would listen to her whispering for a little while, his thin, dark lips curling in disdain.

"How many times have I taught you how you have to pray?" he'd growl at her at tea. "And you keep making it up on your own like some mumbling heretic! You're dumb as an oak! How does God put up with you?"

"He understands," grandmother answered assuredly. "No matter what you say, He sorts it out."

"You're like some Chuvash praying in the woods! . . . Akh, you-u . . ."

Her God was with her all day. She spoke of Him even to animals, and it was clear to me that everything submitted with easy obedience to this God—people, dogs, birds, bees, grass. He was equally kind, equally close to everything on earth.

The tavernkeeper's wife had a cat with green eyes and fur the color of smoke. A spoiled and cunning flatterer, it was the favorite of the courtyard, and it searched constantly for some new morsel to eat. When once it came from the garden carrying a starling in its mouth, grandmother rescued the tormented bird and began to scold the cat:

"You little villain!" she said. "You have no fear of God!"

The tavernkeeper's wife and the yard man laughed at these words, but grandmother shouted at them angrily:

"You think animals don't understand God? They understand no worse than you, who have no hearts. . . ."

As she harnessed him, she often talked things over with Sharap, who'd grown fat and depressed.

"Why so sad, my sweet servant of God, eh? . . . You're getting old. . . ."

The horse would sigh and nod its head.

All the same, she uttered God's name less often than grandfather did. Her God was understandable to me. He wasn't frightening, but it was impossible to lie before Him—the shame was too great. He stirred in me a sense of shame that could not be overcome, and I never lied to grandmother.

It was simply impossible to hide something from that benevolent God, and it seems that even the urge to do so never arose in me.

Once after a quarrel with my grandfather, the tavernkeeper's wife upbraided my grandmother and even threw a carrot at her, despite the fact that grandmother had nothing to do with the earlier dispute.

"You really are a fool, madam," grandmother said to her calmly. I, however, was cruelly offended, and decided to take revenge on the evildoer.

For a long time I contemplated how to wound with maximum pain that fat, red-haired woman who had two chins and no eyes.

From my observations of the internecine conflicts that periodically arose among residents, I knew that they took revenge on one another by chopping off the tails of cats, poisoning dogs, slaughtering chickens and roosters. I knew that sometimes at night they would steal into an enemy's cellar and dump out barrels of *kvas* or pour kerosene into the vats of salted cabbage and cucumbers, but none of this appealed to me. Something more terrible and inspired was called for.

Finally I settled on a plan. Having laid in wait for the tavernkeeper's wife to go down into her cellar, I closed the storm door over her and locked it. I then performed a dance of revenge on top of the door, threw the key onto the roof, and rushed headlong to the kitchen, where grandmother was cooking. She didn't immediately grasp the reason for my elation, but once she did, she swatted me in the appropriate place, dragged me into the courtyard, and sent me onto the roof for the key. Surprised by her reaction, I retrieved the key silently and ran into a corner of the courtyard, from where I watched as she liberated the captive tavernkeeper's wife and they both came walking from the house, chuckling together like friends.

"I'll give you one!" said the tavernkeeper's wife, threatening me with her chubby fist, but a good-natured smile had appeared on her eyeless face. Grandmother grabbed me by the scruff of the neck and hauled me back into the kitchen.

"Why did you do that?"

"She threw a carrot at you."

"You mean—you did this on my account? Why, I should stick you under the stove with the mice till you come to your senses! What a noble defender! Sound as a bubble of soap in the wind! I'll tell your grandfather and he'll strip the skin off your bones! Now go up to the attic—stay there and study your book!"

She refused to talk to me all day, but in the evening, before beginning her prayers, she sat down on the bed and spoke. Her words were memorable, profound:

"I'm going to tell you something now, Lyonka, my soul, and I want you to remember it as a rule: Don't get tangled up in grown-up problems. Grown-ups are spoiled—they've been tested by God. But you haven't yet—so live in your world, a child's world, with a child's mind. You wait, and when God touches your heart, He'll show you your purpose. He'll lead you to your path—understand? And who's guilty of what—that's not for you to consider. It's for God to pass judgment and punish—for Him and not us!"

She fell silent for a moment, snorted a pinch of tobacco, and, narrowing her eyes, added:

"And it must be sometimes even God Himself doesn't have the strength to understand who's to blame for what."

"Doesn't God know everything?" I asked, surprised.

She answered quietly, sadly:

"If He knew everything it seems a lot of people wouldn't do the things they do. It must be sometimes He just looks down from heaven, looks down at all of us on earth and starts to weep, just sobs: 'Oh my darlings,' He cries. 'My darling people, how sorry I am for you all!'"

She began to weep herself, and without wiping her damp cheeks, walked away to pray in the corner. From that point on her God grew even closer, even more understandable to me.

As he instructed me, grandfather also said that God was omniscient and omnipresent, all-seeing—a benevolent being who helps people in all their affairs. But he did not pray the way grandmother did.

Mornings, before approaching that corner of the room where the icons hung, he would wash for a long time, and then, neatly dressed, comb his red hair and his beard with painstaking care, inspect himself in the mirror, straighten his shirt, tuck his black scarf into his waistcoat, and at last make his way cautiously, as if stealing somewhere, to the icons. There was a knot in the floorboards that resembled a horse's eye, and he always stood on that particular spot, his head lowered, his arms along his sides, like a soldier. After a minute of silence, standing thin and straight, he would say imposingly:

"In the name of the Father, the Son, and the Holy Spirit!"

It always seemed to me that a particular silence fell in the room after those words. Even the buzzing of the flies seemed more tentative.

He stands with his head thrown back, his eyebrows raised and bristling, his golden beard jutting straight out. He recites his prayers in a firm, commanding voice, keeping every word distinct and clear, like a pupil answering a teacher in a classroom:

"Suddenly the Judge shall come and the deeds of each shall be revealed. . . ."

He gently beats his fist against his chest and pleads:

"Against Thee I alone have sinned—turn away Thy face from my sins. . . ."

He pronounces every word with sharp precision as he reads the Creed, his right leg quivering as if noiselessly tapping in time to the prayer. His entire body seems to strain and stretch toward the icons, seems to grow, turning thinner and thinner, drier, all of him withered and clean, carefully kept, imploring:

"O bearer of the Healer, heal the perennial passions of my soul. . . . I offer the groans of my heart to thee unceasingly, strive for me, O Sovereign Lady."

With tears in his green eyes, he calls out loudly, supplicates:

"Let faith instead of works be imputed to me, O my God, for Thou wilt find no works which could justify me."

Now he begins to cross himself repeatedly, with sharp and fitful strokes. He nods his head as if butting at something, his voice full of yelps and sobs. Later, after spending some time in synagogues, I understood that grandfather prayed like a Jew.

The samovar has been on the table for a long time, chortling with steam. The smell of rye cakes with *tvorog* drifts through the room. You're dying to eat! Grandmother leans dejectedly against the lintel, sighs, lowers her gaze to the floor. The sun looks in happily through the window from the garden. The dew shines like pearls on the trees. The delicious morning air smells of dill, black currants, and ripening apples—and still grandfather prays, sways on his feet, screeches:

"Quench the flame of my passions, also, for I am poor and wretched."

I know by heart all of the prayers for morning and for bedtime—I know them and I follow tensely: will grandfather make a mistake—miss a word at least?

Such instances were extremely rare and always made me gloat.

Finished with his prayers, grandfather would say to us, "Good morning!"

Grandmother and I would bow and finally sit down at the table. Here I would announce to grandfather:

"You left out 'suffice' today!"

"Are you lying?" he'd ask, nervous, distrustful.

"No, you really left it out. You have to say, 'But may my faith suffice instead of all works,' but you didn't say 'suffice.'"

"Well . . . How? . . ." he exclaims, blinking sheepishly.

Later he'll repay me bitterly for this little demonstration, but for now I revel in his confusion.

Once grandmother said to him jokingly:

"It must be boring for God to listen to your prayers, father. You keep repeating the same thing over and over."

"Whaaaat?" he drawled ominously. "What are you lowing about?"

"I was saying you've never given God the gift of a word from your soul all these times I've listened to you pray!"

He turned purple and began to shake, bounced once in his chair, and threw a saucer at her head—threw it and started screeching like a saw hitting a knot:

"Out, you old witch!"

Describing to me the boundless strength of God, he emphasized the ferocity of that power above all else: here the people sinned and they were drowned; they sinned again and they were burned, their cities destroyed. Here God punished people with hunger and death, and always, everywhere, he is a sword raised above the earth, a scourge for all sinners.

"Whoever disobeys the laws of God will be punished with sorrow and destruction," he said imposingly, tapping the knuckles of his thin fingers on the table.

It was hard for me to believe in the cruelty of God. I suspected that grandfather was deliberately making it all up so that I would be afraid of *him* rather than God. I would ask him openly about this:

"Are you saying these things so I'll listen to you?"

And he would answer just as openly:

"Of course! Just imagine if you stop listening!"

"But what about grandmother?"

"Don't you believe that old fool!" he instructed me firmly. "She was born dumb. She's illiterate, and she's out of her mind. I'll go right now and tell her not to speak to you again about such holy things! Now answer me: how many ranks are there among the angels?"

I answered him, then asked:

"Are they like God's officials—the angels in the ranks? Like bureaucrats?"

"You muddle up everything!" he said, smiling. He chewed on his lip for a moment and hid his eyes, then began to explain reluctantly:

"That doesn't have to do with God. Bureaucrats and officials—that's all human! Those are just people who live off the law. They use it to eat."

"What are laws?"

"Laws—that means habits," the old man answered in a happier, more willing tone of voice, his keen, sharp eyes flashing. "People live and live and after some time they come to an agreement. Basically, they say, 'This is the best way to do it—let's make a rule, a law!' It's like boys getting ready to play a game. First they agree on how the game will be played—what the order of things will be. Well, that kind of agreement—that's a law!"

"And bureaucrats?"

"Bureaucrats are like bullies who come and mess up all the rules."

"Why?"

"That's not for you to know!" he said, frowning sternly. Then he started to preach again: "Above everything human, above all their affairs—God stands alone! They want one thing—He wants another. Nothing human lasts. God blows once and it all turns to dust and ash."

I had many reasons for taking an interest in bureaucrats and wanted to find out more:

"Yakov has a song that goes:

'In heaven angels work as holy clerks,
But here the bureaucrats are Satan's serfs.'"

Grandfather slipped his beard into his mouth with the palm of his hand and closed his eyes, his cheeks trembling. I realized he was laughing inside himself.

"I'd like to tie you and Yakov together by the leg and drop you in a lake!" he said. "He's not to sing those songs—and you're not to listen to them! They come from heretics—Old Believers! Apostates!"

He fell into thought about something, his eyes looking through me to some distant place.

"Akh, you-u . . ." he quietly drawled.

But while grandfather positioned his menacing God high above all of humanity, he—like grandmother—also drew Him and his countless saints into his own personal dealings. Grandmother, on the other hand, seemed hardly to know these saints, other than Nikolai, Yuri, Frol, and Lavr who, like her God, were very kind and close to people, walked among villages and towns, had human traits, and often intervened in their lives. Grandfather's saints were all martyrs. They tore down idols and argued with Roman emperors, and for this they were tortured, flayed, burned alive.

Sometimes grandfather would dream out loud:

"If God would just help me sell this house and make five hundred rubles off the top—what thanks I'd pray to St. Nikolai!"

Grandmother chuckled softly. "As if Nikolai is going to start selling his house for him, the old fool," she said to me. "Holy St. Nikolai has nothing more to worry about!"

For many years I kept grandfather's church calendar with his notes written inside it. The words "Saved from calamity by these benefactors" were written in straight letters and red ink on the day of Joachim and Anna.

I remember that calamity. Worried about supporting his failed children, grandfather had begun to lend money, secretly holding his debtors' possessions in hock. Someone informed against him, and one night the police descended on the house to search it. There was a great commotion, but it all turned out fine. Grandfather prayed until sunrise, and in the morning I watched him write those words in the calendar.

Before dinner he would read with me from the Psalter, the Book of Hours, or the writings of Ephrem the Syrian, a big, heavy book. After dinner he would resume his prayers, their joyless, penitential words reaching us for a long time in the evening quiet.

"What shall I offer Thee, or what shall I give Thee, O greatly gifted, immortal King. . . . And keep us from all dreams. . . . Lord, protect me from evil men. . . . O Lord, grant me tears, remembrance of death. . . ."

Grandmother, on the other hand, would often say, "Oh, I'm so tired today! I'll have to lie down without saying prayers tonight. . . ."

Grandfather took me to church regularly—to night services on Saturdays and late Mass on holidays. Even in church I could tell to whose God they were praying: everything the priests and the deacon read was for grandfather's God, while the singing was always for grandmother's.

Of course, I'm describing very roughly here a child's understanding of the distinctions between those two Gods that divided my soul so disturbingly. But grandfather's God did stir in me powerful feelings of enmity and fear. Loving no one, this God followed everyone with a severe gaze, searching out and finding something foul, evil, and sinful, before all else, in each of us. It was clear he had no faith in people, constantly awaited their repentance, and loved to mete out punishment.

Still, nothing in my life was as beautiful as those thoughts and feelings about God—they were my soul's chief sustenance during a time when everything else about the world only wounded me with its cruelty and its filth, evoked only sorrow and revulsion. God was the best, the most luminous of everything that surrounded me—grandmother's God, that tender friend to every living creature. How could it be that grandfather didn't see a God of kindness? This question disturbed me.

I was not allowed out in the street because it excited me too much—I seemed to grow drunk from the impressions it made on me, and I invariably wound up the guilty party in some outburst or scandal. Friends did not flock to me, and the neighborhood boys viewed me with hostility. I didn't like the way they called me Kashirin, and noticing this, they would call out all the more insistently to one another:

"Hey, look—it's Cadaver Kashirin's little grandson!"

"Get him!"

Then the fighting would start.

I was stronger than usual for a boy my age, and I was a skillful fighter—something that even my enemies, who always attacked in groups, would admit readily. Still, the street left me beaten, and I would usually come home with a bloodied nose, a split lip, and a bruised face, my clothes torn and covered in dust. Grandmother would meet me with alarm and sympathy:

"What now, my little radish, more fighting? What's this all about? What am I supposed to do with you? I'll have to beat you with both hands!"

She would wash my face, press a freshwater sponge to my bruises, daub them in acetate, cover them with copper coins, trying all the while to bring me to my senses:

"Why are you fighting all the time? You're perfectly peaceful at home, but once you get outside you're like nothing I've ever seen! You lose all shame! I'll go and tell your grandfather not to let you out anymore. . . ."

Grandfather saw my bruises but never upbraided me for them. He'd just mutter and quack:

"More medals for you? You must fight like Anika the Warrior. . . . Stop running around in the street! You hear me?"

I wasn't drawn to the street if it was quiet, but when I heard the cheerful racket of boys at play, I'd bolt from the courtyard regardless of grandfather's admonitions. I was not upset by the bruises and scrapes I received, but the cruelty of the street's entertainments invariably kindled in me an indignation that would grow into rage, for cruelty was all too familiar to me. I couldn't stand it when the other boys set roosters and dogs on one another, tortured cats, harassed the goats kept by Jews, or taunted the drunk beggars and the simpleton known as Igosha Death in His Pocket.

He was tall and thin, with skin that looked like it had been smoked, coarse hair growing on a bony face that seemed to be rusting. Wearing a heavy sheepskin coat, he walked the streets hunched over, swaying as he stared silently, intently at the ground under his feet. His cast-iron face and small, sad eyes fostered in me a deferential respect. He seemed to be preoccupied, seemed to be searching for something serious—and therefore it was wrong to bother him.

The neighborhood boys would run after him, pelting his bent back with stones. For a long time it would seem that he didn't notice them or feel the pain of the blows. But then he would stop and lift his head, clumsily raise his hand to straighten his shaggy hat, and look around, as if just waking up.

"Igosha Death in His Pocket! Where are you going Igosha? Look—it's death in your pocket!" shout the boys.

He grabs at his pocket with one hand, then quickly bends down to pick up a stone or a clump of dry dirt, which he brandishes awkwardly with his long arm, muttering curses. His curses always consist of the same three obscenities, and in this regard, the boys are much richer than he. Sometimes he chases them in a limping gait, but his long sheepskin coat hampers him as he tries to run, and he falls to his knees, bracing himself against the ground with hands that look like dry, black twigs. Then the boys drill his back and his side with stones while the boldest run right up to him, crumble fistfuls of dust over his head, and jump away.

The street left in my mind an even more troubling impression with the master craftsman, Grigory Ivanovich. He'd gone completely blind and now wandered as a beggar—tall, striking, silent. A small, grey old woman would hold him by the arm, stopping under windows and calling out in a high-pitched, squeaky voice while looking off to the side:

"In the name of our Lord, give to this blind man, give to this beggar with nothing. . . ."

But Grigory Ivanovich never spoke. His dark glasses would look straight at the wall of a house, a window, the face of someone walking toward him; his hand, completely stained with dye, would quietly stroke his beard; and his lips would remain firmly together. I saw him often, but I never heard a sound from that tightly sealed mouth, and the old man's silence weighed on me painfully. I couldn't approach him and never did—just the opposite: catching sight of him, I'd run home and tell grandmother:

"Grigory's out in the street!"

"He is?" she'd exclaim in a worried, sympathetic voice. "Well, go and give him this. . . ."

I would refuse, angrily, rudely—and she would go herself out past the gate to talk with him for a long time, standing on the sidewalk. Sometimes he'd let out a single, short little laugh, which made his beard tremble, but his words were always brief and few.

Sometimes grandmother would convince him to come into the kitchen, pour him tea and feed him. He once asked where I was, and grandmother called to me, but I ran away and hid behind the firewood. I couldn't go to him—it was unbearably shameful before him, and I knew that grandmother was also ashamed. We spoke about Grigory only once. Having led him through the gate, she was walking quietly back through the yard and crying, her head lowered. I went up to her and took her hand.

"Why do you run away from him? He loves you, and you know he's good."

"Why doesn't grandfather feed him?"

"Grandfather?"

She stopped, pressed me close to her and said prophetically, almost in a whisper:

"Remember my words: God will punish us bitterly for that man. He'll punish us."

She wasn't mistaken. Some ten years later, when grandmother had found her peace forever, my grandfather himself would wander the streets of that town, destitute and insane, begging pathetically before the windows of strangers' homes.

"My good and generous bakers! Give me a little pie! A piece of pie for me! . . . Akh, you-u. . . ."

That bitter, drawn-out, soul-unsettling refrain was all that remained of his former self.

"Akh, you-u . . ."

Besides Igosha and Grigory Ivanovich, there was a degraded, dissolute woman named Voronikha who also troubled me deeply. Huge, disheveled, drunk, she would appear on holidays and send me running from the street. She had a particular way of walking so that instead of moving her feet she seemed to float like a rain cloud without touching the ground as she moved through the town, bellowing out obscene songs and sweeping the streets clear of people, for everyone hid whenever she approached, ducking into shops or courtyards, darting around corners to escape. Her face was almost dark blue, swollen like a bubble, and she held her big, grey eyes wide open in a mocking, terrifying way. Sometimes she would howl and weep:

"Little children! My little children, where did you go?"

I asked grandmother what all this meant. "You shouldn't know such things," she answered gloomily, but all the same explained concisely. The woman once had a husband, a local official named Voronov. He wanted to reach a higher rank, so he sold his wife to his superior, who took her off somewhere, and for two years the woman didn't live at home. When she returned, the children, a boy and a girl, had died, and the husband had been sent to prison for gambling away state money. And so, from grief, the woman started to drink, roam the streets, and riot. The police would take her away in the evening of every holiday.

No, it was better at home than out in the street. Those hours after lunch were particularly good—when grandfather went away to Uncle Yakov's dye shop, and grandmother, sitting by the window, told me interesting stories and tales and talked about my father.

She cut off the broken wing of the starling that she'd saved from the cat, and in place of a leg that had been bitten off, she deftly attached a little wooden stump—and having cured the bird of its injuries, she soon taught it to speak. Sometimes she would stand for an entire hour in front of the cage on the windowsill like some kind of huge, kindhearted beast, repeating a phrase over and over in a deep voice to that coal-black bird, who could imitate almost anything.

"Well, ask for it. Say, '*Kasha* for the bird.'"

The starling watches her from the corner of its round, lively joker's eye, taps its wooden leg on the thin bottom of the cage, stretches out its neck and whistles like an oriole, then copies a jay and a cuckoo, tries to meow like a cat, imitates a dog's howl—but can't quite manage human speech.

"Now, don't you fool around," grandmother says to it seriously. "Just say it: '*Kasha* for the bird.'"

The little black monkey in feathers lets out a deafening cry that resembles grandmother's words, and the old woman laughs joyfully, gives the bird a little of the *kasha* that it's asked for from her finger.

"I know you're just pretending, just putting on a show, you little peacock," she says. "You know how to speak just fine."

And she really did teach the bird to speak. After a little while it could ask for *kasha* quite clearly, and catching sight of grandmother, it would drawl:

"Khel-low."

At first the starling lived in grandfather's room, but he soon banished the bird to the attic, to live with us, for it had learned how to tease him. Grandfather always pronounced the words of his prayers very distinctly, and as he did so, the bird would stick its waxen, yellow beak through the little wooden bars of its cage and whistle a harmony:

"*Tyu, tyu, tyu-irr, tu-irr, tiir, tyu-uu.*"

Grandfather found this highly offensive, and one day he broke off his prayers, stamped his foot, and began to shout threateningly:

"Take this devil out of here! I'll kill it!"

There were many interesting and entertaining things at home, but sometimes a deadening discontent would choke me. Some great weight seemed to settle inside me, and for a long time, I would live as if in the bottom of a deep, dark pit, deprived of hearing and vision, all my feelings—blind, half dead.

VIII

Grandfather unexpectedly sold our house to the tavernkeeper and bought another one on Kanatnaya Street. Unpaved, overgrown with weeds, quiet, and clean, the street was comprised of brightly painted little houses and led directly to the fields.

Our new house was neater, more appealing than the old one. The light blue shutters of the three front windows and the latticework around the dormer stood out brightly against its soothing, dark crimson facade. A lime tree and an elm draped their thick green leaves like a pretty awning over the left side of the roof. In the courtyard and the garden there were many comfortable, secret places; it was as if they'd been specially made for hide and seek. The garden was particularly good: not big, but nicely overgrown and densely tangled, it contained a little bathhouse like a toy in one corner; in the other lay a large, fairly deep pit, where charred logs—the remains of an earlier bathhouse that had burned down—stuck out among the tall, tangled weeds. The garden was enclosed by Colonel Ovsyannikov's stable on the left, and the Betlengs' outbuildings on the right. Its interior reached to the farmstead of a dairymaid named Petrovna, a red, fat, noisy woman who resembled a bell. Sunk deep in the earth and well covered with moss, her dark, dilapidated house had a friendly, genial expression, its two windows looking out onto the open fields, across which cut deep gullies, and in the distance, the dark blue rain cloud of the forest. Soldiers marched and ran across the fields all day, their bayonets flashing like white lightning in the sloping rays of the autumn sun.

The entire house was filled with people whom I'd never seen before. In the front half lived a Tatar soldier with a small, round wife who shouted, laughed, and played a richly decorated guitar from morning until evening, singing in a high-pitched, ringing voice. There was a slightly bawdy song she sang most often of all:

If the first one doesn't hold you tight—
Then find a girl who'll love you right;
Climb the steps where she resides,
And there you'll gain a lovely prize—
Oh, a lovely, sweet surprise! . . .

Round as a ball, the soldier would sit by the window, constantly smoking his pipe and puffing out his dark blue cheeks, his odd, rust-colored eyes held wide open as he gazed contentedly around. He'd cough with a strange, barking sound:

"Vukh, vukh-vukh, vukh."

In the warm annex above the stable and the cellar lived a tall, gloomy, Tatar military servant named Valei and two cart drivers—Uncle Pyotr, who was small and grey, and Styopa, his mute nephew, who was strong and sinewy, and whose face resembled a spotless copper tray. All these people were new to me, a trove of unfamiliarity.

But more than anyone, it was the boarder known as A Fine Business who seized my attention and drew me steadily toward him. He lived in the back of the house, in a long, rented room with two windows—one opening on the garden, the other on the courtyard.

He was a lean, stooped man with kind eyes behind his glasses, a white face, and a black, forked beard. He spoke very little and was easily overlooked. When you called him to lunch or tea, he would invariably respond:

"A fine business. . . ."

Grandmother soon began to call him this by name, both in his presence and his absence:

"Lyonka, call A Fine Business to have tea." "And you, A Fine Business, why are you eating so little?"

His entire room was crammed full of boxes, strewn with thick books printed in Russian type, which I couldn't read. Bottles of variously colored liquids stood everywhere amid pieces of copper and iron, bars of lead. From morning until night, wearing a red leather coat and checkered grey pants spattered with some kind of paint, smelling unpleasantly, clumsy, disheveled, he melted lead and soldered bits of copper, weighed something on a little scale, mumbled, burned his fingers and hurriedly began blowing on them, bumped into things as he approached the plans hanging on his wall, wiped his glasses, and sniffed the pages spread before him, his thin, straight, oddly white nose almost touching the paper. Sometimes he would suddenly stop in the middle of the room or at the window and stay standing there for a long time, his eyes closed, his face lifted, all of him rooted to the spot, silent.

I would climb onto the roof of the barn and from across the courtyard observe him through his open window. I could see the blue flames of the spirit lamp on the table and a dark figure writing something in a tattered notebook, his glasses glinting with the cold blue sheen of ice. The wizard's work he conducted there would captivate me for hours, raise my curiosity to a painful, white-hot pitch.

Sometimes he would stand at the window like a portrait in a frame, his hands behind his back, and stare directly at the roof—but he never seemed to notice me, which hurt my feelings greatly. Then he'd suddenly go jumping back to his table, bend over it, start rummaging around.

I think I would have been afraid of him had he been richer, better dressed—but he was poor. A wrinkled, dirty collar stuck out from the shirt beneath his coat; his pants were covered in patches and spots; and he wore tattered slippers over his bare feet. Poor people are not dangerous or frightening. My grandmother's sympathetic attitude toward them—and my grandfather's disdain—had convinced me of this without my really noticing.

Everyone in the house disliked A Fine Business and spoke of him in a mocking tone. The soldier's merry wife called him "chalk nose" while for Uncle Pyotr he was "The Apothecary" or "The Wizard," and for grandfather "The Black Magician," or "The Free Mason."

"What's he making?" I asked grandmother.

"That's not your business. Learn how to keep quiet," she answered sternly.

One day I gathered my nerve and approached his window.

"What are you making?" I asked, struggling to conceal my apprehension.

He flinched, then looked at me for a long time over the top of his glasses.

"Climb in," he said, extending his hand, which was covered in sores and scars from old burns.

The fact that he proposed entering his room through the window rather than the door raised him even higher in my estimation. He sat down on a box and stood me before him, moved me away, then brought me closer again, and finally said:

"You are—from where?"

This was strange. Four times a day I sat at the table with him in the kitchen.

"I'm the grandson here," I answered.

"Aha, yes," he said, examining one of his fingers. He didn't say anything more.

"I'm not a Kashirin—I'm Peshkov," I said, having decided it was necessary to clarify this point with him.

"Peshkov?" he said uncertainly, emphasizing the wrong syllable. "A fine business."

He moved me aside, rose to his feet, and walked toward his table, saying, "Well, sit quietly."

I sat for a long time, watching as he used a file to scrape a piece of copper held in a vise; the metal filings fell like golden grains onto a piece of cardboard placed beneath it. He gathered up a fistful and dropped them into a thick cup, then added from a jar a white powder that looked like salt, poured in something from a dark bottle, and in the cup it began hissing, started smoking. An acrid smell filled my nose, made me cough and shake my head.

"Smell bad?" the wizard asked proudly.

"Yes."

"Indeed, indeed. But that, brother, is entirely good."

What's he boasting about? I thought to myself, and answered severely:

"If it smells bad, it can't be good."

"Well, brother," he exclaimed, winking, "that isn't always so. . . . Do you play knucklebones?"

"You mean dibs?"

"Yes, dibs then."

"Yes."

"Want me to give your striker a nice lead coat?"

"Yes."

"All right then, bring your striker here. . . ."

He came up to me again, looking with one eye at the smoking cup in his hand.

"I'll give your striker a good solid coat," he said. "And you don't come to see me anymore, all right?"

This hurt me deeply.

"I won't come again, no matter what."

Aggrieved, I went into the garden. Grandfather was there, pottering around, covering the roots of the apple trees with manure. It was autumn; the leaves had begun to fall long ago.

"Come on, then," he said, handing me a pair of shears. "Trim the raspberry cane."

"What's A Fine Business building?" I asked.

"He's ruining his room," grandfather answered angrily. "Burnt the floor, stained the wallpaper—tore it! I'll tell him to move out!"

"You should," I said as I started clipping the withered vines.

But my words were premature.

When grandfather left the house on rainy evenings, grandmother would arrange the most interesting of evenings in the kitchen, inviting all the residents to tea. The cart drivers would come, along with the gloomy military servant. The lively milkmaid Petrovna often appeared; sometimes even the soldier's merry wife joined the group as well. A Fine Business always sat in a corner near the stove, silent, motionless, sticking out like a post while the mute Styopa played a card game with Valei, the Tatar, who'd occasionally slap his cards across the mute's wide nose, muttering:

"Akh, Satan! . . ."

Uncle Pyotr would bring a huge loaf of white bread, which he cut into large, flat slices and generously covered with a special raspberry jam that came in a large clay pot and contained a smattering of fried sunflower seeds. Holding one of these delicious pieces of bread on his outstretched hand, he'd approach each member of the party, bow, and say in a gentle voice:

"Please, have some bread and jam, for me, enjoy. . . ."

When the bread had been received, he would carefully inspect his dark palm, licking away any drops of jam he discovered there.

Petrovna would bring a bottle of cherry brandy; the merry wife came with candy and nuts, and soon a splendid feast would begin, one of grandmother's greatest pleasures.

She arranged such an evening not long after A Fine Business had offered me a bribe never to visit him again. An implacable autumn rain spattered and streamed over the house; the wind whined, and the trees scraped their branches loudly against the walls. But in the kitchen it was warm and comfortable, and there was something particularly endearing about the way that everyone sat close and quietly together. Grandmother was in rare form, telling one elaborate story after the other, each one topping the last.

She was sitting on the stove, her feet resting on the step as she leaned toward her listeners, who were illuminated by a small tin lamp. She always sat this way when she was in the mood for storytelling, explaining, as she climbed up to her perch:

"I have to talk from up above—it's better from up here."

I found a place by her feet on the wide step, almost directly above A Fine Business's head. Grandmother told a good story about Ivan the Warrior and the hermit Miron. Her words were powerful and rich, and they flowed in a steady, lilting stream:

There was an evil warlord, Gordion;
His soul was black, his conscience made of stone.

He persecuted truth and tortured men,
Lived easily in evil as a Great Owl in a tree.
He hated most the hermit called Miron,
Soft-spoken advocate of truth and peace.
And so he called on one who served him faithfully—
Ivan the Warrior, and said: "Ivanka, leave
And find Miron, chop off the old man's head,
Seize it by its withered beard and lug it back
To me: gladly I will feed the dogs."
Ivan obeyed. Off he went, thinking bitterly,
"It isn't I who steps here now, necessity
Is driving me. Why is it I've received
So harsh a lot from God?" Soon he saw
The hermit, hid his sword, bowed low, and said:
"Have you kept well, old man? How do you fare with God?"
The sharp-eyed hermit smiled. "Enough deceit,"
He wisely said. "By God all things are seen.
He holds all good and evil in His hand.
I know, Ivan, why you have come to me."
Ivan was much ashamed before the anchorite,
But still he feared to disobey his lord outright.
From its scabbard he removed his sword,
Upon his coat he wiped the gleaming blade.
"I would have spared you this, Miron," he said
"And killed you quick, before your tired eyes
Had fallen on this steel and you'd begun to pine.
But now—well now you have a chance to pray,
So pray to God a final time
For you, for me, for all the human race:
And when you finish, I'll cut off your head."
The old man knelt beneath a sapling oak.
The young tree bowed to him; he smiled and spoke:
"It must be vast indeed, a prayer for all humanity.
You'd better kill me outright now, Ivan,
And spare yourself the wearisome monotony."
But here the soldier angrily replied,
Here he spoke with foolish pride:
"Oh, no, old man, what's said is said.
You start your prayer. I can wait here for eternity."
The old man prays till dusk descends.

From dusk he prays to dawn.
From dawn he prays until it's night again.
Summer slips into the spring, one year fades
Into the next—and still the hermit prays.
The sapling oak now reaches to the clouds,
Surrounded by a dense and shady copse
That's risen from the acorns that it dropped,
And still the holy prayer resounds!
And so they both remain today,
Quietly the hermit begs for mankind's aid,
Implores the Holy Mother for her grace,
While nearby stands Ivan, his sword blade
Blown away in dust, his heavy armor now
Devoured by rust, his fine attire rotted off.
Through every passing season he remains unclothed,
Untouched by winter storms and snow,
But parched like leather in the summer sun.
The clouds of gnats that drink his blood don't dry
His veins completely out so he might die;
Peaceably the wolves and bears pass by
While he stays rooted to that solitary place,
Lacking any strength to speak or raise his hand,
Punishment, apparently, for that command
He recognized as evil but obeyed,
Believing that his guilt could be allayed
By his subservience to savage power,
And he could hide behind the conscience of another.
Meanwhile the old man's prayer for every sinner
Flows on and on to God, a brilliant river
Flashing as it runs into the sea,
Even now, even at this very hour.

I noticed at the very start of grandmother's story that something was agitating A Fine Business. He jerked his hands in strange little spasms; took his glasses off, waved them to the rhythm of the flowing words and put them on again; nodded his head and pressed his fingers firmly to his eyes; brushed his palm across his forehead and his cheeks again and again, as if wiping away a heavy sweat. If someone stirred or moved his feet, the boarder whispered sternly:

"Shhhhh . . ."

When grandmother stopped speaking, he leaped to his feet and began to whirl around the room, waving his hands unnaturally and muttering:

"You know, that's—that's just astonishing! Someone has to write that down! That's true—terribly true. Our . . ."

It was clear now that he was crying. His eyes filled with tears; the drops clung to his lashes, rising and falling as he blinked. His eyes were bathed in them. It was a strange and very sad sight. He ran around the kitchen, awkward, absurd, jumping up and down, waving his glasses before his nose as he tried to put them on and failed, again and again, to hook the wire over his ears. Uncle Pyotr grinned as he watched him, and everyone fell into an awkward silence.

"Well, write it down—there's no sin in that," said grandmother hurriedly. "I know many more like that one."

"No, no—that one! That one's terribly Russian," the boarder shouted excitedly. He suddenly froze in the middle of the kitchen and began to speak loudly, cleaving the air with his right hand while his glasses trembled in his left. For a long time he spoke heatedly, letting out little yelps and stamping his feet, often repeating the same words:

"You can't hide behind another's conscience—yes, yes!"

Then his voice suddenly seemed to break; he fell silent, looked at everyone in the room and left quietly, sheepishly, with his head lowered.

People smiled and looked around embarrassedly. Grandmother moved farther back onto the stove, into the shadows, and sighed heavily. Petrovna wiped her fat red lips with her hand. "Seems like something made him angry," she said.

"No," Uncle Pyotr answered. "That's just how he is."

Grandmother climbed down from the stove and silently began to heat the samovar.

"Gentry's all like that," Uncle Pyotr went on speaking unhurriedly. "They're all capricious."

"Bachelors are always trouble," Valei muttered gloomily.

Everyone laughed.

"He worked himself right into tears, though," Uncle Pyotr drawled. "That's just how it goes. . . . One day you're pulling pike from every brook, the next your left without a hook."

It all turned dreary. A vague despondency weighed down my heart. A Fine Business had surprised me. I felt sorry for him. The little pools of tears that drowned his eyes stayed vivid in my memory.

He didn't spend the night at home, but he came back the next day after lunch, quiet, wrinkled, and clearly embarrassed.

"Yesterday I made a lot of noise," he said to grandmother like a guilty child. "Are you angry?"

"What for?"

"For me talking so much, getting in the way. . . ."

"You didn't hurt anyone."

I had the sense that grandmother was afraid of him. She didn't look him in the face, and her voice wasn't right—too quiet.

He walked right up to her and said with startling simplicity:

"You see, I'm terribly alone. I don't have anyone! You don't talk, don't talk—and then something starts to boil in your soul, and suddenly it all comes out! All of a sudden you're ready to talk to a stone, a tree. . . ."

Grandmother moved away from him.

"You should get married."

"Ekh," he exclaimed, wrinkling his face. He waved his hand and left.

Grandmother frowned and watched him, snorted a pinch of tobacco.

"Don't you hang around him too much," she instructed me firmly. "God knows what type he is. . . ."

But I was drawn to him again. I had seen how his face changed, how it darkened when he said, "I'm terribly alone." Something in these words was very understandable to me; something in them touched my heart. I went to find him.

From the courtyard I looked into his room. Empty, it resembled a store-room where things that no one really needs had been thrown haphazardly—things as strange and extraneous as their owner. I went into the garden and saw him there, in the pit. He was sitting awkwardly on one of the charred beams, his hands behind his head, his elbows resting on his knees. One end of the beam was sunk in the earth; the other, black and shiny as a piece of coal, stuck out over a patch of withered wormwood, nettles, and burdock. The fact that he sat there so awkwardly drew me to him even more.

For a long time he didn't notice my presence, staring somewhere past me with eyes that seemed as sightless as those of a newly hatched owl. Then he suddenly asked:

"For me?" He sounded annoyed.

"No."

"What then?"

"Just . . ."

He took off his glasses and wiped them with a handkerchief; it was covered with red and black spots.

"Well, climb down here!" he said.

When I sat down next to him, he hugged me firmly around my shoulders.

"Sit here.... We'll just sit and not talk, all right? Just like this.... You're a stubborn one, aren't you?"

"Yes."

"A fine business . . ."

We sat there without talking for a long time. It was quiet, one of those sad and gentle evenings when the weather's warm for the last time in the fall, and all the bright colors around you are fading, growing weaker by the hour. The earth has exhausted all of its pungent summer smells; there's only the scent of cold damp in the strangely transparent air. Jackdaws rise and fall uneasily in the reddening sky and bring sad thoughts to mind. Everything's silent, mute; even the smallest sound—a fallen leaf rising in a slight breeze, a bird fluttering its wings—seems so loud you flinch uneasily, but then go still again, slip back into the silence that has settled over the earth and filled your chest.

Particularly light and pure ideas take shape in such moments, but they're delicate and sheer as gossamer, fragile, ineffable. They spark and quickly disappear, like falling stars. They singe the soul with sorrow about something; they comfort and disturb it. This is when the soul begins to churn and seethe; this is when it's fused, takes shape for all one's life—here its face is formed.

Pressing myself against the boarder's warm side, I looked with him at the red sky through the black branches of the apple trees, followed the flight of bustling redpolls; watched young goldfinches as they tore apart the crowns of dried-up burdock and shook out their astringent seeds; studied woolly, blue-grey clouds with purpled edges that drifted from the fields while beneath them crows flew heavily toward their nests in the graveyard. Everything was good; in some unusual way, everything seemed close and comprehensible.

From time to time my companion sighed deeply and asked:

"Isn't it glorious, brother? . . . Are you warm enough? . . . Is the damp getting to you?"

When the sky darkened and everything around us seemed to swell with the damp twilight, he said:

"Enough now, let's go."

He stopped at the garden gate and said quietly:

"You have a good grandmother. . . . Oh, what earth!" He closed his eyes and recited distinctly:

He lacks the strength to raise his hand,
Punishment for that command
He recognized as evil but obeyed . . .

You remember that, brother—remember it well!"

Nudging me forward, he asked: "Do you know how to write?"

"No."

"Learn. And when you've learned, write down the stories that your grandmother tells. That, brother, will be very useful."

We became friends. From that day on I went to visit A Fine Business whenever I wanted. I would sit in a box filled with rags and observe unfettered as he melted lead and heated copper, brought it to a red-hot glow and used a hammer with a pretty handle to pound it into iron plates on a small anvil; worked with a rasp and file, an emery, a saw with a blade as thin as thread; and all the while weighed everything on a delicate copper scale.... Pouring various liquids into thick white cups, he watches them smolder, filling the room with bitter smoke, then wrinkles his brow, looks something up in his thick book, mumbles and bites his red lips, or quietly drones in a gravelly voice:

"O rose of Sharon . . ."

"What are you making?"

"One thing, brother . . ."

"What kind of thing?"

"Ah, well, you see, I don't know how to say it in a way that you'll understand."

"Grandfather says you might be making false money."

"Grandfather? Hmmm. . . . Well, he's talking about trifles. Money's nothing, brother."

"Then what do you pay for bread with?"

"Well, yes, brother. You have a point there. . . ."

"See? And what about beef?"

"And beef too . . ."

He lets out a quiet, surprisingly tender laugh and tickles me behind my ears the way one would a cat.

"I can't argue with you," he says. "You always outdo me, brother. Let's stay quiet instead."

Sometimes he would interrupt his work and sit down next to me, and together we'd look out the window for a long time, watching the apple tree lose its leaves and grow poorer, rain scattering across the roofs and the high grass in the courtyard. A Fine Business was sparing with his words, but those he did speak were always somehow essential. Usually, if he wanted to direct my attention somewhere, he would gently nudge me and then show me with his eyes, blinking.

At first I wouldn't see anything in particular in the courtyard, but with the nudge of his elbow and a few concise words, everything would seem significant, and all of it would remain a long time in my memory. A cat runs across the courtyard and stops before a bright puddle, sees its own reflection there, raises its soft paw as if to strike it.

"Cats are proud, distrustful," quietly says A Fine Business.

The rooster Mamai, whose feathers are a reddish gold, flies up onto the garden fence, beats his wings to steady himself there but almost falls, then stretches out his neck and mutters angrily, as if affronted.

"An important general, but not the smartest."

Valei comes clumsily toward the house, slopping through the mud like an old horse. His bony face is swollen. He squints and looks up into the sky as a white ray of autumn sunlight falls directly on his chest, and a copper button on his coat begins to burn. The Tatar stops and touches it with his crooked fingers.

"Like he's admiring a medal they just gave him. . . ."

I soon grew deeply attached to A Fine Business. He became crucial to me in both days of bitter injury and hours of joy. Himself disinclined to speak, he allowed me to talk about everything that entered my head, whereas grandfather would cut off my rambling speech with a stern shout:

"Stop talking nonsense! You're a mill for the devil!"

And grandmother was so filled with her own thoughts and impressions that she no longer heard or absorbed those of others.

A Fine Business always listened closely to my chattering, and would often say with a smile:

"Well now, brother, that isn't so. You're making that up yourself."

These sharp, essential observations always came at the exact moment when I needed to hear them. It was as if he saw right through everything that was taking shape in my heart and mind, saw every false and extraneous word before I had time to pronounce it—and seeing it, cut it away with three gentle blows:

"You're lying, brother."

I would deliberately test this magical ability of his quite often by inventing a story and telling it to him as if it had actually occurred. But as soon as he had heard a little, he would shake his head:

"Well, you're lying, brother."

"But how do you know?"

"Well, brother, I can see. . . ."

Grandmother often took me with her to get water on Sennaya Square. Once, while making this trip, we saw five townsmen beating a peasant. They knocked him down and tore at him like dogs setting on another dog.

"Run away!" grandmother shouted. She threw the buckets off her yoke and began swinging it as she charged the townsmen. Frightened, I ran after her and started throwing stones at the attackers while grandmother bravely jabbed at them with the yoke, striking at their shoulders and heads. Some other people interceded then, and the townsmen ran away. Grandmother began to wash the beaten man. His face was smashed, and even now with horror I can see him pressing his dirty fingers to his torn nostril, howling and coughing as blood spurted from behind those fingers, spattering grandmother's face and chest. She too was shouting and trembling all over.

When I got home I ran to the boarder's room to tell him what I'd seen. He stopped his work and stood before me, staring sternly from under his glasses and holding his long file like a saber before him. Suddenly he interrupted me, speaking with unusual force:

"Perfect—that's it exactly! That's how it was!"

Amazed by what I'd seen, I didn't pause to register his words and kept on talking, but he hugged me and began pacing around the room, sputtering:

"That's enough—you don't need to say more! You already said everything that's needed, brother. Understand? That's all!"

I stopped talking and felt hurt, but after thinking about it for a little while, I understood with a very memorable sense of amazement that he had stopped me at just the right moment: I really had said everything.

"Don't you dwell on those things, now, brother," he said. "It's not good to remember things like that."

Sometimes he'd unexpectedly say something that would remain with me all my life. Once I was telling him about my nemesis, Klyushnikov, a fat boy with a big head from New Street with whom I'd repeatedly fought to a draw. A Fine Business listened closely to my troubles and said:

"That's nothing—that kind of strength isn't strength at all. Real strength lies in the speed of movements: the faster the stronger. Follow?"

The next Sunday I tried to work my fists more quickly—and I easily overcame Klyushnikov. This heightened even further my regard for the words of A Fine Business.

"You have to know how to take things. Knowing how to take something—that's very difficult!"

Although I didn't understand anything, I would instinctively remember phrases like this. Some exasperating secret lay hidden in their simplicity, and for this reason, they lodged in my memory. After all, you didn't need any great skill to take a stone or a piece of bread, a hammer, a cup!

Common contempt for A Fine Business grew steadily. Even the merry wife's cat, who was affectionate with everyone, ignored A Fine Business's tender calls, and refused to crawl into his lap the way she would with all the other residents. I beat her for this, twisted her ears, practically broke into tears as I implored her not to be afraid of him.

"My clothes smell of acid. That's why the cat won't come to me," he'd say, but I knew that everyone else, even grandmother, had another explanation, one that was false and malicious.

"Why do you hang around him?" grandmother would ask angrily. "You watch he doesn't start teaching you things."

And grandfather, that redheaded weasel, would soundly beat me every time he learned that I had visited the boarder's room. Of course, I didn't tell A Fine Business that I was forbidden to associate with him, but I did talk openly about the way other people in the house felt about him.

"Grandmother's afraid of you. She says you practice black magic. Grandfather too—he says you're an enemy of God and a danger to people."

He jerked his head as if shaking off a fly. His chalk white cheeks turned pink as a smile flashed across his face and made my heart contract, made everything I saw turn green.

"I saw that already," he said quietly. "It's sad, isn't it, brother?"

"Yes."

"Sad, brother . . ."

In the end they drove him out.

I went to see him one morning after tea and found him sitting on the floor, putting his things into boxes and quietly singing about the rose of Sharon.

"Well, brother, say goodbye. I'm moving away."

"Why?"

He stared at me as he spoke.

"Don't you know? They need the room for your mother."

"Who said that?"

"Your grandfather."

"He's lying!"

A Fine Business drew me toward him by the hand, and when I'd sat down on the floor, he began to speak quietly.

"Don't be angry. I thought you knew, brother—knew and didn't tell me. That's not very good, I thought."

I felt both sad and irritated with him for something.

"Listen," he said, almost in a whisper, smiling. "Remember when I told you not to come to see me anymore?"

I nodded.

"You were upset with me, weren't you?"

"Yes."

"I didn't want to upset you, brother. It's just that I knew, you see, that if we became friends, they'd start to shout at you—right? Isn't that what happened? Do you understand now why I did that?"

He spoke with me as if he were also a child, as if he were my age, and I was terribly glad to hear these words. It seemed to me that I had understood him long ago, even then, when we first met. I told him this:

"I knew a long time ago."

"Well then—there you have it! There it is, dear friend."

My heart ached unbearably.

"Why don't any of them like you?"

He put his arms around me and hugged me. "I'm not like them," he said, blinking. "I'm a stranger to them. Because of that. Just because of that."

I pulled at his sleeve, not knowing what to say, unable to speak.

"Don't be angry," he said again. And whispering in my ear he added, "You shouldn't cry either."

But tears were already running down from behind his clouded glasses.

We sat there for a long time the way we always did—mostly silent, saying just a few short words now and then.

He left in the evening, having hugged me firmly and said goodbye warmly to everyone in the house. I went out beyond the gate and saw him shuddering in the back of a cart as its wheels pounded over the lumps of frozen mud in the road. As soon as he'd left, grandmother began cleaning his dirty room. I deliberately paced from one corner to the other in order to bother her.

"Go away!" she shouted, bumping into me.

"Why did you drive him out?"

"You tell me!"

"You're all fools," I said.

She swatted me with her wet rag, shouting:

"Shame on you! You've lost your mind! . . ."

"Not you—all the others are fools," I corrected myself, but this didn't placate her.

At dinner grandfather said:

"Well, thank God! . . . It got to be like a knife in my heart every time I saw him—'I've got to get him out of here,' I'd think."

I broke my spoon out of spite and endured another beating.

And so ended the first of my many friendships with someone from that endless line of people who are strangers in their homeland—the very best people in their country.

IX

I imagine myself in childhood as a kind of hive to which, like bees, simple, ordinary people bore the honey of their ideas and their knowledge of life, generously enriching my soul with whatever they could offer. The honey was often dirty and bitter, but knowledge of any sort is still honey.

After A Fine Business left, Uncle Pyotr made friends with me. Skinny, clean, and neat, he resembled grandfather, but he was shorter, smaller in every way. He looked like an adolescent who had dressed up as an old man for a joke. His face resembled something made of wicker, a sieve of thin leather strips, and between those plaits, his lively, comical eyes, the whites of which were slightly yellow, darted like siskins in a cage. His grey hair was curly, and his beard grew in ringlets. The smoke from his pipe was the same color as his hair, and it too wreathed around him. Laced with funny phrases and digressions, even his sentences seemed to wind and loop as he talked. He spoke in a droning voice that sounded affectionate, but I always had the sense he was laughing at everyone around him.

"The lady of the estate back then, Countess Tatyan—patronymic Leksevna—she says to me back in the early days, 'You go be a blacksmith.' So—off I go. But soon she tells me, 'Go help the gardener!' Well, fine, I think—no one's found a job a peasant can't get wrong. Another time she says, 'You, Petrushka, need to catch some fish.' All right, I can fish too. But once that gets to be my passion, it's 'Farewell fish, thank you very much,' and they send me off to town to drive a cart, give the wages to the countess. Well, all right then—a cart. What's for me to say? The emancipation came along before she and I could think up any more changes. When it was all said and done, I'd wound up with a horse in place of a countess."

The old animal looked as if a drunken decorator had begun to cover her white coat with different colored paints but never bothered to finish the

109

job. Her legs were out of joint. Her entire body resembled something sewn from rags and her eyes were clouded over. Her bony head drooped sadly; it seemed to be only weakly attached to her torso by a series of swollen tendons and a worn-out hide. Uncle Pytor never beat her, treated her respectfully, and called her Tanka.

"What are you doing calling an animal by a Christian name?" grandfather said to him once.

"Oh no, Vasily Vasilev, not at all, respected sir," Uncle Pyotr said. "There's a Christian name Tatiana—but there's no such name as Tanka, no sir."

Uncle Pyotr was literate, and being well read in the Holy Scripture, he always argued with grandfather about which saints were the holiest, or engaged with him in a kind of contest to see who could condemn the ancient sinners most harshly, with particular ire directed at Absalom. Sometimes these debates took on a purely grammatical bent. Grandfather would say "profaneness," "falseness," and "mendaciousness" while Uncle Pyotr insisted on "profanity," "falsity," and "mendacity."

"It's one thing your way—another mine," grandfather would say hotly, his face turning purple. "You with your itsy-bitsy little words!"

Wreathed in smoke, Uncle Pyotr would ask snidely: "Well, what about yours? You have to hiss like a snake to pronounce them. God must hear you and think, 'Pray all you please, you'll get no reprieve.'"

"Leksey—leave the room!" grandfather would shout fiercely, his green eyes flashing.

Pyotr loved cleanliness and order. If he came across some bit of refuse as he walked through the courtyard—a wood chip, a pottery shard, a bone— he'd kick it aside and say reproachfully:

"Useless junk! You're in the way!"

He was talkative and he seemed happy and kind-hearted, but sometimes his eyes would fill with blood, grow turbid and still, like the eyes of a corpse. At times he'd hide somewhere in a corner, in the dark, hunched over, gloomy, mute as his nephew.

"What's wrong, Uncle Pyotr?"

"Get away," he'd say in a hard, blank voice.

Some sort of *barin* moved into one of the houses on our street. He had a large bump on his head and an exceedingly strange habit: on holidays he would sit at his window and fire small shot from a rifle at dogs, cats, chickens, crows, and even pedestrians whom he didn't like. Once he sprayed A Fine Business with small shot. It didn't penetrate his leather coat, but some of it wound up in his pocket. I remember how attentively A Fine Business peered through his glasses to examine the blue-grey pellets. Grandfather began urging him to complain, but he tossed the small shot into a corner of the kitchen and said, "It isn't worth it."

On another occasion the marksman sprayed several pellets into grandfather's leg. Furious, he petitioned to the justice of the peace and began assembling victims and witnesses, but the *barin* suddenly disappeared somewhere.

Every time those gunshots boomed on the street, Uncle Pyotr—if he was home—would hurry to cover his greying head with a flamboyant peaked cap that had faded from too much sun and go running out the gate. Once on the street, he'd hide his hands under the back of his caftan, raising it like a rooster's tail, stick out his chest, and resolutely stroll past the marksman's house. He'd go past once, turn, come back—and then do it again. Everyone from our house would be standing at the gate while the soldier watched from a window, his wife's blonde head sticking up over his purplish face. Various people would come from the Betlengs' courtyard as well. Only the grey, lifeless home of the Ovsyannikovs revealed no one.

Sometimes Uncle Pyotr's walks were fruitless—apparently the marksman didn't consider him sufficiently worthy game to bother shooting, but occasionally the double barreled gun would boom in quick succession:

"*Bukh-bukh!*"

Without hurrying his steps, Uncle Pyotr would approach us and say with great satisfaction:

"Right through my caftan!"

Once the small shot hit him in the shoulder and neck. Picking it out with a needle, grandmother reproached him:

"What are you encouraging that savage for? And what will you do when he blasts out one of your eyes?"

"No-oo, Akulina Ivanovna," Pyotr drawled scornfully. "He's not nearly that good a shot!"

"But why are you egging him on?"

"Am I egging him on? I wanted to tease him." And looking at the extracted buckshot now lying in his palm, he said:

"No, he can't shoot at all! Now once the Countess Tatyan Leksevna had a fellow fulfilling her conjugal obligations—she changed husbands like butlers—and this fellow, Mamont Ilich, I tell you—he was a military man, and he knew how to shoot! And he, grandmother, used bullets—nothing else! He'd stand the fool Ignashka somewhere far away—maybe forty paces from him, and tie a bottle to the fool's belt so it dangled between his legs.

Ignashka stands there with his legs spread apart, laughing like an idiot while Mamont Ilich aims his pistol and—*bots!*—the bottle shatters! Only one time some kind of gadfly bit Ignashka—he flinched and the bullet hit him in the leg, right in the knee cap! They called a doctor, and he chopped the leg clean off—took no time at all. They buried it. . . ."

"And the fool?"

"He was just fine. A fool doesn't need arms or legs—his stupidity's all it takes to keep him well fed. Everyone loves a fool because stupidity can't hurt your feelings. It's like they say:

Simple folk fear no offense
Where the deacon's dumb
And the bailiff's dense."

Stories like this didn't surprise grandmother—she knew dozens of them. But I was uneasy:

"Can a nobleman just kill someone?"

"Oh, yes. Why not? Of course he can. They even kill each other. Once an *uhlan* came to visit Tatyan Leksevna. He and Mamont have an argument, and right away the two of them are off to the park with pistols in their hands. And there on the road by the pond that *uhlan*—*bots!*—he gives one to Mamont right in the liver. Then the *uhlan's* off to the Caucasus—and Mamont's headed for the churchyard. That's how they do things with each other! There's nothing to say when it comes to common people. Especially now, since we're no longer theirs. Before they might be a little sorry to kill someone off—it was their property, after all. But now we're nothing to them. . . ."

"They were never too sorry," grandmother said.

"Well, yes, that's true too," Pyotr agreed. "It was their property, but it was always cheap. . . ."

He treated me with a certain tenderness, spoke to me in a voice that was kinder than the one he used with others, never hid his eyes from me. But there was something about him I didn't like. Treating everyone to his favorite jam, he always gave my piece of bread the thickest coating, brought me gingerbread cookies and poppy seed treats from town, talked with me in a quiet, serious way:

"Well, little sir, how are we going to get by? As a soldier or a clerk?"

"Soldier."

"That's good. It's not so hard to be a soldier these days. A priest's good too. You just shout, 'God have mercy!' every once in a while, and that's about it. The priesthood's easier than soldiering—but fishing's easiest of all. There no learning anything—it just comes natural."

He could do a funny imitation of a fish circling a hook, a perch, a chub, or a bream struggling on a line.

"Now you get angry when your grandfather switches you," he'd say comfortingly. "But there's no point in getting angry about that, little sir. He switches you for your education. And the beatings he gives you—they're for children! Now my mistress Tatyan Leksevna—her beatings were famous! She had a special person to do it. He was named Khristofor, and he was such a master of his craft that neighbors from other estates would ask to borrow him: 'Please, Lady Tatyan Leksevna, let Khristofor come over and beat some of our house serfs.' She'd let him go. . . ."

Without the slightest sense of outrage he described in detail how the countess, wearing a white muslin dress and an airy, sky-blue shawl, would sit in a red armchair on the columned porch and watch Khristofor whipping men and women.

"That Khristofor, he came from Ryazan, but he looked like a gypsy or some type of Ukrainian. His mustache reached all the way to his ears, and his face was blue—he shaved his beard. He was either a bit dim-witted, or he just pretended to be slow so people didn't ask him a lot of questions. Sometimes he'd fill a cup with water in the kitchen and use a little stick to drown whatever he caught—a fly or a cockroach, some kind of beetle. He'd take a long time drowning them. Sometimes he'd find very good things for drowning right under his own collar . . ."

These kinds of stories were already well known to me. I'd heard them many times from grandmother and grandfather, and although the details varied, they were strangely similar in essence. Someone was always being tormented, humiliated, or harassed. I was tired of these accounts. I didn't want to hear about such things anymore.

"Tell a different story," I asked Uncle Pyotr.

He drew all the wrinkles of his face toward his mouth, then raised them to his eyes and said:

"All right, my greedy little friend. Once we had a cook . . ."

"Who?"

"Countess Tatyan Leksevna . . ."

"Why do you call her Tatyan instead of Tatyana? It makes her sound like a man."

He let out a thin laugh. "She's a lady, of course, although she did have a little black moustache—she came from black Germans, you see—people like Negroes. Anyway, the cook—this is a funny story, little sir . . ."

The funny story consisted of the cook ruining a meat pie, being forced to eat the entire thing himself, and getting sick.

"That's not funny at all!" I said angrily.

"Oh? Well what is funny? You tell me then. Well—you tell me what's funny!"

"I don't know . . ."

"Then keep quiet!"

And again he'd unwind the threads of some tedious story.

Sometimes my cousins would come to visit on holidays. Mikhail's Sasha was still lazy and sad, while Yakov's remained neat and all-knowing as ever. Once the three of us were walking around on the rooftops when we saw a *barin* in the Betlengs' courtyard. He wore a green frock coat lined with fur and sat on a pile of firewood, playing with some puppies. His bald, yellowing little head was uncovered. One of the cousins suggested that we steal one of the puppies, and a clever plan for the theft quickly took shape: the cousins would leave immediately to wait on the street by the Betlengs' gate; I would frighten the nobleman, and when he ran away in alarm, the cousins would steal into the courtyard and make off with one of the puppies.

"How am I going to frighten him?"

"Spit on his head—on his bald patch!" one of the cousins suggested.

Is it a great sin to spit on someone's head? I'd heard many times and seen with my own eyes that far worse things are done to people, and therefore, I resolutely carried out the assignment given me.

Scandal and uproar ensued. Toward us in the courtyard ran an entire army of men and women from the Betlengs' house, led by a handsome young officer. Since the cousins had been walking innocently on the street at the moment of the crime—and knew nothing of my savage behavior— grandfather flogged only me, thoroughly satisfying each member of the Betleng household.

While I lay beaten on the bench above the stove, Uncle Pyotr came climbing up to me, festively dressed and happy.

"That was very skillful thinking, littler sir," he whispered. "That's just what the old goat deserved—spit on them all! Even better—drop a rock on his rotten old head!"

The round, hairless, childlike face of the *barin* rose before me, and I remembered how he'd squealed quietly, pathetically, like a puppy as he wiped his bald, yellow pate with his little hands. The shame I felt was unbearable. I hated my cousins. But all of that disappeared as soon as I glimpsed the cart driver's wattled face above me. It was twitching in the same foul and frightening way that my grandfather's face had trembled as he beat me.

"Go away," I shouted, pushing at him with my feet and hands.

He began to giggle, winked, and climbed down from the stove.

From that time on I lost all desire to talk to Uncle Pyotr. I started to avoid the cart driver while at the same time observing him with suspicion, vaguely expecting something.

Another incident soon followed the episode with the *barin*. The Ovsyannikov house had caught my attention long ago, for it seemed that some kind of secret life, something from a fairy tale was unfolding within those blank and ordinary walls.

They lived happily and noisily at the Betleng house. There were pretty young ladies in the family, and students and officers came to visit them. They were always laughing and shouting, singing, playing instruments. The house's exterior was itself cheerful. The glass on the windows shone cleanly, a rich profusion of green plants visible behind them. Grandfather didn't like the house.

"Heretics! Atheists!" he said of all its residents. He called the women by foul names, which Uncle Pyotr once explained to me with equally disgusting words, gloating as he uttered them.

The Ovsyannikovs' stern and silent house inspired grandfather's respect.

Although it consisted of only one story, the building rose quite high from the clean, bare courtyard that surrounded it, thickly overgrown with grass. In the middle of the courtyard was a well under a little roof that stood on two columns. The house seemed to hold itself back from the street, as if hiding. Its three front windows were arched and narrow, set far above the ground, with cloudy panes of glass that turned all the colors of a rainbow when struck by sunlight. On the other side of the gate stood a storehouse. Its front was identical to that of the main house, but its three windows were false: the casings had been pounded into the wall, and the white window frames were simply painted onto the grey facade. These blind windows were unpleasant, and the storehouse reinforced a sense that the entire household wished to hide away, exist unnoticed. There was an air of either quiet pride or quiet injury to everything about the place, its empty stables, its deserted sheds and huge gates.

Sometimes a tall old man would come limping into the courtyard, his chin clean shaven, the hair of his white mustache bristling like needles. Sometimes another old man with sideburns and a crooked nose would lead from the stable a grey horse with a long head. The horse's chest was narrow and its legs delicate. Entering the courtyard, it would bow to everyone present, like a meek and humble nun. The old man with the limp would loudly slap the horse with his palm, whistle, sigh loudly—and then they'd hide the horse away again in the dark stable. I had the idea that the old man wanted to leave the house but couldn't because of a spell that had been cast on him.

Three boys played in the courtyard almost every day from early afternoon to evening. Dressed alike in grey coats and pants, with identical hats, round faces, and grey eyes, they so closely resembled one another that I could tell them apart only by height.

I would watch them through a crack in the fence. I wanted them to notice me, but they never did. I liked the happy, friendly way they played together at games I didn't know. I liked their clothes and their concern for one another, which was especially apparent in the way the older brothers treated the youngest, a funny, lively, little sprig. If he fell, they'd laugh the way one always laughs if someone falls, but their laughter had no gloating to it, and they'd help him up right away. If he got his hands or his knees dirty, they'd wipe his pants or his hands with their handkerchiefs and burdock leaves, and the middle one would say kindheartedly:

"Such a cwumsy won!"

They never fought or deceived one another, and each was graceful, strong, and tireless.

Once I climbed into a tree and whistled at them—they stopped where they were and calmly gathered together, discussing something, glancing up at me from time to time. I thought they would start throwing rocks at me, so I climbed down, put some stones in my pockets for ammunition, and returned to my perch in the tree. But by then they were playing in a faraway corner of the courtyard and, apparently, had forgotten my presence. This was disappointing, but I didn't want to be the one to start a war, and soon someone shouted from one of the windows:

"Children—straight home! Now!"

Unhurriedly, obediently, they started toward the house like geese.

I sat in the tree above the fence many times and watched them, thinking, "Now, now they'll call me down to play with them"—but they never did. In my mind, I would join them in their games, at times getting so carried away that I'd shout or laugh loudly. Then the three of them would look up at me, quietly discussing something, and I would sheepishly climb down to the ground.

Once they were playing hide and seek. It was the middle boy's turn to search, so he stood in a corner behind the storehouse, covering his eyes with his hands, not peeking as his brothers ran to hide. The oldest boy quickly and skillfully climbed into a wide sledge parked under the storehouse awning, but the little one began to panic, running comically around the well and finding nowhere to hide.

"One," shouted the middle boy. "Two!"

The youngest brother jumped onto the well's wooden railing, grabbed the rope, stuck his feet into the empty bucket—and disappeared, the bucket knocking dully against the well's side as it dropped. The pulley was well greased; it spun rapidly, silently releasing more and more rope. I froze for a moment, watching it. But then I fully grasped what could happen next, and leaped down into the courtyard, shouting:

"He fell in the well!"

The middle boy reached the well's railing together with me and grabbed the rope. It pulled him off the ground and burned his hands, but then I managed to catch hold of it, and a moment later, the oldest brother had come running.

"Careful, careful, please," he said as he helped me pull.

We quickly hauled the youngest brother up in the bucket. He too was frightened. Blood was dripping from the fingers of his right hand, his cheek was badly grazed, and he was wet from the waist down. His face had a blue tinge, but he was smiling as he shuddered, his eyes held wide, and drawled:

"I fell a loo-ong way . . ."

"You wost your mind, that's what!" said the middle one, embracing him and using a handkerchief to wipe the blood from his face. The oldest brother frowned and said:

"Let's go. There's no hiding it."

"Will you get a beating?" I asked.

He nodded, then extended his hand to me, saying:

"You came running fast!"

Gladdened by this praise, I didn't have time to take his hand before he'd turned to the middle brother again.

"Let's go," he said. "He's going to catch cold. We'll say he fell—but nothing about the well."

"Yes, let's not say anything about that," agreed the youngest brother, still shivering. "I fell in a puddle—right?"

They left.

It had all taken place so quickly that when I looked back to the tree branch where I'd been, I saw that it was still rocking, dropping yellow leaves.

The brothers didn't come out into the courtyard for a week, then they reappeared, noisier than before. When the oldest one saw me, he shouted warmly:

"Come over here!"

We gathered in the sledge under the storehouse awning and sat there for a long time, sizing each other up as we talked.

"Did you get a beating?" I asked.

"There was no way around it," the oldest one answered.

It was hard to believe that someone beat these boys the same way they beat me. I felt angry and hurt for them.

"Why do you catch birds?" the youngest one asked me.

"They sing nice," I said.

"No, don't catch them anymore," he said. "Let them fly where they want."

"Well, all right. I won't catch them anymore."

"Only, first, catch me one."

"What kind do you want?"

"One that's happy. Even in the cage."

"Probably a siskin . . ."

"The cat will eat it," said the middle brother. "And papa won't let you."

The oldest boy agreed. "He won't."

"Do you have a mother?"

"No," said the oldest brother, but the middle one corrected him:

"We do, only she's another one, not ours. We don't have ours. She died."

"The other one's called a stepmother," I said.

"Yes," the older brother nodded.

The three of them grew pensive, gloomy. Knowing from grandmother's stories what a stepmother meant, I understood their preoccupation. They sat huddled close together, identical, like chicks.

"Your mother will still come back—just wait a little," I promised them, thinking of the stepmother witch who used trickery to take the place of a natural mother.

The oldest boy shrugged. "But if she died? It doesn't happen like that."

Doesn't happen like that? How many times have the dead—even those who were chopped into pieces—risen anew when sprinkled with living water? How many times has death proven false, been revealed as the work of a wizard or a witch rather than something true and divine?

I began excitedly telling them grandmother's stories. The oldest one smiled at first, saying quietly:

"We know that, those are all stories. . . ."

His brothers listened silently. The smallest one pressed his lips together and puffed out his cheeks, while the middle brother leaned toward me, one elbow resting on his knee, the other arm draped around his brother's neck, pulling him forward.

The twilight was already deep and red clouds were hanging over the rooftops when the old man with a white mustache appeared near us, wearing a long brown cloak like a priest's vestments and a shaggy fur hat.

"Who's that?" he asked, pointing at me.

The oldest brother stood up and nodded toward grandfather's house.

"He's from over there."

"Who asked him here?"

The three boys immediately climbed out of the sledge without speaking and started home, reminding me again of well-behaved geese.

The old man grabbed me firmly by the shoulder and led me through the courtyard to the gate. I felt the urge to cry from fear, but he took such long, quick steps that I found myself in the street before I had the chance. Stopping at the gate, he shook his finger at me and said:

"Don't dare come on my property again!"

My temper flared. "I wouldn't go near you, you old devil!"

With his long arm he seized me again and began leading me down the sidewalk, asking:

"Is your grandfather home?"

His words fell like hammer blows on my head.

Much to my dismay, grandfather did turn out to be at home. He stood before the threatening old man with his head raised and his beard thrust out before him, speaking hurriedly as he stared into a pair of eyes as round and lifeless as two cheap coins.

"His mother's away, and I'm a busy man. There's no one to keep an eye on him. Forgive us, please, colonel."

The colonel filled the house with his quacking, then turned and left, straight as a wooden post. A little later I was thrown out into the courtyard, to Uncle Pyotr's cart.

"Another outburst, little sir?" he asked, harnessing his horse. "What did you get beaten for this time?"

When I told him, his face flushed and he started hissing:

"What did you make friends with them for? Little *barins*—they're all snakes! Look what you got for talking to them! You should show them how it feels! Let them see what it's like."

Embittered by the beating I'd just endured, I listened at first with sympathy to Uncle Pyotr, but his wicker face trembled ever more unpleasantly, and it reminded me that the three brothers would also be beaten—and that I had nothing to reproach them for.

"There's no reason to beat them. They're good people—and you lie about everything," I said.

He peered at me, then suddenly began to shout:

"Get off the cart!"

"You're a fool!" I shouted and jumped down to the ground.

He began to chase me around the courtyard, shouting unnaturally as he ran and tried to catch me:

"I'm a fool, am I? I lie? I'll show you a fool! . . ."

Grandmother came out onto the porch, and I rushed toward her as he began denouncing me:

"He won't give me any peace! I'm five times his age and he calls me a liar! Curses at me—uses swear words!"

Whenever people lied to my face, I'd grow completely flustered, turn stupid—and so it was at that moment. I was completely lost. But grandmother said firmly:

"No, Pyotr, really—you're lying outright now. He'd never say use such shameful words!"

Grandfather would have believed him.

From that moment on, a quiet, malicious little war ensued between the two of us. He'd try to bump into me or catch me with his reins as if by accident. He let my birds out of their cages and once set a cat on them. And he constantly appealed to grandfather with false or exaggerated complaints against me. More and more it seemed that he was a boy just like me—that he'd only dressed up to look like an old man. I would undo the weaving on his bast shoes, cut their straps slightly so they'd break when he went to lace them up. Once I put pepper in his hat and made him sneeze for an entire hour. In general, I made it a point to use everything within the powers of my strength and intellect to even the score with him on every count. He watched me very closely on holidays and more than once came upon me talking with the three brothers—a forbidden activity for which he promptly denounced me to grandfather.

My acquaintance with the three boys continued, and I took more and more pleasure in it. There was a secluded little corner between one wall of grandfather's house and the Ovsyannikovs' fence where a lime tree, an elm, and a dense elder bush grew. I cut a half circle in the fence under the bush, and the brothers would come there, either in pairs or individually, and we would talk quietly, squatting or kneeling on the ground. One of them would always keep watch so that the colonel didn't catch us unaware.

They told me about their unhappy life, which deeply saddened me. We discussed the lives of my captured birds and many children's things, but they never said a word about their father or their stepmother—at least, I don't remember them doing so. Mostly they just asked me to tell a story. I would very carefully repeat one of grandmother's tales, and if I forgot something, I would ask them to wait while I ran off to her for help, which always seemed to please her.

I told them a great deal about grandmother, and once the oldest brother sighed deeply, and said:

"It seems like all grandmothers are good. Ours was good too. . . ."

He spoke so often and so sadly about what was, what used to be, that it seemed he'd already lived on this earth for a hundred years rather than just eleven. I remember that he had very narrow palms and delicate fingers—he was altogether thin and frail while his eyes were both bright and mild, like the glow of an icon lamp. His brothers were very endearing; I trusted them deeply and instinctively, and I always wanted to do something to make them happy, but I liked the oldest of the three the most.

Carried away with the conversation, I often failed to notice Uncle Pyotr until he suddenly appeared and drove us apart, drawling:

"Ag-ai-n?"

I could see that his bouts of deep depression were recurring with increasing frequency, and even learned to determine his mood beforehand as he returned from work: usually he would open the gate unhurriedly, and its hinges would release a long, leisurely groan. But if the cart driver was in a bad mood, they yelped, sharply and briefly, as if gasping in pain.

His mute nephew went away to get married in the countryside, and Uncle Pyotr lived alone above the stables. His room was like a kennel, with a low ceiling, a tiny window, and the heavy odor of musty leather, tar, sweat, and tobacco—a smell that always kept me from visiting him. He slept without ever putting out his lamp, which grandfather didn't like at all:

"You're going to burn us down, Pyotr!"

"Not at all, don't worry! I put the light in a glass of water at night," he'd answer, looking off to the side.

He was always looking off to the side now, and he had long ago stopped coming to grandmother's evenings in the kitchen. He didn't treat anyone to jam anymore. His face had shrunk, his wrinkles grown deeper, and he swayed while he walked, dragging his feet as if ill.

One weekday morning I was helping grandfather shovel the snow that had fallen thickly in our courtyard when the catch on the gate opened with a particularly sharp click: a policeman entered from the street, closed the gate with his back, and motioned to grandfather with his fat, grey finger. Grandfather approached him, and the policeman began speaking inaudibly, leaning his face so close that his large nose seemed to be poking the old man's forehead.

"Here! When? Let me think . . ." grandfather answered hurriedly.

Suddenly he made a funny little jump and said: "God almighty, really?"

"Quiet," said the policeman sharply.

Grandfather looked around and caught sight of me.

"Put the shovels away and get in the house."

I hid around the corner. They went to the cart driver's kennel. The policeman took the glove off his right hand and slapped it against the palm of his left, saying:

"He knows. He left the horse and went into hiding somewhere. . . ."

I ran to the kitchen to tell grandmother everything I'd seen and heard. Her hair was dusted with flour as she kneaded dough for bread, shaking her head slightly.

"He must have stolen something," she said matter-of-factly after hearing what I had to say. "What's it to you? Go play outside."

When I hurried back into the courtyard, grandfather was standing by the gate. He took off his hat and crossed himself, looking up at the sky. His face was angry, bristling, and one of his legs was trembling.

"I said 'go home'!" he shouted at me, stamping his foot.

He followed me back and called out as soon as he entered the kitchen:

"Come here, mother."

They went into the next room and whispered there for a long time. When grandmother came back into the kitchen it was clear to me that something terrible had happened.

"What's frightened you?"

"Learn to keep quiet," she answered softly.

All day the mood at home was grim and anxious. Grandmother and grandfather glanced at each other uneasily, exchanged brief, incomprehensible words that deepened the sense of alarm.

"Keep the icon lamps burning everywhere, now, mother," grandfather ordered, coughing.

We ate lunch unwillingly, hurriedly, as if expecting someone. Grandfather puffed out his cheeks wearily, grumbled and wheezed.

"The devil's strong in his machinations against man. . . . He seemed all pious, eh? A churchgoer . . ."

Grandmother sighed.

The murky, silver-matted winter day stretched on and on in its tedium while everything at home grew only more unsettled and oppressive.

Another policeman came toward evening. This one was red-haired and fat. He sat on the bench in the kitchen and dozed off, breathing heavily and bending forward, as if bowing in his sleep.

"How was all of this uncovered?" grandmother asked.

He paused, then answered huskily:

"Don't you be afraid! We'll uncover everything!"

I remember how I sat by the window, trying to warm up a coin in my mouth so that I could press it into the ice on the glass and make an impression there of St. George killing the dragon.

Suddenly there was a heavy banging in the vestibule, the door flew open, and from the threshold Petrovna shouted deafeningly:

"Look in your courtyard! What's back there?"

Catching sight of the policeman, she tried to dart back into the vestibule, but he caught her by her skirt and began to yell with equal alarm:

"Stop! Who are you? Look at what?"

She stumbled on the threshold, fell to her knees, and started wailing, choking on her words and tears:

"I'm going out to milk the cows and I look—what's that in Kashirin's garden? It looks like a boot. . . ."

Grandfather began to stamp his feet.

"You're lying! You fool," he bellowed. "You couldn't see anything in our garden from there! There's a high fence there, and it's got no gaps! There's nothing there!"

"You're right," cried Petrovna, stretching one hand toward him, clutching her head with the other. "You're right, sir. . . . I was going to milk the cows and I see tracks to your fence, and the snow's all beaten down in one place. So I look over the fence and I see him! See him lying there!"

"Who-oo-oo?"

This shout lasted a terribly long time, and it was impossible to make the slightest sense of it, but as it receded, all the people in the house seemed to lose their minds, shoving each other as they ran from the kitchen to the garden—and there, in the snow that had softly covered the bottom of the pit, lay Uncle Pyotr, his back leaning against one of the charred beams, his head drooping down to his chest. Under his right ear was a deep gash, like a large red mouth. Little, dark blue pieces of something stuck out of it like teeth. Frightened, I closed my eyes partway, but through my lashes I could still see in Pyotr's lap the knife I knew he used for cutting leather; his right hand lay near the blade, its dark fingers tightly knotted in a ball. He'd flung his left hand out to the side, and now it was buried in the snow. The snow beneath him was melting, and his small body was sinking deeper into the soft, light down, which made him seem even more like a child. A strange red pattern in the shape of a bird had spread out over the snow to his right, while to the left it was smooth, untouched, blindingly bright. He seemed to bow his head in submission, his chin flattening his thick and curly beard against his bare chest, where a large copper cross lay in the streams of congealed blood. My head was spinning heavily from the noise of all the voices around me. Petrovna shouted ceaselessly. The policeman shouted. Grandfather shouted at Valei, ordering him to go somewhere:

"And don't walk over the tracks!"

But then he frowned and, staring at his feet, grandfather said to the policeman with sudden force and authority:

"There's no reason for you to be shouting here, officer! This is God's affair, God's judgment! And you come here with your trash! Akh, you-u . . ."

Right away everyone fell silent; everyone stared at the dead man, crossing themselves, sighing. People were running toward us from the courtyard. They climbed over the fence from Petrovna's, fell, rumbled in the distance, but it stayed quiet where we were until grandfather suddenly looked around and began to wail in despair:

"People! Neighbors! Look where you're running—you're destroying our raspberry patch! Aren't you ashamed?"

Grandmother took me by the hand and, sobbing, led me home.

"What did he do?" I asked, and she answered:

"Couldn't you see?"

All evening, until late that night, strangers crowded into our kitchen and the room next to it, shouting while a policeman gave orders and a man who resembled a deacon wrote something, quacking like a duck as he asked:

"What? What?"

Grandmother gave tea to everyone in the kitchen. At the table sat a chubby man with a mustache, a pockmarked face, and a rasping voice.

"His real name is still unknown to us," he said. "We only know that he was born in Elatma. And the mute is not mute at all—he's confessed to everything. A third's confessed as well—there's a third person in this too. They'd been robbing churches for a long time—that was their specialty."

"Oh, God," sighed Petrovna, wet and red.

I lay on the bench over the stove, looking down. All the people looked very short to me, looked fat and horrible.

X

Early one Saturday morning I went into Petrovna's garden to catch bull-finches. I tried to catch them for a long time, but none would enter my trap. They seemed to be flaunting their beauty as they paced along the snow's silvery crust with amusing self-importance or flew up into the bushes, where the branches were warmly coated in frost, and the red-breasted birds rocked up and down, like flowers with beating hearts, scattering snow in blue sparks. It was so beautiful that I felt no frustration with my unsuccessful hunt. In general, I was an unenthusiastic hunter, always preferring the process to the result. I liked just thinking about the birds, watching how they went about their lives.

It's good to sit alone at the edge of a snowy field, listening to birds chirp in the crystalline silence of a frost-bound day while somewhere far away the bell of a passing troika sings as it flies into the distance, sad lark of the Russian winter.

Feeling my ears grow numb, I jumped around in the snow to warm myself, then gathered up my snares and cages, climbed into grandfather's garden, and headed home. The gate to the street was open, and a huge peasant was leading three horses harnessed to a large, closed sleigh from the courtyard. Steam rose thickly from the horses, and the driver whistled happily. My heart leaped.

"Who did you bring?"

He turned, looked at me under his arm, jumped up to the driver's seat, and said:

"A priest."

Well, this had nothing to do with me. If it's a priest, he must be coming to the boarders.

"Ekh, my little chicks!" the driver shouted. He whistled and touched the horses with his reins, filling the silence with his happy noise. The horses strained good naturedly toward the field. I looked after them and closed the gate. But when I went into the empty kitchen, my mother's powerful voice was ringing out in the next room, her words precise and clear:

"Well, what now then—kill me?"

I dropped my cages and rushed into the vestibule without taking off my coat—and ran straight into grandfather. He grabbed me by the shoulder, looked me in the face with wild eyes, and swallowed hard.

"Your mother's here—go on!" he wheezed. "Wait!" He shook me so hard I tottered on my feet. Then he pushed me toward the door. "Go on!"

I fumbled with the door—it was covered in felt and oil-cloth for insulation, and for a long time, I couldn't find the latch, my hands trembling from cold and excitement. Finally I managed to open it, quietly. I stood blind at the room's threshold.

"There he is!" said my mother. "My goodness you're big! What, don't you recognize me? But just look how you're dressing him, what a . . . And his ears are white! *Mamasha*, get the goose fat, quickly. . . ."

She stood in the center of the room, bending over me, peeling off my clothes, turning me like a ball. Her large body was wrapped in a soft, warm red dress, wide as a man's coat with a row of big black buttons on the side that went all the way from the neck to the hem. I'd never seen such a dress.

Her face looked smaller than before, smaller and paler, while her eyes seemed to have grown larger and deeper. There was more gold in her hair. She threw my clothes toward the room's threshold as she undressed me, her dark red lips curling squeamishly. Her commanding voice filled the room:

"Why aren't you saying anything? Are you glad? Ugh, what a dirty shirt! . . ."

Then she rubbed the goose fat on my ears. It hurt, but from her came a sweet, refreshing smell, and this eased the pain. I pressed myself to her, glancing at her eyes, speechless with excitement.

Through her voice I could hear grandmother speaking quietly, unhappily:

"He's full of his own will. Doesn't listen to anyone. Isn't even afraid of grandfather. . . . Akh, Varya, Varya . . ."

"All right, *mamasha*, all right. Don't whine. It will all work out."

Compared to my mother, everything was old, small, and pathetic. I too felt old—old as grandfather. She pressed me between her strong knees, stroked my hair with her warm and heavy hand, said:

"You need a haircut. And it's time to start school. Do you want to go to school to learn?"

"I already learned everything."

"There's still a little more you need to learn. No, just look how strong you are, eh?"

And she laughed in a rich, warm voice as she played with me.

Grandfather came into the room, grey, red-eyed, bristling. She moved me aside with her hand.

"Well then, *papasha*—should I leave?"

He stopped at the window, scratched at the ice on the glass with his fingernail. He didn't speak for a long time. Everything grew strained, turned terrible—and as always in such moments of extreme tension, it seemed my body was covered with eyes and ears. Something rose inside my chest and made it swell, made me long to shout.

"Leksey, get out," grandfather said blankly.

"Why?" said mother, again drawing me toward her.

"You're not going anywhere. I forbid it."

Mother rose and drifted across the room like some kind of luminous cloud, then stopped behind him.

"*Papasha*, listen . . ."

He turned toward her and screamed: "Quiet!"

"Well, that I won't allow," my mother said softly. "I won't let you shout at me."

Grandmother got up from the couch and shook her finger.

"Varvara!"

"Wait, wait—who am I? Eh?" Grandfather muttered, dropping into a chair. "Who am I?"

Suddenly he roared in a voice that wasn't his:

"You shamed me, Varvara!"

"Leave," grandmother ordered me. Crushed, I went into the kitchen, climbed onto the stove, and listened for a long time to them talking on the other side of the partition. Sometimes they spoke all at once and interrupted each other; other times they all went silent, as if they'd suddenly fallen asleep. They were talking about a child that mother had given away to someone, but it was impossible to understand why grandfather was angry—because mother had the baby without asking him, or because she didn't bring the baby to him.

Then he came into the kitchen, disheveled, purple, spent. Grandmother followed him, wiping tears from her cheeks with the hem of her jacket. Grandfather sat down on the bench, bracing himself with his arms, hunched over, trembling, biting his grey lips. Grandmother knelt before him and began to speak in a quiet but urgent whisper:

"Forgive her, father; forgive her in Christ's name. Even the strongest sled can be broken. Do you really think this doesn't happen with the gentry?

With the merchants? Look what a woman she is! Please now, forgive her. None of us is free of sin. . . ."

Grandfather leaned back against the wall, looked at her face and smiled crookedly as he growled and sobbed:

"Well, of course—what else! Who don't you want to forgive? You forgive everyone! It's always the same! Akh, you-u . . ."

He leaned over and grabbed her by the shoulder, began to shake her, whispering rapidly:

"And God, meanwhile—He doesn't forgive a thing, does He! The grave's about to swallow us both and He keeps right on punishing us through our last days. There'll be no peace, no joy for us. And mark my words—we'll die beggars, beggars!"

Grandmother took his hands, sat down next to him, and began to laugh softly.

"What's the harm in that? So we'll be beggars. What are you so afraid of? You'll sit at home and I'll go out to the people for help. They'll give plenty to me. We'll be well fed! You let all that go. . . ."

He suddenly began to laugh, turning his head like a goat and grabbing grandmother by the neck, pressing himself to her, small, wrinkled, sobbing.

"Ekh, you fool—you holy fool, my last true person. There's nothing you regret, little fool—nothing you wouldn't give away. And you don't understand a thing! Think of how we've struggled, how I've sinned for them. . . . If we just had a little now—just the slightest bit to show for it. . . ."

Unable to endure any more, I burst into tears, jumped down from the stove, and rushed to them, sobbing. I sobbed out of sorrow for them, and out of joy from their words, for I'd never heard them speak so well to each other. I sobbed because my mother had come, and because they didn't question my right to join them in weeping, hugging me, squeezing me, shedding their tears on me while grandfather whispered in my ears and eyes:

"Akh, and you're here too, are you?—you little fiend! Now your mother's come you'll spend all your time with her. No need for grandfather anymore, the cranky old devil, eh? And grandmother too—your indulger, your spoiler—no need for her anymore either, eh? Akh, you-u . . ."

He spread his arms apart, moving us aside, and rose to his feet.

"Everyone's leaving. Everyone's straining to get away. It's all coming apart . . ." he said loudly and angrily. "Well, go on—call her here. . . . Let's get this over with!"

Grandmother left the kitchen. He bowed his head and spoke toward the icon corner:

"All merciful God, well, now You'll see—now!"

He struck his fist hard against his chest with an audible thud. I didn't like this—in general, I didn't like the way grandfather spoke to God. He always seemed to be boasting before Him.

Mother came, and the kitchen grew brighter from her red clothes. She sat down on the bench at the table with grandmother and grandfather on either side of her, the wide sleeves of her dress draped over their shoulders. She quietly and seriously told them about something, and they listened without speaking or interrupting. They both turned into children then, and it seemed she was their mother.

Worn out from worry and excitement, I fell asleep on the stove. In the evening grandmother and grandfather dressed up for evening services. Seeing grandfather in the full uniform of the guild elder, a raccoon coat, and pants specially cut to be worn outside one's boots, grandmother winked happily at him and said to my mother:

"Just look at what a father you have—such a neat little goat."

My mother laughed lightheartedly.

When I was left alone with her in her room, she sat on the couch and folded her legs under her.

"Come sit with me," she said, patting the place beside her with her palm. "How are you doing here? Pretty bad, eh?"

How was I doing?

"I don't know."

"Does grandfather beat you?"

"Not so much anymore."

"Really? Well, tell me about something—whatever you want. Well?"

I didn't want to talk about grandfather, so I started to tell her how a very nice man once lived in this room, but no one liked him and grandfather forced him to leave. I could see that mother didn't like this story.

"Well," she said, "what else?"

I told her about the three boys and how the colonel dragged me from their courtyard. She hugged me tightly.

"What trash. . . . What stupid trash. . . ."

She fell silent and stared at the floor, narrowing her eyes, shaking her head.

"Why was grandfather angry with you?" I asked.

"I'm to blame before him."

"You should have brought the baby. . . ."

She jerked back sharply, frowning, biting her lips—and burst out laughing, started squeezing me.

"Oh, you little monster! You don't talk about that anymore, do you hear? Don't talk about it—don't even think about it!"

For a long time she spoke quietly, sternly, and incomprehensibly, then rose and began to pace around the room, tapping her fingers on her chin, moving her thick eyebrows up and down.

A tallow candle burned and guttered on the table, its light reflected in the emptiness of a mirror, dirty shadows crawling around the floor. The icon lamp flickered in the corner. The moonlight silvered the ice on the windows. Mother looked around as if searching for something on the walls and the ceiling.

"What time do you go to bed?"

"A little later."

"You slept during the day, too," she remembered and sighed.

"Do you want to leave?" I asked.

"To go where?" she exclaimed with surprise. She raised my head and looked for a long time at my face—so long that tears welled up in my eyes.

"What's that about?"

"My neck hurts."

My heart hurt as well. I could tell right away that she wouldn't live in that house, that she would leave.

"You're going to look like your father," she said, moving the floor mat aside with her foot. "Has grandmother told you about him?"

"Yes."

"She loved Maksim very much—very much! And he loved her as well. . . ."

"I know."

Mother looked at the candle, squinted, and snuffed it out.

"That's better," she said.

Yes, it was fresher and cleaner that way. The dark and grimy shadows no longer fussed around the room. Light blue spots illuminated the floor. Golden sparks flashed on the window panes.

"Where did you live?"

As if remembering something that had been forgotten long ago, she named several towns, circling the room all the while, silent as a hawk.

"Where did you get a dress like that?"

"I sewed it myself. I make everything I wear."

She was unlike anyone, and this was pleasant. But it was sad that she spoke so little—if you didn't ask a question, she'd go completely silent.

She sat down next to me again on the couch. Pressed close to each other, wordless, we remained there until the old people came home, their hair and clothes permeated with the scent of candle wax and incense, their movements solemn, quiet, calm.

Dinner was elaborate and formal. Everyone spoke very little, spoke carefully, as if afraid of waking someone from a light sleep.

Mother soon began to teach me "secular" reading and writing with great energy. She bought books and with one of them, *The Native Word*, I mastered the subtleties of standard Russian. But mother immediately proposed that I begin to memorize poetry, and with this began our mutual affliction.

The poem said:

Majestic road, so straight and true,
No small expanse God's granted you,
Leveled not by axe or spade,
Rich with dust and softly splayed
For weary hoof or well-worn shoe.

But I read "magic" instead of "majestic," "pants" instead of "expanse," and "paid" instead of "splayed."

"Well, just think a little, you monster," my mother would demand. "What pants? Ex-panse. Ex-panse. Understand?"

I understood, but all the same would recite "pants," surprising even myself.

She'd grow angry then, say I was stubborn and slow-witted. These were bitter words for me, for I tried very conscientiously to learn the cursed poem, and in my mind I read it correctly, but when reciting it out loud, I invariably garbled the words. I grew to hate those elusive lines and out of rage began to mangle them deliberately, stringing together senseless words with similar sounds. I liked it when that enchanted poem was completely deprived of all meaning.

But this entertainment came with a cost. Once, after a successful lesson, mother asked if I'd at last learned the poem. Against my will I began to mutter,

A fancy road, a priest, some shoes,
Curds and two-horned toads in stew,
A pig trough full of slops for you . . .

I realized what I was doing too late. Mother rose, bracing herself with her hands on the table.

"What is that?" she asked, pronouncing each word very distinctly.

"I don't know," I said, stupefied.

"But still—what is it?"

"It's just . . ."

"Just what?"

"Funny."

"Go in the corner."

"What for?"

She repeated it in a quiet but threatening voice:

"The corner!"

"What corner?"

Without answering, she looked at my face in such a way that I became completely flustered—what did she want? A round table with a vase of flowers and fragrant, dried grasses jutted out from the corner under the icons; a trunk covered with a rug stood in the other front corner; one of the back corners was occupied by the bed; and there was no fourth corner—the doorway stood flush against the wall.

"I don't know what you want," I said, in despair of ever understanding her.

She sat back down and wiped her forehead and her cheek without speaking.

"Did grandfather put you in the corner?" she asked.

"When?"

"In general—ever!" she shouted, slapping her palm twice against the table.

"No. I don't remember."

"Do you know it's a kind of punishment—standing in the corner?"

"No. Why? A punishment?"

She sighed.

"Akh . . . come here."

I went up to her and asked:

"Why are you shouting at me?"

"Why are you ruining the poem on purpose?"

I explained as well as I could that when I closed my eyes I could remember the poem exactly the way it was printed, but when I went to recite it, different words would sprout up.

"You're not just pretending?"

I answered "no," but right away I thought to myself: "But maybe I am pretending?" And suddenly, unhurriedly, I recited the poem perfectly. This amazed me. Destroyed me.

My face felt as if it had suddenly swollen up. My ears filled with blood and turned heavy. An unpleasant noise roared inside my head. I burned with shame, standing there, watching my mother through my tears. Her face darkened with sadness, and she pressed her lips together, raised her eyebrows:

"What? How could you . . ." she asked in a stranger's voice. "You mean—you were just pretending?"

"I don't know. I didn't want . . ."

"It's hard with you," she said, lowering hear head. "Go away."

She began to demand that I learn more and more poetry, but my memory only grew worse at preserving those flat and even lines while the bitter urge to change them, to replace their words with new ones, grew ever more overpowering. I was able to make such changes all too easily—the unneeded words would appear in swarms and quickly entangle themselves with the required words from the book. Entire lines would often be obscured from my sight in this way, and no matter how hard I tried, the correct lines would not surrender to my memory's eye. One mournful poem—written, it seems, by Vyazemsky—was a particular source of misery for me:

As morning breaks or evening falls,
Old men and widows, orphans plead
For help in Jesus' memory . . .

But the fourth line:

And softly pass outside our walls

I neatly dropped from the poem. Exasperated, my mother told grandfather about my performance.

"He's just messing around," the old man answered menacingly. "His memory's fine—he knows his prayers better than I do! He lies—his memory's firm as a rock! Whatever's chiseled into it will stay for good. Beat him!"

Grandmother added to the evidence against me:

"Stories he remembers fine. Songs he remembers—and aren't poems just another kind of song?"

All of this was true, and I felt guilty for my failures, but as soon as I set out to memorize a poem, different words would appear out of nowhere, come crawling like cockroaches and arrange themselves into new lines:

All these beggars in the street,
Acting like they want to eat;
Once the get a little bread,
They go and sell it off instead,
Take it to Petrovna for her cows,
And use the profits to get soused
On vodka that they guzzle down
Loafing in a gulley outside town.

Lying on the stove bench with grandmother at night, I would endlessly repeat everything I'd learned from the books and everything I'd composed myself. Sometimes she would laugh, but more often she'd reproach me:

"See that—just look, you know you can learn it. But you shouldn't laugh at beggars, may God be with them. Jesus was a beggar, and all the saints as well. . . ."

I muttered:

I'm sick of beggars everywhere
And grandfather lurking at the stairs.
"How can I be so cruel?" you say.
Well please forgive me Lord above,
The old man's got just one true love,
And that's to beat me night and day.

"What are you saying! Your tongue should wither up!" grandmother said angrily. "What if grandfather heard you saying such a thing?"

"Let him hear."

"You'll be sorry you acted so badly and upset your mother. Things aren't easy for her here as it is, let alone with you acting up," she said, her voice pensive and gentle.

"Why is it hard for her here?"

"Learn to keep quiet. That's not for you to understand."

"I know that grandfather . . ."

"I said 'keep quiet!'"

I lived badly, experiencing something close to despair, but I wanted to hide it, so I acted up or pretended to be in high spirits. Mother's lessons grew ever more abundant and incomprehensible. I mastered arithmetic easily but couldn't stand writing, and didn't understand a thing about grammar. But what weighed most heavily on me was seeing and sensing how hard it was for my mother to live in grandfather's house. She seemed more and more depressed, looking at everyone with a vacant stare, often sitting silently for long periods by the window that opened onto the garden, all the life and color seeming to drain out of her. When she'd first arrived, she was graceful and fresh, but now dark circles lay under her eyes, and she spent entire days walking around the house in a wrinkled dress, her hair uncombed, her jacket left unbuttoned. This ruined her appearance and offended me. She was supposed to be beautiful all the time, reserved, always dressed in perfect clothes—better than anyone!

With sunken eyes she looked through me to the window or the wall during our lessons, asked me questions in a tired voice and forgot my answers, grew angry with increasing frequency, shouted more and more. This too was painful and offensive—mother ought to be the most fair-minded of all, just like in the stories!

Sometimes I would ask her:

"Is it hard for you with us?"

She'd answer angrily:

"Worry about yourself!"

I saw too that grandfather was preparing something frightening for mother and grandmother. He often locked himself in mother's room, whined and began screeching there. He sounded like a wooden pipe that a shepherd with a deformed side, Nikanor, used to play, and which I always found obnoxious. During one of these discussions, mother started shouting all over the house:

"That will never be! Never!"

Then the door slammed and grandfather started howling.

That was in the evening. Sitting at the kitchen table, grandmother whispered something to herself as she sewed one of grandfather's shirts. When the door slammed, she stopped to listen.

"Oh God," she said. "She's gone to the lodgers!"

Suddenly grandfather appeared in the kitchen, ran up to grandmother, and hit her on the head.

"Don't jabber when you shouldn't, you witch!" he hissed, shaking his hand, which he'd apparently hurt when he struck her.

"You're an old fool," grandmother said calmly, straightening her headscarf. "How could I not speak? I'll tell her everything I can about your schemes!"

He threw himself at her and began beating his fists rapidly against her head. She didn't defend herself, didn't push him away.

"Beat me, go ahead," she said. "Go ahead, you little fool."

I started throwing pillows and blankets, even boots at them from the stove bench, but in his rage grandfather didn't notice. Grandmother collapsed on the floor, and he began to kick at her head until, at last, he stumbled and fell, overturning a bucket of water. He quickly got back on his feet, spitting and snorting, and looked around the room with the eyes of a wild animal, then ran away to the attic. Groaning, grandmother got up and sat on the bench, started to arrange her tousled hair. I jumped down from the stove.

"Pick up the pillows and all the rest and put it back on the stove," she said to me angrily. "That's a brilliant plan—throwing pillows on the floor! Is this even any of your business? And here I am with that old demon all worked up, the fool. . . ."

She gasped suddenly, and lowering her head, called me over to her:

"What hurts so much back there? Take a look, eh?"

I sorted through her heavy hair and found that one of her hairpins had gone deep into her scalp. I pulled it out and found another one, but my fingers went numb:

"I'd better get mother. I'm afraid . . ."

She waved her hand.

"What are you saying, 'Get mother'! Thank God she didn't see any of this!—and now you want to go and get her! Go away. . . ."

With a lacemaker's skillful fingers she began sifting through her full, black mane. I collected myself and helped her pull out two more thick, bent pins.

"Does it hurt?"

"It's nothing. I'm going to heat the bathhouse up tomorrow. I'll wash and it'll all be fine."

In a tender voice she began to implore me:

"You won't tell your mother that he beat me, will you now, my soul? They're already angry with each other. Will you keep it secret just for us?"

"Yes."

"Well, don't forget. Now, let's clean this up. Is my face bruised? Well, good, then we can keep all this to ourselves!"

She began to dry the floor with a rag.

"You're like a saint," I said with conviction. "They torture you and torture you, and you just say it's nothing."

"What nonsense, a saint! Where could you find a saint around here!"

She grumbled for a long time, crawling on all fours as she wiped the floor, and I sat on the stove step, trying to devise a way to take revenge against grandfather.

It was the first time he'd beaten her so violently and disgustingly before my eyes. Now his flushed face and his disheveled red hair seemed to glow before me in the twilight. His offense burned and boiled inside my heart, but I couldn't think of a worthy form of revenge, and this exasperated me.

Some two days later I went into his room in the attic for something. He was sitting on the floor, sorting through some papers before an open trunk, while on the table lay his beloved church calendar—twelve sheets of thick, grey paper marked into squares for each day of the month, and in every square a picture of the day's saints. Grandfather cherished that calendar. I was permitted to look at it only on rare occasions when he was highly pleased with me for some reason. As I studied them, the small, grey, endearing figures drawn so closely together within each square always stirred a particular feeling in me. I knew many of their stories—Kirik and Ulita, Varvara the Great Martyr, Panteleimon, and many more. I especially liked the sad story of the Holy Man Aleksey and the wonderful poem about him that grandmother often recited movingly. Sometimes you would look at those hundreds of people and take quiet comfort in the thought that there had always been martyrs.

But now I resolved to cut the church calendar into pieces, and as grandfather turned toward the window, reading a piece of blue stationery with eagles on it, I grabbed several sheets and quickly ran downstairs, where I stole grandmother's scissors from the table, climbed up to the stove bench, and began cutting the heads off the saints. I had decapitated one row when I began feeling badly about the calendar and decided to cut along the lines marking the squares. I hadn't finished the second row before grandfather appeared.

"Who gave you permission to take the calendar?" he asked, standing on the step below the bench. When he saw the squares of paper lying on the planks, he started grabbing them, lifting them up to his face, throwing them down and picking them up again. His jaw went crooked and his beard jumped. He was breathing so hard the pieces of paper blew down to the floor.

"What did you do?" he finally shouted and started to pull me toward him by my leg. As I twisted in the air, grandmother seized me in her arms, and he began to strike us both with his fist, wailing:

"I'll kill you!"

Mother appeared. I found myself in the corner near the stove as she shielded me with her body, catching grandfather's hands, knocking them away as they flew at her face.

"What is this insanity?" she said. "Control yourself!"

Grandfather collapsed on the bench under the window, howling:

"They've killed me! Everyone's against me. Everyone! Ahaaaa! . . ."

"Aren't you ashamed of yourself?" mother said flatly. "Why do you pretend all the time?"

Grandfather shouted and kicked his feet against the bench. His beard was sticking up toward the ceiling in a funny way, and his eyes were squeezed shut. It seemed to me that he felt embarrassed before my mother; the way he closed his eyes made me think he really was pretending.

"I'll glue all these pieces onto some calico. It'll be even better—stronger," said mother, examining the sheets and bits I'd cut apart. "Look how wrinkled it's all gotten in storage. The paper's falling apart. . . ."

She spoke to him in just the same way she spoke to me when I didn't understand something during one of our lessons. Grandfather suddenly rose to his feet, straightened his shirt and his waistcoat in a businesslike way, and cleared his throat.

"Glue them today! I'll bring you the rest of the pages now."

He started toward the door but at the threshold turned and pointed at me with his crooked finger:

"And he gets a beating!"

"That follows," my mother agreed. "Why did you do this?" she asked, leaning over me.

"I did it on purpose. He'd better stop beating grandmother or I'll cut off his beard."

Removing her torn jacket, grandmother shook her head and said reproachfully:

"You should have kept quiet! You promised!" She spit on the floor. "May your tongue swell in your mouth! Maybe then you won't wag it!"

Mother looked at her, walked through the kitchen, came back to me: "When did he beat her?"

"You should be ashamed asking that, Varvara! Is it any of your business?" grandmother said angrily.

Mother hugged her.

"Ekhh, *mamasha*, my darling . . ."

"Get away from me! '*Mamasha!*'"

They looked at each other silently, then moved apart. The sound of grandfather's steps came from the vestibule.

During the early days of her arrival, mother made friends with the soldier's merry wife, and almost every evening she went to the front half of the house, where even people from the Betlengs' house—officers and pretty ladies—would sometimes come to visit. Grandfather didn't like this at all. Having dinner in the kitchen, he'd shake his spoon and grumble:

"Those hedonists have gathered again! Now they'll keep us up all night. . . ."

He soon cleared the lodgers out of the apartment, and once they'd left, he had two loads of different furniture delivered from somewhere. He arranged it all in the front rooms, then closed it off with a padlock.

"We don't need any tenants. I'll have my own guests."

And it wasn't long before guests began to come on holidays. Among them was grandmother's sister, Martryona Ivanovna, a washerwoman with a big nose and a tendency to shout. Wearing a silk striped dress and a gold-colored headscarf, she came with her two sons, Vasily, a long-haired, kind, and happy draftsman dressed all in grey, and Viktor, who came in brightly colored clothes and had a head shaped like a horse's, his narrow face flecked with freckles. While still taking off his galoshes in the vestibule he began to sing in a squeaking, high-pitched voice like Petrushka the clown:

"Andrei—papa, Andrei—papa . . ."

This greatly surprised and alarmed me.

Uncle Yakov also came, bringing both his guitar and a bald, one-eyed watchmaker who was quiet, wore a long, black frock coat, and resembled a monk. He would always sit in the corner, smiling as he leaned his head to the side, supporting it, strangely, with one finger stuck into the cleft of his clean-shaven chin. He had a dark complexion, and his one good eye seemed to stare at everyone with particular intensity. He spoke little and often repeated the same words:

"Don't trouble yourself. . . . It is all the same."

When I first saw him, I suddenly remembered a day long ago, when we still lived on New Street, and loud, alarming drumbeats rang out beyond the gate as a tall, black cart surrounded by people and soldiers made its way along the street from the prison to the square. In it sat a small man in chains on a bench, a round, cloth hat on his head and a black board on his chest with words written in large white letters. The man hung his head as if reading them, his body swaying, the chains dimly rattling. When mother said to the watchmaker, "This is my son," I stepped back from him in alarm, my hands hidden.

"Don't trouble yourself," he said, moving his entire mouth toward his right ear in a terrible way. He caught me by the belt, drew me toward him, deftly turned me in a circle, and let me go, saying with approval.

"A fine boy—a good and strong boy."

I climbed into the leather armchair in the corner, which was so big that I could lie down in it, and which, on account of its size, grandfather boastfully called "Prince Gruzinsky's chair." From there I observed the boring ways in which big people tried to enjoy themselves and the strange, suspicious manner in which the watchmaker's face seemed to alter and reshape itself. His face seemed to be made of liquid; it melted, oozed like oil. If he smiled, his fat lips rode up on his right cheek. His little nose slid around like a ravioli on a plate. His large, protruding ears also moved strangely, either rising with the brow of his one good eye, or bending in toward his cheekbones. It seemed that if he wanted to, he could fold them over his nose like the palms of two hands. Occasionally the watchmaker would sigh, stick out his dark little tongue, which was round as a pestle, and make a neat, perfect circle as he quickly licked his fat, greasy lips. None of this was funny, but it was so startling that I was forced to watch him constantly.

They had tea with rum, which smelled like burnt onions, and drank liquors that grandmother had made—one that was yellow as gold, another dark as tar, a third that was green. They ate thick fermented milk and wheatcakes made with poppy seeds and honey. They sweated, panted, praised grandmother. And having eaten their fill, they moved decorously from the benches at the table to individual chairs, and lazily began imploring Uncle Yakov to play. He bent over his guitar, strumming and singing in an unpleasant monotone:

Akh, we lived the best we could,
Made noise in every neighborhood,
Told our stories all day long
To the pretty countess from Kazan.

This struck me as a very sad song, but grandmother said:
"You might play something else, Yasha. A real song, eh? Remember, Motrya, the songs they used to sing?"
The washerwoman straightened her rustling dress and said weightily:
"They have different tastes today, sister."
My uncle squinted at grandmother as if she were far away and stubbornly kept on singing, scattering sad sounds and intrusive little words around the room.
Grandfather was secretly discussing something with the watchmaker, showing him something on his fingers. The watchmaker raised his eyebrow and looked in mother's direction, nodding, his liquid face faintly changing shape again.
Mother always sat between her cousins, talking quietly and seriously with Vasily, who often sighed and said:
"Ye-es, that's got to be considered. . . ."
Viktor, meanwhile, smiled contentedly, tapped his heels, and suddenly began to sing in his squeaky voice:
"Andrei—papa, Andrei—papa . . ."
Everyone fell silent and looked at him with surprise.
"He got that from the tee-ater," the washerwoman explained in an important voice. "They sing that there. . . ."
There were two or three such evenings, memorable for their oppressive boredom, and then the watchmaker appeared on a Sunday afternoon, just after morning services. I was in mother's room, helping her unstitch an old beaded embroidery when grandmother opened the door slightly and thrust her frightened face into the room.
"Varvara, he's here," she whispered loudly, then vanished as abruptly as she'd appeared.

Mother didn't flinch, didn't stir. The door opened again, and grandfather stood at the threshold.

"Get dressed, Varvara," he said solemnly. "Get dressed and go."

Without getting up or looking at him, mother asked:

"Go where?"

"Go with God! Don't argue. He's an even-tempered man and he's a master in his profession. He'll be a good father to Leksey. . . ."

Grandfather pronounced these words with unusual portentousness. He ran his hands along his sides as he spoke, his bent elbows sticking out behind him and twitching the entire time. It was as if his arms wanted to stretch our before him and he was struggling to keep them in check.

Mother interrupted him calmly:

"I'm telling you: this will not be."

Bristling, hunched over, grandfather stepped toward her and reached out his hands like a blind man.

"Go, or I'll lead you there by your braids," he wheezed.

"You'll lead me there?" mother asked, rising to her feet. Her face turned pale, and her eyes narrowed terribly as she tore off her blouse and her skirt, and wearing just her undershirt, went up to grandfather.

"Lead me where you like."

He bared his teeth and threatened her with his fist.

"Varvara, get dressed!"

She pushed his hand aside and grabbed the door latch.

"Well, are we going?"

"I'll curse you," grandfather whispered.

"I'm not afraid of that. Well?"

She opened the door, but grandfather grabbed the hem of her shirt, fell to his knees, and began to whisper:

"Varvara, you devil, you'll be destroyed. Don't humiliate . . ." Then he began to whine quietly, pathetically: "Mo-other . . . Mo-other . . ."

Grandmother was already blocking the corridor, waving her hands as if driving a chicken somewhere. She forced mother back into the doorway and growled through her clenched teeth:

"Varka, you fool, what are you doing? Go back! You're a disgrace!"

She pushed her into the room, latched the door, and bent over grandfather.

"Oh, you dense old devil!" she said, lifting him with one hand and threatening him with the other. When she put him on the couch he plopped down like a rag doll, opened his mouth, and began to shake his head.

"You get dressed!" grandmother shouted at my mother.

"I won't go to him—do you hear me?" mother said, picking her dress up from the floor.

Grandmother pushed me down from the couch:

"Get some water, quick."

Her voice was calm and commanding, almost a whisper. I ran out to the vestibule; the sound of level footsteps came from the front of the house, and my mother's voice droned from her room:

"I'm leaving tomorrow!"

I went into the kitchen and sat down at the window as if moving in my sleep.

Grandfather moaned and sobbed. Grandmother muttered angrily. A door slammed. A frightening silence filled the house. Remembering what I'd been sent for, I dipped the copper jug into the water and went back to the vestibule. The watchmaker appeared from the front room, stroking his fur hat as he held it in his hand, wheezing, his head lowered. Grandmother pressed her hands to her stomach and bowed from the waist, saying softly:

"You yourself know—love cannot be forced."

He tripped over the threshold and stumbled into the courtyard. As she crossed herself, all of grandmother's body began to tremble. She was either crying silently or laughing.

"What is it?" I asked as I ran up to her.

"Where'd you wander off to?" she shouted, snatching the jug from me and splashing water on my feet. "Lock the door."

She went back to mother's room and I returned to the kitchen, where once again I listened while they groaned and gasped and sighed as if struggling to move a weight beyond their strength from one place to another.

It was a bright day. Winter sunlight fell in sloping rays through the ice-covered glass of two windows. The table had been set for lunch, and on it dimly shone the tin plates, the carafes filled with red *kvas*, and grandfather's dark green vodka made from betony and St. John's wort. Through the thawed patches on the windows you could see blinding snow on the roofs, glittering silver bonnets spread over the tops of the fence posts and the birdhouse. On the windowsills, in cages filled with light, my birds were playing. The siskins I'd tamed were chirping happily. The bullfinches were squeaking. The goldfinch was pouring out its song. But I took no joy in that happy, bright, sweet-sounding day. I had no use for it—had no use for anything. I felt the urge to let all my birds go and started taking down their cages when grandmother ran into the room. Cursing, slapping her hands against her sides, she rushed toward the stove.

"Akh, may the wind blow you all away! You fool, Akulina! You old fool!"

She pulled a pie from the oven, began tapping its crust with her fingers—and spit bitterly on the floor.

"Well, it's all dried out! Cooked right through! You demons! May you all be torn to bits! And what are your eyes popping out about? I'd like to pound you all like cracked pots!"

She pouted, then began to cry, her big tears plopping heavily on the pie's crust as she turned it from side to side and poked at it.

Mother and grandfather came into the room. She flung the pie onto the table with such force that all the dishes jumped.

"There, look how it came out thanks to you all, may you have no rest!"

Happy and calm, my mother embraced her, began cajoling her while grandfather sat down at the table looking haggard and tired. He tied a napkin around his neck and squinted, his eyes tearing up in the sun.

"All right, all right, it's fine," he muttered. "We've had good pies in the past. God's stingy. He pays you for years with a few minutes. And He pays no interest. Sit down, Varvara, it's fine . . ."

He seemed to have lost his mind. He talked all through lunch about God, about profane Ahab, about the heavy lot of fatherhood.

Grandmother stopped him angrily:

"Be quiet and eat!"

Mother joked with me, her clear eyes flashing:

"Were you scared before?"

No, I wasn't scared. But now everything was awkward, impossible to understand.

The meal was the same as always on a holiday—large and tediously long. And it seemed that these could not possibly be the same people as those who half an hour earlier had shouted at one another, had seethed with tears and sobs, had been ready to fight with their fists. Somehow it was no longer possible to believe that they did these things in earnest, or that it was difficult for them to cry. All their sobs and their tears, their mutual torture, which flared up so often and died down so quickly—it had all become commonplace to me. It moved me less and less. Touched my heart less and less.

Many years later I understood that because of the privations and the poverty of their lives, Russians in general liked to entertain themselves with misery; they played with it like children, and they were rarely ashamed to be wretched.

In the endless tedium of daily life, grief becomes a holiday; a fire's an entertaining show. On a blank face even a scratch is a beauty mark.

XI

After that episode, mother grew in both strength and resolve—and soon she commanded the household, while grandfather receded farther and farther from view, turned pensive and quiet, no longer resembled himself.

He hardly left his room anymore, sitting alone all the time in the attic, reading a secret book called *Notes of My Father*. He kept the book in a locked trunk; many times I'd seen him wash his hands before taking it out. It was small and thick, bound in reddish leather. A strikingly ornate inscription in faded ink appeared on the bluish page before the title: "For the honorable Vasily Kashirin, with gratitude and heartfelt remembrance." Some kind of strange last name was written below it, signed with a flourish that looked like a bird in flight. Grandfather would carefully open the book's heavy cover, put on a pair of silver-framed glasses, and gaze at that signature, wiggling his nose for a long time to adjust his spectacles. "What is that book?" I asked him many times, and he always answered solemnly:

"You don't need to know. Just wait a little. I'll die and leave it to you. I'll leave you my raccoon coat too . . ."

He began to speak less often with mother; his words for her were softer, and he listened carefully to the things she said, his eyes gleaming like Uncle Pyotr's as he grumbled and waved his hand:

"Fine, do what you want. . . ."

In his trunks lay all kinds of strange and wonderful apparel: brocade skirts and sleeveless satin jackets, silk *sarafans* sewn with silver thread, head-dresses decorated with pearls and fringe, bright kerchiefs and scarves, strands of colored stones, heavy Mordvinian necklaces made of coins. He'd carry it all in armloads to mother's room, spread it out on the tables and chairs, and mother would look with delight at all this finery while he said:

"In our time clothes were prettier, finer than they are today. The clothes were finer but our lives were simpler, calmer. . . . Those times are gone—gone for good. . . . Well, try something on. . . . Get dressed up a little."

Once mother went into the next room for a little while and reappeared in a dark blue *sarafan* with golden thread, a headdress of pearls. She curtsied low before grandfather and asked:

"Does it please you, father sir?"

Grandfather wheezed as he walked in a circle around her, all of him somehow seeming to shine. He spread his arms apart and fluttered his fingers.

"Ekh, Varvara—if we just had more money, and the right people around you. . . ." he said quietly, indistinctly, as if speaking in his sleep.

Now mother was living in two rooms in the front of the house. She had many guests, chief among them the two Maksimov brothers: Pyotr, a strong, handsome officer with a big light beard and blue eyes—the same officer before whom grandfather had flogged me for spitting on the *barin's* head—and Evgeny, who was also tall, with thin legs, a pale face, and a sharp little black beard. His large eyes resembled plums and he wore a greenish uniform with gold buttons and gold lettering on his narrow shoulders. He had a graceful way of tossing his head to flip the long, curly hair back from his forehead. He would smile condescendingly, and he always told stories in a muted voice, starting each with some disarming phrase:

"But you see—here's how I look at it . . ."

Mother would screw up her eyes and smile as she listened to him, often interrupting:

"You are a child, Evgeny Vasilevich, forgive me. . . ."

The officer would slap his wide palm on his knee and shout:

"Exactly! A child!"

The Christmas holidays were noisy and festive. People came in costume almost every night to mother's rooms. She would dress up too—always better than the others—and drive away with her visitors.

Every time she passed beyond the gate with another group of guests in brightly colored clothes, the house would seem to plunge into the earth. Everywhere turned silent, lifeless, ill at ease. Grandmother drifted from room to room like an old goose as she straightened and cleaned while grandfather stood with his back pressed against the warm tiles of the stove and talked to himself:

"Well fine, good. . . . Let's see where this smoke is coming from. . . ."

After Christmastide, mother put me and Sasha, Uncle Mikhail's son, in school. Sasha's father had recently married. The new stepmother had taken no liking to the boy and started beating him from her first day in the house until grandmother finally insisted that grandfather bring him to live with us. From everything that we'd been taught during our first month at school, I could remember only that in answer to the question, "What is your name?" you could not simply answer "Peshkov" but rather had to say, "My name is Peshkov." I had also learned that you shouldn't say to the teacher, "You, brother, can just stop shouting—I'm not afraid of you."

I disliked school from the start, but my cousin made friends easily there and in the early days was very satisfied. But once during class he dozed off and started shouting in his sleep:

"I w-o-o-o-o-n't!"

Awoken, he asked to use the bathroom, for which he was cruelly derided. As we walked down into the gully in Sennaya Square on our way to school the next day, Sasha stopped and said:

"You go ahead. I'm not going. I'll take a walk around instead."

He squatted, carefully buried his bundle of books in the snow, and left. It was a clear January day. The silver sun was shining everywhere, and I envied my cousin terribly. But against my will, I continued on to school—I didn't want to disappoint my mother. Of course, the books that Sasha had buried in the snow were lost for good, and therefore, he had good reason not to go to school the next day as well. But on the third day grandfather learned of his behavior.

A kind of trial was convened. Mother, grandfather, and grandmother sat at the kitchen table to interrogate us. I still remember how comically Sasha answered grandfather's questions:

"Why can't you seem to get to school?"

Looking grandfather right in the face with his gentle eyes, Sasha said unhurriedly:

"I forgot where it is."

"You forgot?"

"Yes. I tried to find it. I looked hard, but . . ."

"You could have followed Leksey—he remembers where it is."

"I lost him."

"Leksey?"

"Yeah."

"How's that?"

Sasha thought a little, then said with a sigh:

"There was a blizzard. You couldn't see a thing."

Everyone laughed. The weather had been clear and calm. Sasha also smiled cautiously, but grandfather bared his teeth and asked sarcastically:

"Why didn't you hold his hand, or grab on to his belt?"

"I was holding on for a little while," Sasha explained, "but the wind pulled us apart."

His words were torpid, hopeless. I was both uncomfortable listening to his awkward, useless lies and amazed at his persistence.

We were both flogged, and an old man with a broken arm who'd once been a fireman was hired as our escort. It was his responsibility to ensure that Sasha no longer strayed from the path of learning. But this didn't help: as we approached the gully the next day, my cousin suddenly bent down, pulled off one of his felt boots, and threw it as far as he could. Then he took off the other boot, flung it in the opposite direction, and bolted across the square in just his socks. The gasping old man went trotting after the shoes, then timidly led me home.

Mother, grandmother, and grandfather went around town all day searching for the runaway, and it was only toward evening that they found Sasha at Chirkov's Inn, near the monastery, where he was entertaining the guests with his dancing. They brought him home but didn't even beat him, astounded by the boy's stubborn silence. Lying with me on the stove bench, he lifted his feet and shuffled them along the ceiling as he quietly said:

"My stepmother doesn't love me. My father doesn't love me, and grandfather doesn't love me. So why should I live with them? I'm going to find out from grandmother where the robbers hide. I'll run away—join up with them, then you'll all be sorry. Want to come with me?"

I couldn't run away with him. Those days I had an undertaking of my own: I'd decided to become an officer with a big, light beard, and you had to go to school for things like that. I explained my plan to Sasha, who approved it after some consideration.

"That's good too. When you become an officer, I'll already be a robber chief, and you'll have to catch me. And one of us will have to kill the other or else take him prisoner. But I won't kill you."

"I won't kill you either."

We settled on this.

Grandmother came and climbed up to the top of the stove.

"Now, my little mice," she said, looking at us. "Ekh, my little orphans, my poor little shards."

She tried to comfort us and started to upbraid Sasha's stepmother, Nadezhda, the innkeeper's fat daughter. Then she upbraided all stepmothers and stepfathers, and in passing told the story of the wise hermit Iona, who sought God's judgment against his stepmother when he was still an adolescent. Iona's father was from Uglich, a fisherman on the White Lake.

148

His young wife destroyed him:
Made him drunk on strong stout,
Made him drowse with a potion she'd brewed,
And lay him asleep in a dugout canoe,
Which closed like a coffin around him.
She took up the maplewood paddle herself,
And guided that craft to the lake's silent depths
Where no one would see her foul deed.
Far from the banks she set the boat rocking,
Heaved at its sides till it tipped
And down the drugged body fell through the black,
Down like an anchor it sank,
While quickly she swam to the shore, and collapsed there,
Raised her woman's lament—
Displayed before all her false grief.
The people believed her and wept:
"Young widow," they cried, "Few are your years
And great is the sorrow you bear.
But God is the giver of life,
And God is the maker of death."
Only the stepson Iona
Doubted his stepmother's tears.
Pressing his hand to her heart,
He spoke in a voice calm and clear:
"Treacherous bird of the night,
Mother whose blood I don't share,
Your weeping is false—I can feel
Joy in your quickening heart.
Let us be judged then by God,
Let the powers of heaven decide:
Give anyone here a knife of true steel,
High let him hurl it above us:
If truth lies with you, the knife will slay me;
But if I own the truth—the blade will seek you."
An evil flame flared in her eyes
As the stepmother stared at the boy
And firm on her feet decried:
"You, little beast with no brain,
Sloughed premature from the womb—
How do you utter such lies?"

Hearing these words, the people grow somber.
They see a dark business at hand,
And murmuring turn to each other
To search for some sense in it all.
Then an old fisherman comes from the crowd.
He bows to all sides and declares:
"Give me, good people, a knife of true steel:
From my right hand it will sail to the sky,
Then plummet to earth and reveal
The teller of truth and the maker of lies."
They give the old man a sharp blade:
He casts it far over his head of grey hair—
Like a bird to the heavens it flies.
And then they all wait—but the knife doesn't fall.
They gaze at the shimmering vault of the sky;
They take off their hats and crowd close.
Silent they stand in the soundless night,
And mute the blade hangs in the air.
A scarlet dawn breaks on the lake;
Flushed in its light, the stepmother scoffs—
And then the knife plunges to earth:
Quick as a swallow it darts
Straight to the stepmother's heart.
All the good people kneel down to pray:
"Glory to You, God! Glory to Your truth!"
The old man took Iona away
To a monastery far from that place.
It stands on the banks of the bright river Kerzhenets,
Near the invisible city, Kitezh.*

The next day I woke up covered in red spots—I'd come down with
chicken pox. They moved me into the back of the attic, where I lay for a
long time with my arms and legs tightly bound in wide bandages, blind and
plagued with savage nightmares, one of which almost destroyed me completely. Only grandmother came to see me. She fed me with a spoon like a
little child and told me endless stories, none of which I'd heard before. I'd
already begun to recover—only my fingers were still covered, wrapped up
in bandages like mittens so I couldn't scratch my face—when one evening

*In the village of Kolyupanovka, in the Tambov Region, I heard a different version of this legend,
in which the knife kills the stepson, who has slandered his stepmother [author's note].

grandmother didn't come at her usual time. This stirred in me a great unease. Suddenly I saw her. She was lying on the dusty floor outside the attic door, her arms thrown wide apart, her face down, her neck cut half open like Uncle Pyotr's. A large cat was moving toward her from the corner, from the dusty twilight, its green eyes wide with hunger.

I jumped up from the bed, smashed out both of the window's frames with my shoulders and my feet, and threw myself into a snowdrift in the courtyard below. My mother had guests that evening, and no one heard me smashing the glass and breaking the window frames, and I wound up lying in the snow for quite a long time. I hadn't broken anything, just dislocated my shoulder and cut myself badly on the glass, but my legs were paralyzed, and for three months I lay in bed, unable to move them—lay there and listened to the noise that grew ever stronger in the house, the frequent slamming of the doors downstairs, the countless footsteps of the people there.

The rustling of dismal snowstorms as they sweep across the roof; the wind moaning while it roams around the attic space beyond the door; rattling dampers and a mournful singing from the chimney; crows cawing through the afternoons; and on quiet nights, the desolate howls of wolves drifting in from the fields—to this music grew my heart. Then spring began to appear at the window, the March sun like a single, radiant eye glancing through the glass. It was timorous and quiet at first, but its caresses grew stronger every day. Cats began to sing and caterwaul from the attic and the roof. The sounds of the season's stirrings seeped through the walls. Icicles smashed like shimmering glass; melting snow slid from the roof's peak. The sound of ringing bells took on a fullness that it never had in winter.

Grandmother came to see me, her words smelling more and more of vodka. Then she started to carry with her a large, white kettle, which she hid under my bed, winking as she said:

"Don't tell grandfather please, my soul—let's keep this a secret from the old house spirit."

"Why are you drinking?"

"Hush, hush. . . . You'll find out when you grow up."

She sucked on the kettle spout, wiped her lips with her sleeve and smiled sweetly.

"Well, then, you, my good sir—what was I telling you about yesterday?" she asks.

"My father."

"But where was I?"

I reminded her, and again her words began to flow in graceful, even streams.

She'd started these stories about my father herself, after coming to the attic sober one day and saying sadly, tiredly:

"I saw your father in my sleep. He seemed to be going through a field, carrying a walking stick made of walnut and whistling. A spotted dog was running behind him with its tongue hanging out. Maksim Savvateich has been coming often in my dreams for some reason lately. His restless soul must still be searching for its proper shelter."

And now she'd been telling me the story of my father for several nights in a row. It was no less fascinating than all her other stories: He was the son of a soldier who rose to an officer's rank and was then exiled to Siberia for cruelty to his subordinates. There, somewhere in Siberia, my father was born. He lived badly and began to run away from home while still a small child. Once his father used dogs to hunt him down like a rabbit in the forest; another time, he beat my father so badly after catching him that the neighbors took him away and hid him.

"Do they always beat children?" I asked.

Grandmother answered matter-of-factly:

"Always."

My father's mother died early, and when he was nine, his father died as well. His godfather, a joiner, took him in, registered him in the guild cities of Perm, and began to teach the boy his craft. But my father ran away. He made money leading blind people around the market fairs and at sixteen came to Nizhny, where he began working for a joiner on the Kolchin line of steamboats. By the age of twenty he was already a good cabinetmaker and upholsterer. The shop where he worked was next to the houses that grandfather owned on Kovalikha.

"We had low fences," grandmother said, laughing, "And very boisterous people all around! Varvara and I are there picking raspberries in the garden one day and *shast!* over the fence comes your father. I was afraid at first: here comes this great fellow through the apple trees in a white shirt and velveteen pants—but no shoes—he's barefoot, and no hat—his long hair's tied back with just a leather band. That's how he came to propose! I'd seen him before—he'd pass by our windows sometimes, and I'd always think to my-self—'What a fine looking fellow.' Now here he comes and I ask, 'Why can't you keep to the footpaths?' He drops to his knees: 'Akulina,' he says, 'Ivanovna, here I am before you, all of me, with a full soul, and here is Varya—help us, please, in God's name. We want to be married.' I was stunned, couldn't even move my tongue. I looked over and there was your mother hiding behind the apple tree—red as a raspberry—and she's giving him signs, the little schemer, with tears in her eyes. 'Akh, you two,' I say. 'May they blast you both from the mountain! What have you started? Are you out of your mind, Varvara? And you, my fine fellow,' I say to him. 'You better think a little. Aren't you aiming awfully high?' Your grandfather was rich back then, after all. The children hadn't split anything up. He still had four houses. He had money and he was very much in favor—not long before then they'd given him a hat with a braid and a uniform because he'd served nine years straight as head of the guild. He was proud back then! I tell them everything the way I should, but I'm trembling myself with fear as I speak, and I'm sorry for them both, they look so sad and gloomy. Here your father says, 'I know Vasily Vasilev won't give me Varvara's hand by choice—that's why I'm going to steal her away. But you must help us.' They were telling me all this so I would help! I even raised my hand to him, but he didn't move away. 'You can beat me with a stone if you like, just help us,' he says. 'I won't back down.' Here Varvara comes up and puts her hand on his shoulder, says, 'We've already been husband and wife for a long time—since May,' she says. 'We just need to be married.' Oh, father! That almost knocked me off my feet!"

All her body shook as grandmother began to laugh. She snorted a pinch of snuff, wiped the tears from her eyes, and let out a sigh of contentment.

"You can't yet understand what that means—'to be husband and wife' and 'to be married.' Only it's a terrible thing if a girl has a baby without being married! You remember that, and when you grow up, don't lead girls into trouble like that. That would be a great sin for you, and the girl will be wretched—and the baby will be unlawful. You remember now—don't forget! You live and take pity on girls, love them with your heart, and not just to fool around. These are good words—you remember them."

She fell to thinking about something, and sat silently, rocking back and forth, then roused herself and started once again:

"Well, what can you do with that? I yanked on Varvara's braid, slapped Maksim on the head. But he says, fair enough, 'You won't fix this by hitting us.' And she chimes in too: 'First think about what's to be done,' she says. 'Then you can beat us.' 'Do you have money?' I ask him. 'I did,' he says. 'I bought Varvara a ring with it.' 'What was it—three rubles?' I ask. 'No,' he says. 'About a hundred silver.' And in those days money bought a great deal—things were cheap! I look at them, look at your mother and father, and I think, what children, what childish little fools. 'I hid the ring under the floor so you wouldn't see it,' says your mother. 'We can still sell it!' Children, complete children! Still, somehow or other we agreed that they'd get married in a week, and I'd make arrangements with the priest myself. But I'm all in pieces, all in tears, and my heart's fluttering. I was afraid of grandfather, and it was terrifying for Varvara. But still, we'd worked out a plan.

"Only, your father had an enemy. He was a master craftsman, an evil man—and he'd guessed everything a long time before then, started watching us closely. Well, when the day came, I dressed my daughter up in the best clothes I could find and led her out past the gate, where a troika was waiting around the corner. She climbed in, Maksim whistled to the driver, and off they went! I'm going home all in tears when suddenly I run into this man and he, the villain, says, 'Being kind, I won't interfere with fate, but you, Akulina Ivanovna, you'll have to give me fifty rubles.' But I don't have any money—I don't care for money and never tried to keep it—and I say to him stupidly: 'I don't have any money, and I won't give you a thing.' 'Then promise me for later,' he says. 'How can I promise? Where would I get it later?' 'Well,' he says, 'Is it so hard to steal from a rich husband?' If I wasn't a fool, I'd have kept talking and held him up, but I spit in his face and started home—and he ran to our courtyard before me and called everyone out, told them everything—raised a riot!"

She closed her eyes and smiled as she spoke:

"Even now it's terrifying to think about the risks we took! Grandfather howled like a beast: Is this some kind of joke? He used to look at Varvara and boast, 'I'll give her away to a nobleman, to a *barin*!' Well, here's what you get instead of a *barin*! The Holy Mother knows better than us what marriages to make! He rushes around the courtyard like he's on fire, calls out Yakov and Mikhail. Your father's freckle-faced enemy—the master craftsman—he agrees to go with them too, and so does the driver, Klim. I see your grandfather pick up a flail—a big weight attached to a belt, and Mikhail gets out a gun. We have good, spirited horses and a light *drozhky*. 'Well,' I think, 'They'll catch them easily!' But here Varvara's guardian angel gave me a thought. I got hold of a knife and started cutting at the strap that holds the harness shaft, thinking it might break along the road. And that's exactly what it did—the harness snapped apart. It almost killed grandfather and Mikhail along with Klim, and it held them up—when they finally fixed it and came flying into the churchyard, Varya and Maksim were standing on the portico, already married—glory to You, God!

"Our group wanted to start fighting with Maksim, but he was big and powerful—his strength was rare! He threw Mikhail from the portico and hurt his arm—knocked his shoulder out of joint. He hurt Klim too and those other three—Yakov and your grandfather and that master—they were scared of him. But even in his anger, Maksim kept his head. 'Drop the flail,' he says to grandfather. 'Don't swing at me. I'm a peaceful man. I took what God gave me, and no on can take that away. I don't need anything else from you.' They backed away from him. Grandfather got back in the *drozhky* and shouted, 'Farewell, now, Varvara. You are not a daughter to me anymore and I don't want to see you. You can live or you can die of hunger, it makes no difference to me now.' He came back and started beating me, started cursing me, but I just groaned and held my words. What is to be is what remains: the rest just falls away. Afterward he says, 'Well, Akulina, take heed: you have no daughter anymore, remember that!' But I have just one thought: 'Keep talking nonsense, you redheaded fool. Anger fades like ice.'"

I listen closely—listen greedily. Her story surprises me at times. Grandfather depicted my mother's wedding completely differently. He'd opposed the marriage, and after the wedding he refused to let my mother enter his house. But according to his story, she hadn't married in secret, and grandfather had been present at the church. But I don't want to ask grandmother which account is closer to the truth because her story is more beautiful, and I like it more. She never stops rocking back and forth as she tells her stories—it's like she's riding in a boat. When she speaks about something sad or terrible, she rocks more urgently, one arm stretched out in front of her, as if holding something back in the air. She often closes her eyes, a blind smile hidden away in the deep creases of her cheeks, her thick eyebrows trembling just slightly. Sometimes her blind and all accepting kindness touches me to the heart; sometimes I wish she'd say something stronger, shout.

"I didn't know where they were at first, for two weeks or so, and then Varvara sent a lively little boy who came and told me. I waited until Saturday and pretended I was going to the all-night service, but instead I went to them! They're living far away, in an outbuilding on Suetinsky Street. All the people in the courtyard were from the workshops. It was littered and dirty, noisy—but they were just fine, both of them happy, purring and playing with each other like two kittens. I took them whatever I could—tea, sugar, different groats, jam and flour, some dried mushrooms, a little money. I don't remember how much; I'd been collecting it little by little from grandfather—you're allowed to steal if it's for someone else. But your father won't accept anything. He takes offense, says 'What are we, two beggars?' And Varvara starts singing the same song. 'Akh, *mamasha*, what's all this for?' I scolded them: 'My little simpletons,' I said. 'Who am I to you? I'm the God-given mother of one of you—the mother by blood of the other! Are you really going to insult me? Do you know how bitterly the Holy Mother weeps in heaven when a mother on earth is insulted?' Well, here Maksim just grabbed me in his arms and started carrying me around the room— carrying me and even dancing. He was strong as a bear! And Varka struts around like a peahen, showing off her husband like a new doll. She's just a little girl, but she rolls her eyes all the time and talks very seriously about keeping the household like some old woman who's been doing it for years—you could die from laughing watching her! And then the tarts she brings with tea are hard enough to break a wolf's tooth—the curds spill out of them like gravel!

"A long time passed that way. You were ready to be born already, and grandfather was still silent all the time. He's a stubborn old house spirit! He knew that I was visiting them on the quiet, but he pretended he didn't. Everyone in the house was forbidden to speak of Varvara, and everyone kept silent. I kept quiet too, but I knew a father's heart cannot stay mute for long. Then came one of those secret hours when everything's unsettled and waiting fills the air. Night. A snowstorm howling. It seems like bears are crawling through the windows. The stovepipes sing. All the demons have broken loose from their chains. Grandfather and I lie in bed, but we can't sleep, and I say: 'Awful to be poor on a night like this. . . . Even worse if your heart's ill at ease.' Suddenly he asks: 'How are they getting by?' 'Fine,' I say. 'They're getting by just fine.' 'Who did I ask about?' he says. 'You asked about your daughter, Varvara, and your son-in-law, Maksim,' I say. 'How do you know I was talking about them?' 'Enough, already, father,' I say to him. 'Stop acting like a fool. Quit this game already. Who's it helping after all?' He sighs. 'Akh, you devils,' he says. 'You bunch of grey devils.' And then he asks: 'That great big one—is it true he's a fool?' I say, 'A fool's the one who doesn't want to work—who hangs off someone else's neck. If you're looking for a fool, maybe you should look at Yakov and Mikhail. Don't they live like fools? Who works in this house? Who gives us bread? You do. And are they any help?' Here he starts upbraiding me: I'm an idiot, a villain, a madam— and I don't know what else! But I don't answer back. 'How could you be taken in by someone like that?' he says. 'You don't know what he is, where he's from. . . .' I keep quiet until grandfather gets tired. Then I say, 'You should go and see how they're getting by. It seems like they're doing just fine.' 'That's too big an honor for them,' he says. 'Let them come to me. . . .' And here I started weeping out of joy while he let down my hair—he loved to play with my hair, and he mutters, 'Stop sniveling, you fool. Do you think I have no soul?' He was awfully good back then, our grandfather. It was only when he decided he was smarter than everyone else that he started getting stupid and grew mean.

"And so they came, your mother and your father, on a holy day, on the Sunday of Forgiveness, both of them big and clean and sleek. Maksim's so tall grandfather only reaches to his shoulder when he stands up across from the old man and says: 'Please God, Vasily Vasilevich—don't think that I've come to you for a dowry. I've come here to pay honor to the father of my

156

wife.' Grandfather liked that. He smiles, says, 'Well, you lanky thief. Enough messing around—come live here with us.' Maksim frowns. 'Well, whatever Varya wants,' he says. 'It's all the same to me.' And from then on the two of them went at it tooth to tooth; they just couldn't find a way to get along. I wink at your father; I kick him under the table—and he just keeps saying what he thinks is right. He had fine eyes, clear and full of joy—but his eyebrows were dark and he had a way of drawing them together so his eyes were hidden and his face went stubborn, turned to stone—and then he wouldn't listen to anyone but me. I loved him more than my own children! He knew that, and he loved me too. He'd nestle up against me, hug me, pick me up in his arms and carry me around the room, saying: 'You're my true mother, you're like the earth for me—I love you more than Varvara!' Your mother was very happy at that time, full of mischief and pranks, and she'd throw herself at Maksim, shouting, 'How can you say such things! *Permyak!* Your brains have been pickled!' The three of us would romp around the rooms, play like children! We lived well then, my little soul. Your father's dancing was remarkable as well. And he knew good songs. He learned them from the blind—no one sings better than them!

"They moved into an outbuilding in the garden, and that's where you were born, right at noon. Your father came home for lunch and you were there to meet him! Oh, how he rejoiced! And what a commotion he raised! He wore your mother out with fussing over her, as if it's some great trouble for a young bride to bear a child! He put me on his shoulders and carried me right through the courtyard to inform your grandfather that a new grandchild had appeared—and even grandfather started laughing. 'Akh, Maksim,' he said, 'You're wild as a wood goblin.'

"But your uncles, they didn't like Maksim. He didn't drink and he didn't hold back with his words. And he was always coming up with pranks. They came back on him, though, all those tricks he played; he paid bitterly for them. Once, during the great fast, the wind started up and suddenly the whole house was singing, droning terribly in every room. All of us were stunned. What evil's come upon us? Grandfather was completely terrified. He ordered that all the icon lamps be lit and began to run around the house, shouting, 'We need a priest! We have to have him pray for us!' And then it stopped all at once, which made everyone even more afraid. But Uncle Yakov guessed what it was—'That's Maksim up to something,' he says. And later Maksim told us himself that he'd stuck different bottles and vials in the dormer window. When the wind blew in their necks, they all started droning, each with its own sound. Grandfather warned him, 'You look out Maksim, or those tricks will take you back to Siberia!'

"We had a very cold winter one year, and the wolves started coming into town from the fields. They'd kill a dog or frighten a horse, once they even ate a watchman who'd passed out drunk. They caused quite a panic! But your father, he takes a gun, puts on his skis, and goes into the field at night. And next time you look, he's hauling a wolf back—and then he'd got two! He skinned them, cleaned out their heads, put in glass eyes—they turned out good! And so, one night Uncle Mikhail went to the vestibule to do his business and all of a sudden he came running back, his hair all standing on end, his eyes bugging out, his throat stopped—he couldn't say a word! His pants fell down and he got all tangled up in them, fell over, gasped: 'Wolf!' Everyone grabbed whatever was nearest and rushed to the vestibule with a light. They look—and there it is, a wolf's head coming right out from the trunk! They start beating at it, shooting—and it couldn't care less! They look again—it's just a skin and an empty head! The front paws are nailed to the trunk! Grandfather got very angry with Maksim after that—he was white-hot furious! Soon Yakov started joining in. Maksim would glue together a head out of cardboard, give it eyes, a mouth, and a nose. For hair, he'd paste on oakum, and then he and Yakov would go around the street, sticking that terrible face in people's windows. And the people would be frightened, of course—they'd shout! At night the two of them would walk around in sheets too. They frightened a priest once, and he went running to the policeman's booth. The policeman took fright too and started shouting for help! They got into a great deal of trouble, and there was no talking sense to them. I told them to stop, and Varya did too, but no, they wouldn't settle down. Maksim just laughed. 'It's so funny, watching people run away, breaking their heads over nothing!' You just try telling him. . . .

"But all that nearly led to his destruction. Just like your grandfather, your Uncle Mikhail takes offense very easily, and he remembers his injuries a long, long time. He got the idea he'd do your father in. And one night they're coming back from someone's house. There's four of them—Maksim, the two uncles, and a fellow who was a deacon at the time, although later the church threw him out because he beat a driver to death. They're walking from Yamskaya Street, and the others lure Maksim down to Dyukov Pond, acting like they want to slide on the ice in their shoes, the way boys do. They lure him down there and knock him into a hole in the ice—I told you about that before. . . ."

"What makes the uncles evil?"

"They aren't evil," grandmother says calmly, snorting a pinch of tobacco. "They're just—stupid. Mishka is stupid in a cunning way, and Yakov's just middling, a simpleton really. . . . Well, they knock him in the water and he

158

comes back up, grabs the edge of the ice—and they start stamping on his hands, smash up all his fingers with their boot heels. But it's his good luck to be sober while they're all drunk, and somehow, with God's help, he stretches out along the ice, holds his face up in the middle of the hole to breath, where they can't get to him. They throw chunks of ice at his head for a little while, then leave—let him drown on his own! But he climbs out and runs to the police—you know, right there on the square. The policeman happens to know Maksim and all our family. 'How did this happen?' he asks."

Grandmother crosses herself and says with gratitude:

"Dear God, give peace to Maksim Savvateich with Your saints, for he is worthy! You see, he kept it all from the police. He says to them, 'I got drunk and wandered down to the pond, fell in the hole myself.' But the policeman says, 'Not true—you don't drink!' Well, sooner or later they rubbed him down with vodka, put him in dry clothes, and wrapped him up in a sheepskin coat. The same policeman brought him home, along with two others. But Yashka and Mishka hadn't yet come back—they were going round the taverns still, bringing more glory to their mother and father. Varvara and I looked at Maksim and he's not like himself anymore, all purple, his fingers all broken and seeping blood. It looks like there's snow in the hair at his temples, but it doesn't melt—he's gone grey there!

"Varya starts wailing, 'What have they done to you?' The policeman starts nosing around everyone, and I can feel it in my heart—Oh, this is bad. I set Varya onto the policeman to keep him busy and start asking Maksim on the quiet—what happened? 'Meet Yakov and Mikhail at the gate first,' he whispers. 'Tell them to say they left me at Yamskaya and went on to Pokrovka, while I turned onto Pryadilny Alley. Keep it straight or it'll be disaster with the police.' I run to grandfather. 'You go start talking to the policeman. I'll wait for our sons past the gate,' I say, and then I tell him what evil's occurred. He starts getting dressed, trembling, muttering, 'I just knew it, I could feel this was coming!'—but he's making all that up, he didn't know anything. Well, I greeted the children with my palm to their faces. Mishka sobered up right away from fear, while Yashenka, the dear, couldn't put two words together and just kept mumbling, 'I don't know anything— that's all Mikhail, he's oldest!' We quieted the policeman somehow or other—he was a good fellow. 'Oh,' he said, 'You all look out—if something happens here, I'll know who's to blame'—and with that he left. Then grandfather goes up to Maksim and says, 'Well, thank you. A different person wouldn't have done that. I understand that. And you, daughter, thank you for bringing a good man to your father's house.' He could speak so well, grandfather could, when he wanted to. It wasn't until later that he locked up his heart out of stupidity. Then the three of us were left alone. Maksim Savvateich started crying and sort of raving: 'Why did they do that to me? Why? What did I ever do to them? Mama, why?' He always called me mama instead of *mamasha*—just like a little boy, and he himself was like a boy in nature. 'Why? What for?' he asks, and I just sob. What else was left for me to do? My children—how sorry I was for them. Your mother rips all the buttons off her jacket, sits there all disheveled, like she just had a fight, growls, 'We're leaving, Maksim! My brothers are our enemies. I'm afraid of them— we're leaving!' I try to shut her up right away—don't throw garbage in the stove when it's already full of smoke! And then grandfather sends in those two morons to ask forgiveness. She flies at Mishka and slaps his face—there's your forgiveness! And your father says to them: 'How could you, brothers? You almost left me a cripple. How would I work without hands?' Well, they made peace somehow or other. Your father took ill for a little while afterwards—seven weeks he lay in bed. He says to me from time to time, 'Come away with us to some other town. It's too gloomy here!' Soon it worked out for him to go to Astrakhan. They were expecting the Tsar there that summer, and your father was given a commission to help build the triumphal arch. They left on the first steamboat after the thaw. It was like parting with my own soul to say goodbye to them, and he too was sad, tried all the time to convince me—'Come away with us to Astrakhan!' But Varvara was glad and didn't even try to hide her joy, the shameless girl. . . . And so they left. . . . And that was all. . . .''

She took a swallow of vodka and a pinch of snuff, looked out the window at the dove grey sky.

"Your father and I didn't share the same blood," she said. "But we had the same soul."

Grandfather would come into the room sometimes during her stories. He'd raise his little polecat face, sniff the air with his sharp nose, stare suspiciously at grandmother while he listened to her talk.

"Keep lying, keep lying," he'd mutter.

Sometimes he'd suddenly ask:

"Leksey—has she been drinking vodka here?"

"No."

"You're lying. I can see it in your eyes."

Then he'd leave reluctantly. Grandmother would wink as he went and say some kind of funny phrase:

"Do as you please—just leave us in peace."

Once, as he stood in the middle of the room and stared at the floor, grandfather asked quietly:

160

"Mother?"

"Ai?"

"You see what's going on?"

"I see."

"What do you think about it?"

"Fate, father. Remember how you always talked about a nobleman?"

"I suppose."

"Well, here he is."

"Without a shirt on his back."

"Well, that's for her to worry about."

Grandfather left. Sensing something bad, I asked grandmother:

"What were you talking about?"

"You always want to know everything," she said gruffly, massaging my legs. "If you know everything when you're young, there'll be nothing left to ask when you're old!" She began to laugh and shake her head.

"Akh, grandfather, you're just a little speck of dust in God's eye! Lyonka, don't you talk about this, but your grandfather's gone bankrupt. He gave a *barin* big money—thousands—and the *barin* lost it all, left grandfather with nothing but ash. . . ."

She fell into thought, smiling. She sat there for a long time and didn't speak, her forehead and her cheeks all wrinkled, her big face darkening, turning sad.

"What are you thinking about?"

"I'm just wondering what story to tell you," she said, drawing herself up. "Well, I'll tell you about Evstigney, all right? Here's how it goes."

The deacon Evstigney believed
No one was as smart as he—
No nobleman or ancient priest,
No cunning hound who roamed the street.
Proud and fancy as a peacock,
He strutted like a turkey when he walked,
Explaining endlessly the flaws he found
In everyone and everything around:
This apple skin's a bit too light,
That alleyway is awfully tight!
The morning sun is much too bright,
That church dome wasn't sculpted right!
Point out anything you like to him,
You'd hear the same refrain

She puffs out her cheeks and goes bug-eyed, makes her kind face look silly and stupid as she speaks the next lines in a lazy voice:

Oh, what a mess they made!
I could do it twice as well in half the time.
They ought to be ashamed,
Such sloppiness is just a crime!

She pauses for a moment, then smiles as she goes on:

Then one night the devils came to call.
"You don't like it here at all,
Now do you, friend?" they said.
"Then come away with us to hell.
For you we'll make the coals burn well!"
Before the deacon donned his hat
The demons seized him in their paws,
Began to scratch and tickle with their claws
Until two raised him on their shoulders high
And thrust him deep into the flames.
"Well," they asked triumphantly. "How's that?"
Even as he roasts and fries,
The deacon looks around with scornful eyes,
Then props his hands against his sides,
Puffs out his lips and loudly sighs:
"What dirty fires you use to heat this place!
The smoke and fumes are a disgrace!"

She speaks the last line in an insolent and idle, low-pitched voice, then laughs as she explains to me:

"Evstigney wouldn't give up! He's stubborn, wants everything his way—just like our grandfather! Well, now its time to go to sleep . . ."

Mother came to see me rarely in the attic. She didn't stay for long, and she spoke hurriedly whenever she visited. She was always more beautiful, always better dressed than before, but just as I sensed it in grandmother, I could tell there was something new about her, something hidden from me. I was ever more certain of this, ever more suspicious.

Grandmother's tales absorbed me less and less. Even her stories about my father could not calm the vague unease that grew each day within me.

"What's bothering my father's soul?" I asked her.

"Who could know?" she answered, closing her eyes slightly, "That's a thing for God in heaven, unknown to us."

162

Unable to sleep at night, I made up sad stories as I stared out the dark blue window and watched the stars slowly drifting in the sky. My father was always at the center of these stories. He was always going somewhere alone with a stick in his hand, a shaggy dog at his heels.

XII

One day I fell asleep toward evening and, waking up, discovered that my legs had woken up as well. I lowered them to the floor and they again gave out, but the certainty that they were whole and I would walk once more had already taken hold. This realization was so bright and good that I shouted from joy. I pressed my feet with all my weight against the floor, collapsed, and immediately started crawling toward the door and down the stairs, imagining the sheer amazement I'd cause when I appeared below.

I don't remember how I found myself in grandmother's lap. We were in mother's room. Before her stood some sort of strangers. A dried-up, green old woman was speaking sternly, her voice drowning everyone out:

"Give him tea with raspberry jam and wrap him up from head to . . ."

She was completely green—her dress, her hat, her face with a wart under one eye—even the little tuft of hair on that wart was like grass. She lowered her bottom lip and drew the upper one back to look at me with green teeth, one hand in a fingerless glove of black lace covering her eyes.

"Who is that?" I asked, grown timid.

Grandfather answered in an unpleasant voice:

"This is another grandmother for you."

With a slight laugh, mother moved Evgeny Maksimov toward me.

"And here is your father."

She began to say something quickly, incomprehensively. Maksimov bowed to me, squinting, and said:

"I will give you some paints."

It was very bright in the room. The silver candelabra with five candles were burning on the table in the front corner. Grandfather's favorite icon, "Weep Not for Me, O Mother," stood between them, its inlaid pearls flashing and melting in the light of the flames, the raspberry garnets glittering

165

on the golden halos. From the street outside, silent, vague, round faces were pressed like pancakes to the dark windowpanes, stuck to the glass with their noses flattened. Everything around me began floating away somewhere while the green old woman felt behind my ear with her cold fingers:

"Without fail. . . . Without fail. . . ."

"He's dropped off," grandmother said and carried me toward the door. But I hadn't fallen asleep. I'd just closed my eyes, and as she carried me up the stairs, I asked her:

"Why didn't you tell me?"

"Akh, you. Enough. Be quiet now."

"You're all cheaters."

She laid me on the bed, buried her face in the pillow, and began to sob, her shoulders heaving, all her body trembling.

"You cry too, cry," she sputtered, choking on her tears.

I didn't feel like crying. It was gloomy and cold in the attic. I shivered and the bed rocked and squeaked. The green old woman rose before my eyes. I pretended to fall asleep, and grandmother left.

Several empty days passed in a thin, monotonous stream. After the betrothal, mother went away somewhere and a deadening quiet filled the house.

One morning grandfather came with a chisel in his hand and started knocking the putty out from the frame of the storm window. Grandmother appeared with rags and water in a washtub.

"Well, old lady?" he asked her quietly.

"Well, what?"

"Are you glad?"

She answered him the way she'd answered me on the stairs:

"Akh, you. Enough. Be quiet."

Simple words now possessed a particular meaning; something large and sad was hidden behind them—something you shouldn't talk about, something everyone knew.

Grandfather carefully removed the storm window and carried it away. Grandmother threw open the window—a starling was shouting in the garden; sparrows chirped. The drunken scent of thawing earth came flooding into the room. The bluish tiles of the stove turned a confusing white; it made you cold to look at them. I climbed down to the floor.

"Don't go around barefoot," grandmother said.

"I'm going to the garden."

"It's still damp there. Wait a little!"

I didn't feel like listening to her. Just being around big people was unpleasant.

Light green shoots of young grass had already pushed up through the earth in the garden. The buds of the apple trees had swollen and burst. The moss on the roof of Petrovna's house was a pleasant green. There were birds everywhere. The happy noise and the fresh air made my head spin pleasantly. In the pit where Uncle Pyotr had cut his throat lay a thick bed of rust colored weeds, tangled and matted by the snow. It was unpleasant to look at them, so devoid of spring. The charred black beams shone sadly, and the entire pit seemed annoyingly useless. I had the angry urge to tear out all the weeds—eradicate them, gather up the shards of brick, drag out the charred, black beams, take away everything dirty and useless, and create there a clean little place where I could live alone all summer, without any big people. I immediately set to work at this project, and it turned my attention away from the house, distracted me for a long time. Everything at home remained very painful, but I thought about it less and less.

"What are you puffing out your lips about?" my mother or grandmother would say. It was awkward that they asked this; I wasn't angry with them. It was just that everything at home had become foreign to me. During dinner, lunch, and evening tea the green old woman often sat with us at the table like a rotting post in an old fence. Sewn to her face with invisible thread, her eyes protruded slightly from their bony sockets and swiveled rapidly from place to place, seeing everything, catching everything. They rose up to the ceiling when she spoke of God and dropped down to her cheeks when the talk turned domestic. Her eyebrows seemed to have been made of bran and somehow stuck onto her face. Her large, bare teeth bit silently through everything she stuck in her mouth, her hand bent in a funny way, her pinky poking out. Her ears wiggled and little balls of bone rolled around beside them. Even the green hair on her wart stirred, sliding along her wrinkled, yellow, and revoltingly clean skin. Just like her son, she was scrubbed completely clean, and it was awkward—wrong somehow, to touch them. Soon after she first saw me she tried to stick her lifeless hand, which smelled of frankincense and yellow Kazan soap, toward my mouth, but I turned and ran away.

She often said to her son:

"You must absolutely discipline the boy. Do you understand, Zhenya? Absolutely."

He'd lower his head obediently, pinch his eyebrows together, and stay silent. Everyone kept silent in that green thing's presence.

I hated the old woman and her son with a concentrated kind of hatred. This troublesome state of mind cost me many beatings. Once at lunch she said as she opened her eyes terrifyingly wide:

"Akh, Alyoshenka, why do you eat so quickly? And why take such big bites? You'll choke yourself, dear."

I pulled the piece of food I'd been chewing out of my mouth, stuck it back on my fork, and extended it to her:

"Here. You can have it if you need it."

Mother yanked me away from the table, and I was taken away in shame to the attic. Grandmother came and burst into laughter, stopping her mouth:

"Oh my gracious, what unruliness! May Christ be with you always!"

I didn't like that she stopped her mouth, so I ran away from her, climbed onto the roof, and sat there for a long time behind the chimney. I wanted very much to behave badly, to say angry things to everyone—and it was hard to overcome that desire. But soon I had to overcome it. Once I smeared cherry glue all over the chairs that my future stepfather and the new grandmother used. They both stuck and it was very funny, but after grandfather had beaten me, mother came to the attic, drew me toward her, firmly pressed me between her knees, and said:

"Listen, why are you being so evil? If you only knew what misery it is for me."

Her eyes filled with bright tears and she pressed my head to her cheek—and this was harder than a beating. I said that I would never hurt the Maksimovs again, never—if she just wouldn't cry anymore.

"Yes, yes," she said quietly. "You shouldn't misbehave anymore. Soon we'll be married. Then we'll go to Moscow, and then we'll return and you'll live with me. Evgeny Vasilevich is very kind and smart. You'll like it with him. You'll study in high school and then you'll become a university student—just like he is now, and then you'll become a doctor. Whatever you want—an educated person can be whatever he wants. Well, go outside now and play. . . ."

Those "then's," which she placed one after the other in her sentences, seemed to form a long ladder descending somewhere far away from her, somewhere far down into darkness and loneliness. Such a ladder didn't gladden me. I wanted very much to say to her:

"Don't get married, please! I'll take care of you myself!"

But those words would not be spoken. My mother always stirred in me many tender thoughts about her, but I never brought myself to utter them.

Things were going well in the garden. I cut down all the weeds with a heavy knife, tore them out. I lay pieces of brick along the sides of the pit where the earth had fallen in. I made a wide seat out of brick as well, and it was so large you could even lie down on it. I collected many pieces of colored glass and pottery shards and used clay to stick them between the brick so that when the sun glanced into the pit, it all flared up with the joyful kind of light you find inside a church.

"You thought this up well!" grandfather said as he looked at my work. "Only the weeds are going to poke you—you left the roots. Go get a spade and I'll dig them out."

I brought him an iron spade. He spit on his hands and, wheezing, began to drive the blade deep into the rich soil with his foot.

"You throw out all the roots and I'll plant sunflowers here, mallow. It'll be good! Good . . ."

He suddenly fell silent as he bent over the spade—went completely still. I looked closely at him: his small, shrewd eyes, which resembled those of a dog, were sprinkling the dirt with rapid little tears.

"What's wrong?"

He roused himself, wiped his face with his palm, and looked at me dimly.

"I broke a sweat! Look at all those worms!"

He started digging again, then suddenly said:

"You shouldn't have built all this! It's pointless, brother. I'm going to sell the house soon, after all. Toward fall, probably, I'll sell it. We need the money for your mother's dowry. Let her have a good life, at least, may God be with her!"

He dropped the spade, waved his hand, and walked off past the bath-house, to a corner of the garden where he kept his seedbeds. I started digging myself and immediately broke my toe with the spade.

This kept me from going with mother to the church for her wedding. I could only walk out past the courtyard gate, from where I saw her holding Maksimov's arm and bowing her head as she carefully placed her feet on the brick sidewalk and the green grass that poked up through the cracks as if walking on nails.

The wedding was quiet. Returning from the church, they drank tea cheerlessly. Mother changed her clothes right away and went to her bedroom to pack her trunk. My stepfather sat down next to me and said:

"I promised to give you some paints, but they don't have any good ones here, and I can't give mine away. So, I'll send you some paints from Moscow."

"What am I going to do with them?"

"Don't you like to draw?"

"I don't know how."

"Well, I'll send you something else then."

Mother came up to us.

"We'll be back soon, after all. Your father will pass his exams, finish his studies—and we'll come right back."

It was pleasant that they talked to me like an adult, but it was strange, somehow, to hear that a man with a beard was still a student.

"What are you studying?" I asked.

"Surveying."

I didn't care enough to bother asking what that meant. An unpleasant silence filled the house, like the sound of rustling wool. I wanted it to be night. Grandfather stood with his back pressed to the stove and looked out the window, squinting. The green old woman helped mother pack, grumbling and gasping. Grandmother had been drunk since noon. Out of shame they'd taken her to the attic and shut her up there.

Mother left early the next day. She hugged me in parting, lifting me lightly from the ground and kissing me, her eyes somehow unfamiliar as they looked into mine.

"Well, goodbye," she said.

"Tell him to listen to me," grandfather said gloomily, looking into the still pink sky.

"Listen to grandfather," she said as she made the sign of the cross over me. I'd been waiting for her to say something else and now was angry with grandfather, for he'd prevented her.

They got into the horse cab and for a long time mother struggled angrily to free her hem, which had caught on something.

"Help her—can't you see?" grandfather said to me.

I didn't help her; by sorrow I was tightly bound.

Dressed in narrow, dark blue slacks, Maksimov unhurriedly arranged his long legs in the cab. Grandmother began thrusting various bundles into his arms, which he piled on his knees and held in place with his chin, his pale face wincing in alarm as he drawled:

"Ee-nou-gh!"

The green old lady took her seat in the other carriage with her older son, an officer. She sat there like something painted on a canvass while he scratched his beard with the handle of his saber and yawned.

"So—you're off to the war?" asked grandfather.

"Absolutely."

"It's a good thing. The Turks need a beating."

They drove away. Mother turned around several times, waving her handkerchief. Steadying herself against a wall of the house, grandmother also shook her hand in the air, tears streaming down her face. Grandfather squeezed tears from his eyes with his fingers and muttered in bursts:

"There'll be nothing good there. . . . Nothing good."

I sat on the curbstone and watched the cabs bobbing up and down as they drove down the street. They turned a corner and something slammed shut in my chest, closed tight.

It was early. The shutters were still drawn over the windows of the houses. The street was deserted—I'd never seen it so lifeless and empty. Somewhere in the distance, a shepherd was playing insistently on a wooden pipe.

"Let's go have tea," said grandfather, taking me by the shoulder. "Looks like it's fate for you to live with me. You're going to scratch at me like a matchstick on an old brick!"

Silently we busied ourselves from morning until evening in the garden. He dug seedbeds, bound the raspberry cane, picked lichens from the apple trees, crushed caterpillars while I worked constantly on my new abode, fixing it up, decorating. Grandfather chopped off the end of the charred beam and put sticks in the ground for me to hang my birdcages. I wove the weeds we'd cut into a thick wattle fencing, and made an awning to protect the sitting space from the sun and the dew. Everything there was just right.

"It's useful—you knowing how to set things up for yourself," grandfather said.

I valued his words very much. Sometimes he would recline on the seat, which I'd recently covered with turf, and instruct me, speaking unhurriedly, as if it were hard to drag out his words.

"You're separate from your mother now—a slice cut off the loaf. She'll have different children now; they'll be closer to her than you are. And here's grandmother drinking again. . . ."

He goes silent for a long time, as if listening for something. Then he starts again, reluctantly letting fall his heavy words.

"That's the second time she's gone on a binge. She started one when Mikhail was called up for the army too. And she talked me into buying him a recruiter's pass, the fool! Maybe if he'd gone soldiering he'd be different now. . . . Akh, you-u . . . But I'll die soon. And that means you'll be left alone. Just you—your own provider all your life—understand? Learn to be a worker for yourself, and never give in to others! Live quiet and calm—but stubborn. Listen to everyone, and do what's best for you."

Except for days of bad weather, I spent the entire summer living in the garden. On warm nights I even slept there on a large piece of felt that grandmother had given me. She herself would often spend the night there too, carrying an armload of hay to the pit and spreading it out near my sleeping place. She'd lie there and tell stories for a long time, constantly interrupting her own speech with sudden interjections:

"Look there—a star just fell! Someone's pure soul up in heaven's started longing for its mother Earth. That means a good person's being born somewhere right now."

Or she would point something out for me:

"A new star came out—look there! Oh, what a beautiful bright eye! Oh, sweet heaven, light raiment of our Lord. . . ."

"You'll catch cold, you fools!" grandfather would mutter. "You'll get sick—come down with lumbago. You'll be strangled by thieves!"

This is how it was sometimes: The sun goes down and pours rivers of fire into the heavens. The rivers burn out, drop red and golden ash on the velvety green of the garden. In the warm, enveloping dusk, you feel everything before you darken, swell, expand. The leaves have had their fill of sunlight; they slacken now. The grass bends toward the earth. Everything grows softer, airier, exudes its many scents, each as tender as the music that drifts now from the distant field, where someone plays reveille. Night comes, and with it something pours into your chest, something powerful, reviving as a mother's gentle touch. With its warm and fleecy hand, the silence strokes your heart, washes from your memory everything that needs to be forgotten, wipes away those small and bitter grains of dust the day has left. It's lovely to lie on your back and watch the stars begin to burn, adding endless depth to the sky. As it recedes ever farther above you, exposing still more stars, that depth gently lifts you from the ground, and it seems—most strangely—that either the earth has diminished to your size or you have grown and spread, melted, merged with everything surrounding you. It grows darker, quieter, but invisible, sensitive strings are everywhere drawn taut, and every sound—a bird singing in its sleep, a hedgehog running past, a human voice flaring up somewhere in the distance—each of them takes on a resonance that comes only at night, when everything is heightened by that keen and tender quiet.

An accordion begins to play. A woman's laugh rings out. A saber scrapes along the brick sidewalk. A dog squeals. All of it's extraneous. The last few petals dropping from the faded day.

There were nights when suddenly a drunken shout would fly up from the street or the field, or someone would run, stamping his feet heavily on the walkway. These were ordinary sounds and drew no notice.

Grandmother would stay awake for a long time, lying with her hands behind her head as she told me a story with quiet excitement, not caring in the least, it seemed, if I was listening or not. She always knew how to choose a story that heightened even more the beauty and the moment of the night.

172

Imperceptibly I'd fall asleep to the steady rhythm of her speech, waking up together with the birds, the sun peering into my face, the quiet streams of morning air growing warmer. The leaves of the apple trees shook off the dew. The damp grass shone ever more brightly, a crystalline transparency spreading through its blades as a delicate mist gathered like smoke above it. The sun's rays spread out like a fan, turning blue the lilac sky. High and out of sight, a lark rang out its song. Every color, every sound seemed to seep into my chest like dew, stirring an easy joy within me, urging me to get up now and do something and live in friendship with every living thing around me.

That was the quietest, most contemplative time of my life. It was during this summer that a certainty in my strengths began to take hold and grow inside me. I became solitary, unsociable, almost wild. I heard the shouts of the Ovsyannikov children, but I wasn't drawn to them. And the appearance of my cousins didn't stir the slightest joy in me—only fear that they'd destroy the dwelling place I'd made in the garden, the first thing I'd ever done on my own.

Grandfather's speeches grew only more petulant, captious, and dull, and I soon stopped paying attention to them. He began to quarrel more with grandmother, often forcing her out of the house. She would go to Uncle Yakov or Mikhail, sometimes not returning for several days, during which grandfather cooked, burned his hands, howled, cursed, smashed dishes, and grew noticeably stingier.

Sometimes he would come to my little abode and sit comfortably on the turf, wordlessly observing me for a long time, and then suddenly asking:

"Why don't you talk?"

"I just don't. What?"

He'd begin to instruct me:

"We're not *barins*. There's no one to teach us. We have to understand everything ourselves. They wrote books for other people, built schools for them. But none of that's for us. Take everything yourself . . ."

Then he'd fall deep into thought. Mute, motionless, withered—it was almost frightening to look at him.

In the fall he sold the house. Not long before that, at morning tea, he'd announced to grandmother with grim finality:

"Well, mother, I've fed you and fed you—fed you enough! You win your own bread from now on!"

Grandmother reacted to these words with complete calm, as if she'd known for a long time that they'd be spoken and had been waiting for them. She unhurriedly took out her snuff box, filled her spongy nose, and said:

"Well, if it's so, then so it is . . ."

Grandfather rented two dark basement rooms in an old house that stood in a cul de sac at the bottom of a hill. When we were moving to the apartment, grandmother took an old bast shoe with a long lace and tossed it into the space under the stove. Then she squatted down beside it and started calling out the house spirit:

"House spirit, house spirit, here is your sleigh. Come away with us now, dear member of our clan, to a new place, a different happiness."

Grandfather glanced in through the window from the courtyard outside:

"Don't you dare start that, you heretic! Don't you dare humiliate me!"

"But things will go bad, father," she warned him. But grandfather grew fierce and forbade her from moving the house spirit with us.

In three days' time he'd sold the furniture and various other things to some Tatar dealers of used goods, furiously haggling and cursing while grandmother watched from the window, alternately laughing and weeping.

"Steal it! Break it!" she cried out softly.

I was ready to weep as well, distraught over the garden and my hideaway.

We drove off in two carts. The one in which I sat, surrounded by our things, shook violently, as if trying to throw me out. I would live with that shuddering, that stubborn shaking meant to cast me off, for the next two years—right up to my mother's death.

Soon after grandfather had settled into the basement, mother appeared, pale and emaciated, her huge eyes shining with the hot light of astonishment. She seemed to peer at everything around her, as if looking at her father, her mother, and me for the first time—she peered and peered without speaking, while my stepfather paced constantly around the room, whistling softly and coughing, fidgeting with his fingers as he held his hands behind his back.

"Goodness, how terribly you've grown!" mother said to me, pressing her hot palms to my cheeks. She was wearing a wide, reddish, ugly dress that bulged over her stomach.

My stepfather stretched out his hand to me:

"Hello, brother! How are you, eh?"

He sniffed the air and said:

"You know, it's awfully damp in here!"

It was as if they'd both run a great distance. They seemed exhausted. Everything they wore was wrinkled, worn out. All they wanted was to lie down and rest.

We drank tea dully. Watching the rain washing over the windows, grandfather said:

"So—everything was burned?"

"Everything," my stepfather answered decisively. "We barely got out."

"Yes, indeed. Fire doesn't play games."

Mother pressed against grandmother's shoulder and whispered something in her ear. Grandmother narrowed her eyes, as if a light were shining into them. Everything grew even duller.

Then grandfather suddenly spoke, his words calm, biting, and very loud:

"But a rumor reached me, Evgeny Vasilev, sir, that there was no fire, and you just lost it all at cards. . . ."

It grew silent as a cellar. The samovar chortled. The rain lashed at the windowpanes. Then mother started to speak:

"*Papasha* . . ."

"What *papasha*!" grandfather shouted deafeningly. "What'll be next? Didn't I tell you! Didn't I say thirty doesn't go with twenty? Here he is—the delicate one! Nobility, eh? What, dear daughter?"

All four of them began to shout, my stepfather loudest of all. I went into the vestibule and sat down, stunned, on a pile of firewood. They must have switched my mother with someone else. This one was nothing like the earlier one. It was less noticeable inside, but here in the dusk it all came back very easily—the way she'd been before.

Then I found myself in a house in Sormov. I don't remember how I wound up there. Everything was unfamiliar. The walls had no paper; the cracks between the beams were filled with hemp containing hordes of cockroaches. Mother and my stepfather lived in two rooms with windows looking onto the street. Grandmother and I lived in the kitchen with one window opening onto the rooftops. The factory's black smokestacks rose into the air from behind the roofs, each like a thumb thrust between the first two fingers of a fist. From them curled a thick smoke, which the winter wind blew through the village. The heavy stench of something burning hung in all of our cold rooms. A siren howled like a wolf early in the morning:

Khva-ooo, aa-oo, a-oo-oo.

If you stood on the bench and looked across the roofs from the top window, you could see the factory gates, lit up by the streetlamps and opened wide, like the toothless mouth of an old beggar, as throngs of little people crawled in. At noon there was another siren. The black lips of the gate slipped back to reveal a deep hole. Sickened by the people it had chewed up, the factory now spewed them out in a long, dark stream, and they poured along the streets, the white fringe of the wind whipping them on, scattering them among the buildings. The sky was very rarely visible above the village, for day after day, over the rooftops and the soot-stained mounds of snow there hung another roof. Flat and grey, it extinguished all imagining, made us blind with its single, dismal, never-changing hue.

Evenings a dim red glow swayed above the factory, lighting up the ends of the smokestacks. It looked as if the chimneys didn't rise up, but instead, descended to the earth from that smoky cloud—descended and breathed red, howled, droned. Looking at all of this was unbearably sickening. A bitter tedium began to eat away my heart. Grandmother worked as housekeeper and cook. She prepared all the meals, washed the floors, split firewood, hauled water. She worked from early morning until evening, went to bed exhausted, gasping and wheezing. Sometimes when she'd finished cooking, she'd put on a short padded coat, tuck her skirt up high, and leave for town:

"I'll go see how the old man's getting along."

"Take me!"

"You'll freeze. Look how it's blowing out there!"

And then she set out walking seven *versts* on a road buried under snow in the fields.

Forever cold, jaundiced, pregnant, my mother wrapped herself in a torn grey shawl with fringe along its edges. I hated that shawl for disfiguring her large and graceful body. I hated the little pieces of fringe that I ripped from it. I hated the house, the factory, the village. Mother walked around the rooms in worn-out felt boots, her big, ugly belly shaking as she coughed, her blue-grey eyes flashing with a distant, angry light, often stopping on the bare walls, as if stuck to them. Sometimes she would look for an entire hour out the window at the street. It resembled a jaw with some of its teeth gone crooked and black from age, while others had fallen out completely and been replaced by new teeth that were far too big for the mouth.

"Why are we living here?" I would ask. And she would answer:

"Akh—just shut your mouth."

She spoke little to me, and when she did, it was always with a command:

"Go and get . . . bring me . . . give me . . ."

I was rarely allowed on the street, and when I was, I always returned beaten up by other boys. Fighting was my only real pleasure then, and I gave myself to it with a passion. Mother lashed me with a belt, but this punishment only irritated me further, so that I fought even more savagely the next day—and mother punished me still more harshly. Once I warned her that if she didn't stop beating me, I would bite her hand and run out into the fields to freeze to death. She shoved me away with surprise, paced around the room, and sighed with exhaustion:

"Little beast!"

That animated, trembling rainbow of emotions known as love was fading from my soul, while the fuming, dark blue flame of universal hatred flared ever more often within me, and my heart smoldered with bitter discontent, a sense of utter isolation among lifeless, grey absurdities.

My stepfather was strict with me and taciturn with mother. He whistled constantly, coughed, and after lunch stood before the mirror for a long time, carefully picking his uneven teeth with a splinter of kindling. He fought more and more with mother, angrily addressing her with formal "you"—a tendency that never failed to plunge me into utter rage. During their arguments, he always closed the kitchen door tightly, apparently not wanting me to hear his words, but I still listened carefully to the rumbling bass of his muffled voice.

Once he stamped his foot and shouted:

"I can't invite anyone here because of your stupid gut! You're such a cow!"

Outraged and amazed, I sat up sharply on the bench above the stove and struck my head against the ceiling, bit my tongue so hard it bled.

On Saturdays the workers came in dozens to sell to my stepfather the tickets for provisions they were supposed to take to the factory store. They were paid with these tickets instead of money; my stepfather bought them at half value. He received the workers in the kitchen. Sitting behind the table, self-important, sullen, he'd take a ticket, say:

"A ruble and a half."

"Evgeny Vasilev, have some fear of God. . . ."

"Ruble and a half."

That dark and senseless life did not continue long. Shortly before mother was to give birth, they took me away to grandfather. He was living in Kunavino then, in a two-story house on a sandy road that descended down a hill to the fence of the Napolnaya Church cemetery. His cramped room had a Russian stove and two windows looking out on the courtyard.

"Wha-at?" he said when he saw me, starting to laugh and squeal. "They used to say, 'No other friend could be as true as she who gave your life to you.' But now they'll have to say, 'No other friend could be as true as that damned old man who beat some sense in you.' . . . Akh, you-u . . ."

I didn't have time to look around the new place before mother and grandmother came with the new baby. My stepfather had been driven out of the factory for swindling the workers, but he went somewhere else and right away they hired him to work as a cashier, selling tickets at a train station.

A long stretch of empty time passed. Then they moved me again to live with mother in the basement floor of a stone house. She stuck me in school right away, and I found it repugnant from the start.

177

I arrived there in my mother's shoes, a sorry little coat sewn from grandmother's jacket, a yellow shirt, and pants worn over my boot tops. All of this was quickly derided and on account of the yellow shirt I was dubbed "The Ace of Diamonds." I soon made my peace with the other boys, but the teacher and the priest took no liking to me at all.

The teacher was yellow and bald. Blood never stopped running from his nose, and he came to class with cotton wool stuffed up his nostrils. He'd sit down at the table, start to quiz us on the lesson in a nasal voice, then suddenly go silent, pull the cotton wadding out, and start shaking his head as he inspected it. His face was flat, and it seemed to me made of tarnished copper; there was something green growing in the folds of his skin. That face was made particularly ugly by its completely incongruous eyes of tin, which always fastened so unpleasantly on my face that I had the urge to wipe my cheeks clean with my palm every time the teacher looked in my direction.

For several days I sat in the front section, my desk almost flush against the teacher's table. It was unbearable. He seemed to see no one but me, constantly droning like a goose:

"Pes-kov, change your shirt next time! Pes-kov, stop shuffling your feet! Pes-kov, your boots have left a puddle under the desk again!"

I repaid him with wild acts of mischief. Once I found half a frozen watermelon, hollowed it out, and tied it with a string to the door's pulley, so that when the door opened, the watermelon rose in the dark foyer. When the teacher closed the door behind him, the watermelon settled neatly on his bald head like a hat. The school guard led me home with a note from the teacher, and I paid for that prank with my hide.

Another time I sprinkled snuff in his desk drawer, and he started to sneeze so violently that he had to leave the class. In his place he sent his son-in-law, an officer who made the class sing "God Save the Tsar" and "Oh You, My Freedom." Those who sang badly he slapped on the forehead with a ruler; he did this in a way that was particularly loud and funny, but not painful.

The religion teacher, a young and handsome priest with lavish hair, disliked me because I didn't have a copy of *The Sacred History of the Old and New Testaments* and because I mocked his speech.

The first thing he did when entering the classroom was to ask me:

"Peshkov, did you bring your book or not? Yes. Your book?"

I'd answer:

"No, I didn't bring it. Yes."

"What do you mean, 'yes'?"

"No."

"Well, go home then! Yes. Home. I have no intention of teaching you. Yes. No intention."

This didn't disappoint me very much. I'd leave and wander around the settlement's dirty streets, observing its noisy life until my lessons were over.

The priest had a pleasant, Christ-like face and gentle, feminine eyes. His little hands were also very gentle with everything that came into them. He would pick up everything—a book, a ruler, a pen—with surprising delicacy, as if the object were alive and fragile, as if it were something he loved very much and feared breaking with a careless touch. He was not so gentle with the boys, but they loved him all the same.

Although I studied tolerably well, I was soon informed that I would be expelled for unacceptable behavior. I was distraught: this news would make my life even more unpleasant, for mother was already increasingly irritated—and more and more prone to beating me.

But help arrived when Bishop Khrisanf* suddenly appeared at our school. He was a hunchback, if I remember correctly, and he looked like a wizard.

Small, dressed in wide black robes and a funny hat shaped like a bucket, he sat down at the table, removed his hands from his sleeves, and said, "Well, let's have a little talk, my children"—and the classroom immediately grew warm and happy, turned pleasant in a way I'd never known before.

He called me to the table after many others.

"How old are you? So young? What a long fellow you are, brother! Have you been standing out in the rain a lot?"

He laid one of his hands on the table; it was thin, and the nails on his fingers were long and sharp. He took his sparse beard between the fingers of his other hand and fixed his kind eyes on me.

"Well, then. Tell me something from the sacred history. What parts do you like?"

When I told him that I didn't have the book and wasn't studying the sacred history, he straightened his monk's hat and asked:

"How can that be? After all, these are things you have to study. Maybe you know some of them? Maybe you've heard some? You know the Psalter? That's good. And you know prayers? Well, then—just look! And you know *The Lives of the Saints*? In verse? Well, now, just look how much you know!"

---

*Author of the well-known three-volume work *Religions of the Ancient World*, as well as the articles "Egyptian Metempsychosis" and "About Marriage and Women." This article made a powerful impression on me when I read it in my youth. It seems I've probably remembered the latter title incorrectly. It was printed in some sort of religious journal in the 1870s [author's note].

Our priest appeared, red-faced and out of breath. The bishop blessed him, but when the priest began to speak about me, the bishop raised his hand and said:

"Allow me a moment. . . . Well, then, tell us about Aleksey the Holy Man."

"Superb poetry, isn't it brother?" he said when I stopped, having forgotten one of the lines. "And what else? About King David? I'll listen with great pleasure."

I could see that he truly was listening, and he did like the poems. He quizzed me for a long time about them. Then he started asking quickly about other things:

"You studied the Psalter? Who taught you? Kind old grandfather? He's cruel? Really? And do you often misbehave?"

I hesitated but said yes. The priest and the teacher confirmed my confession at length. The bishop listened to them with his head lowered.

"Hear what they say about you?" he asked with a sigh. "Well, come here."

His hand smelled of cypress as he laid it on my head.

"Why do you behave so badly?" he asked.

"It's boring in school."

"Boring? Something's wrong there, brother. If it were boring, you'd do badly at your lessons. But you do just fine. So, it must be something else."

He took a small book from his breast pocket and wrote:

"Peshkov, Aleksey. There. And now you, brother, restrain yourself a little. Don't misbehave too much. A little you can get away with. But a lot begins to irritate people. Am I right, children?"

A chorus of voices rang out happily:

"That's right!"

"You yourselves only misbehave a little bit, right?"

The boys all grinned and began to talk:

"No, no, a lot! We act up a lot!"

The bishop leaned back in his chair, pressed me to his side, and said so surprisingly that even the priest and the teacher laughed:

"Well, brothers, that's just the thing—after all, I was a terrible troublemaker at your age! But why do we behave so badly, brothers?"

The children laughed, and he began asking them questions, cleverly tangling them up in their own words, making one contradict the other and deepening all the time their exuberance. Finally he rose and said:

"It's nice here with you troublemakers, but it's time for me to go."

He pulled back his sleeves and raised his hand to make the sign of the cross with wide strokes as he blessed us:

"In the name of the Father, the Son, and the Holy Spirit I bless you now in your good labor! Goodbye!"

Everyone shouted:

"Goodbye, Holy Father! Come back again!"

Nodding in his monk's high hat, he said:

"I will, I will come again—and I'll bring you all some books!"

Sailing from the classroom he said to the teacher:

"Let them all go home today."

He led me by the hand to the vestibule and, bowing over me, said quietly:

"Now, you restrain yourself, all right? After all, I understand why you misbehave! Well, goodbye, brother!"

I was very moved. Some kind of new emotion was boiling in my chest, and even when the teacher held me back after releasing the rest of the class, I listened carefully, gladly as he said that from now on I should be more silent than water, more pliant than grass.

Putting on his coat, the priest gently droned:

"From now on you should be in my class. Yes. You should. But sit quietly. Yes. Quietly."

While things settled down at school, an ugly incident took place at home: I stole a ruble from my mother. It was a crime without premeditation. One evening she went out somewhere and left me to take care of the baby at home. Bored, I started leafing through one of my stepfather's books—*The Notes of a Physician*, by Alexandre Dumas—and between the pages found a ten-ruble bill and a one-ruble bill. The book was incomprehensible. I closed it and suddenly realized that for a ruble I could buy not only *The Sacred History*, but probably the book about Robinson as well. I'd learned that such a book existed only recently at school. During recess on a very cold day, I'd been telling some other boys a tale when one of them commented scornfully:

"Folktales are worthless. Now Robinson—that's a real story!"

Several others were discovered to have read Robinson, and they all praised the book. I was greatly offended that they didn't like grandmother's tales, and I determined then to read this Robinson in order to pronounce before them: Robinson is worthless!

The next day I brought to school *The Sacred History*, and two dog-eared collections of stories by Andersen, as well as three pounds of white bread and a pound of sausage. I had found Robinson in a dark little shop by the fence surrounding the Church of the Vladimir Holy Mother. It was a scrawny book with a yellow cover; on the inside page was a picture of a man wearing a fur hat, animal skins draped over his shoulder. I didn't like this at all. The covers of the Andersen stories seemed much nicer, even if they were tattered.

During the main recess I shared the bread and sausage with the other boys. We began to read the remarkable story "Nightingale"—and right away it gripped our hearts.

"Everyone who lives in China is Chinese, and the Emperor himself's a Chinaman." I remember how pleasantly that phrase surprised me with its simple, ebullient music and something else uniquely good.

I didn't manage to finish "Nightingale." There wasn't enough time at school, and when I came home, mother asked me in a strange, strangled voice:

"Did you take the ruble?" She was standing at the hearth, frying eggs, a wooden pot-lifter in her hand.

"Yes. I bought books—here."

She beat me diligently with the pot-lifter. And she took away the Andersen books, hid them forever, which was even more bitter than her blows.

I didn't go to school for several days, and during that time my stepfather must have described my deed to his coworkers, who in turn told their children, one of whom brought the story to school. And so, when I returned there, I was greeted with a new nickname—"Thief." It was short and clear, but wrong, for I'd never sought to hide the fact that it was I who took the ruble. I tried to explain this, but no one believed me. I went home and told my mother that I wouldn't be going to school anymore.

Sitting at the window, pregnant again, grey, her eyes tormented and delirious, she fed my brother Sasha and looked at me with her mouth hanging open, like a fish.

"You lie," she said quietly. "No one could know you took that ruble."

"Go ask."

"You bragged about it yourself, didn't you? It was you—am I right? Answer me, am I right? You watch—I'll go to school myself and ask."

I named the boy at school who'd told. Her face seemed to crumple, dissolve in tears.

I went into the kitchen and lay down on my bed, which had been arranged on some crates behind the stove. I lay there and listened to her quietly moaning:

"Oh God, Oh God . . ."

The stench of greasy, damp rags made it impossible to lie there long. I got up and started to the courtyard, but mother shouted:

"Where are you going? Where? Come here!"

We sat on the floor. Sasha lay in mother's lap and grabbed at the buttons on her dress, bending forward as he said:

"Buppon," which meant "button."

I sat pressed close to my mother's side. She put her arms around me, saying:

"We're poor. . . . For us, every kopek, every kopek . . ."

But she never finished whatever she'd started to say, squeezing me in her hot hands.

"What trash . . . trash . . ." she said suddenly, using a word I'd heard before from her.

Sasha repeated it: "Tash!"

He was a strange little boy: clumsy, with a big head, he looked around at everything with lovely blue eyes and a quiet smile, as if expecting something. He started talking unusually early and never cried, living in an uninterrupted state of quiet happiness. He was weak and barely crawled. He always seemed to be delighted to see me, and immediately asked to be picked up. He liked to crumple and fold my ears with his soft little fingers, which smelled of violets for some reason. He died unexpectedly, without being sick. In the morning he was quiet and happy as always, and in the evening, when the church bells rang for night-time services, he was already lying on the table. This happened soon after the birth of the second child, Nikolai.

Mother did as she had promised, and I was able to go back to school, but soon they shipped me off to grandfather again.

One evening, coming from the courtyard for tea, I heard my mother's broken shout:

"Evgeny, I'm begging you. I'm begging."

"Stu-pid-it-y!" said my stepfather.

"But I know you're going to her!"

"Well?"

They both fell silent for several seconds. My mother started coughing and said:

"What trash. What a vicious piece of trash you are."

I heard him hit her, rushed into the room, and saw mother on her knees, her back and elbows braced against a chair, her breast arched high as she wheezed, her eyes flashing terribly while he, neatly dressed in a new uniform, kicked her in the chest with his long foot. From the table I took a knife that we used to cut bread. It had a silver and bone handle, and it was the last thing that had remained with mother since my father's death: I grabbed it and with all my strength I struck at my stepfather's side.

Fortunately, mother managed to shove Maksimov away and the knife slid along his side, cutting a wide gash in his uniform but only grazing his flesh. He gasped and rushed from the room, clutching his side, while mother seized me in her hands, lifted me, and threw me on the floor with a cry. Then my stepfather came back from the courtyard and took me away.

Later that evening, after he'd left the house all the same, mother came to me behind the stove, hugged me carefully, kissed me, wept.

"Forgive me. It's my fault. Oh, darling, how could you? A knife?"

With absolute sincerity and a full understanding of my words, I told her that I would cut my stepfather's throat and then my own. And I believe I would have done this, or at least, I would have tried. Even now I see that long, despicable leg with a bright stripe down the side of the slacks—see it swing through the air and drive the toe of a boot into a woman's breast.

Remembering these leaden abominations from a savage Russian life, I ask myself for a moment: is it worth discussing this? And with renewed certainty I answer myself: yes, it is. For that wretched, stubborn truth has yet to die, even in the present day. And it is this truth that must be known to its roots so that we can tear it from our memory by those roots, tear it from the human soul, from all our hard and shameful life.

There is another, more positive reason as well for me to recount these abominations. Although they are foul, although they weigh us down and even crush many rare souls to death—the Russian individual is still so healthy, still so young in spirit, that he can overcome these horrors—and he will.

This life of ours is staggering not only because the layer of bestial waste that stretches through it is so rich and fetid, but also because something else, something bright and creative, something healthy, something kind and decent still forces its way up through that layer, still grows and stirs an everlasting hope for our eventual rebirth into a life that's filled with light—into one that's human.

XIII

At grandfather's again . . .

"What now, you little vandal?" he said when he met me, rapping his hand on the table. "I'm not feeding you. Let your grandmother do that!"

"And I will," said grandmother. "As if it's such a task."

"Then feed him!" grandfather began to shout, but then calmed down, explaining to me:

"She and I have separated completely. Everything we have is separate now."

Grandmother was sitting at the window, deftly weaving lace, her bobbins clicking happily. A little cushion thickly covered with copper pins shone like a golden hedgehog in the spring sun. She herself seemed to be cast in bronze. She was unchanging! But grandfather was still more wrinkled and withered, his red hair gone grey, the calm self-assurance of his movements replaced by a kind of febrile fussiness, his green eyes filled with suspicion. Grandmother laughed as she described to me the division of their property. Grandfather had given her all the pots, the saucers, and the dishes, saying:

"This is yours—now don't ask me for anything else!"

Then he took away all her old-fashioned dresses, her fox fur cloak, and her other things. These he sold for seven hundred rubles and then gave the money to his godson, a converted Jew who sold fruit and offered interest on the loan. He'd fallen conclusively ill with greed and lost all sense of shame, appealing to rich merchants and his former associates from the guild, complaining that his children had bankrupted him, and asking them for money in his poverty. He took advantage of their respect, and they gave to him generously—gave him large banknotes, which he would then wave under grandmother's nose, boasting and teasing her like a child:

"See that, old fool? They wouldn't give you a hundredth of this!"

185

He loaned the money at interest to a new friend, a tall, bald furrier known in town as the Whip and to the Whip's sister, a chubby shopkeeper who had red cheeks and brown eyes and was languid and sweet, like molasses.

Everything in the house was strictly divided. Grandmother would prepare lunch from food purchased with her money on one day, and on the next, grandfather would buy bread and provisions. Lunch was always worse on grandfather's days. Grandmother bought good meat, but he was always buying entrails, liver, lungs, calves' stomachs. Tea and sugar were kept separately, but they used one pot for making tea. Grandfather would say with alarm:

"Stop, wait—how many did you put in?"

He'd pour the dry tea leaves onto his palm, and after carefully counting them, he'd say:

"Yours are smaller than mine. So I should put in less—mine are bigger, they'll brew better."

He watched grandmother very closely to make sure she drank no more than he did, and to verify that the tea she poured for him was as strong as that she gave herself.

"One last cup?" grandmother would ask, before emptying the teapot. Grandfather would peer inside it. "Well, all right—last one."

They even bought separate supplies of oil for the icon lamps—this after fifty years of shared labor!

To me, grandfather's tricks were as galling as they were funny, but grandmother found them merely amusing.

"That's enough, now," she'd say, calming me down. "What's it really matter? The old man's old, and now he getting stubborn. He's lived eight decades, after all. You try dragging yourself that far! Let him fuss and be stubborn—who does it hurt? I'll earn a piece of bread for you and me, don't worry."

I also began to earn a little money. Early in the morning on Sundays I went into the courtyards and the streets with a bag to collect bones, rags, paper, and nails. The junk dealers would give you twenty kopeks for a *pood* of paper or rags; they gave the same for iron, while a *pood* of bones would bring eight or ten kopeks. I'd go collecting during the week after school as well as on weekends, selling my goods on Saturday for thirty or fifty kopeks, sometimes more on good weeks. Grandmother would take my earnings and hurriedly put them in the pocket of her skirt.

"Thank you, my soul!" she'd say. "Who could doubt that you and I'd get by together? As if it's hard to manage!"

Once I watched her secretly as she held on her palm the five-kopek pieces I'd given her, looking at them and weeping silently, her nose so full of pores, it resembled pumice stone, a single cloudy tear hanging on its tip.

A more profitable occupation lay in stealing firewood and planks from the lumberyards along the Oka's banks and on Peski Island, where people traded iron from booths hurriedly erected during the market fairs. After the fairs, they'd take apart the booths and stack up the planks and stakes—on Peski they'd remain lying there almost to the start of the spring floods. A homeowner in town would pay ten kopeks for a good plank, and it was possible to steal two or three a day. It was essential for our success that bad weather—heavy rain or blowing snow—force the watchmen to take shelter and withdraw.

A friendly gang formed: the ten-year-old son of a Mordvinian beggar woman, Sanka the Pigeon, who was sweet, gentle, and always calmly happy; a gaunt and shaggy-headed boy named Kostroma, who had huge black eyes and no family, and who later hanged himself at the age of thirteen after being sent to a children's prison camp for stealing two pigeons; a twelve-year-old Tatar named Khabi, who was extremely strong, openhearted, and kind; the son of the local cemetery watchman and gravedigger, a blunt-nosed boy of about eight named Yaz, who suffered the Falling Sickness and kept silent as a fish; and the group's oldest member, Grishka Churka, who was sober minded, fair, and passionately devoted to fistfighting, and whose mother was a widowed dressmaker. We all lived on the same street.

Stealing wasn't considered a sin in town—it was more a local custom, providing the half-hungry residents one of their only means of survival. A month and a half of trade fairs weren't enough to feed the locals for an entire year, and therefore, many respected homeowners "worked on the side" on the river. This might mean that they fished out logs and firewood that had been carried away by the spring flood waters, or transported small loads of cargo in flat bottom boats, but usually it meant they stole from the barges on the Oka and the Volga, grabbing anything that wasn't carefully secured. It was in this fashion that most "made their livelihoods," and on Sundays the grown-ups boasted about their successes while the children listened and learned.

In the spring, during the busy time before the market fairs, the streets were richly sown with drunken cab drivers, master craftsmen, and other various workers—and the town's children invariably rummaged through their pockets. They did so openly before the eyes of their elders, for this was a sanctioned industry. They stole tools from carpenters, wrenches from cab drivers, and axle pins from draymen. But our group didn't participate in this. Churka once announced decisively:

"I'm not going to start stealing. My mother doesn't let me."

"And I'm afraid to do it!" said Khabi.

Kostroma had a deep disgust for thieves. He pronounced the word "thief" with particular force, and if he saw other children robbing a drunk, he'd chase them off, cruelly beating any of those he managed to catch. With his big eyes and unhappy demeanor, Kostroma fashioned himself an adult, walking with a special gait—a kind of waddle that made him look like a stevedore—and always trying to talk in a heavy, crude voice. Everything about him was somehow strained, contrived, prematurely aged. The Pigeon was convinced that stealing was a sin.

But dragging planks and stakes from Peski Island didn't seem to be a sin, and none of us was afraid of doing it. We even developed several maneuvers that very successfully simplified this process. As it grew dark in the evenings, or during bad weather, the Pigeon and Yaz headed out to Peski over the wet, swollen ice of the backwater, walking openly, deliberately drawing the attention of the watchmen, while the rest of us would separate and make our way unnoticed to the island. Alarmed by Yaz and the Pigeon, the watchmen would follow them while we gathered at a previously agreed-upon stack of wood and chose our loads. Our quick-footed comrades would still be teasing the watchmen—forcing them to chase the two of them aimlessly—when we started back across the ice. Each of us had a rope with a nail bent like a hook at its end; we'd attach this to a board or stake and drag it over the ice and snow. The watchmen almost never noticed us, and when they did, they couldn't catch up. Having sold our takings, we divided the money into six parts. It usually came out to five kopeks per person, sometimes seven.

You could stay well fed for a day on that money, but the Pigeon's mother would beat him if he didn't bring her money for vodka. Kostroma dreamed of one day raising homing pigeons and saved his money toward this end. Since Churka's mother was sick, he always tried to keep as much money as he could, and Khabi was saving his money in order to one day return to the town where he was born, and from where his uncle had brought him to Nizhny shortly before drowning. Khabi had forgotten the town's name; he remembered only that it was on the Kama's banks, not far from the Volga.

We found this town very funny for some reason and teased the squint-eyed Tatar, singing:

A city on the Kama stands
We don't remember where,
It's impossible to walk there,
Or touch it with your hands.

At first, Khabi took great offense at this, but once the Pigeon said to him in the cooing voice that earned his nickname:

"What are you about? How can you be angry at your friends?"

This flustered the Tatar, and he soon began himself to sing the song about the town on the Kama.

Still, we preferred gathering rags and bones to stealing planks. The work was particularly interesting in the spring, when the snow had melted or it had rained, and the paved streets of the empty trade fair were washed clean. In the ditches you could always collect a lot of nails and iron fragments, and we often found money there—both copper and silver coins. But you had to either grovel at the watchmen's feet for a long time or pay them two-kopek coins to keep them from chasing you out of the rows or taking away your bags. In general, money didn't come to us easily, but we lived very amicably, and although we quarreled a little at times, I don't remember a single fight among us.

The Pigeon was our peacemaker. He always knew how to say just the right words at the right moment—simple words that left us surprised and off balance. He himself would be surprised as he said them. Yaz's angry outbursts did not hurt or frighten the Pigeon. He found everything bad simply extraneous, and he dismissed it with a calm, easy certitude:

"What good does that do still?" he'd ask. And we'd all see clearly: none at all!

He called his mother "my Mordvinian," for which we never laughed at him.

"My Mordvinian toppled home all drunk again yesterday," he would tell us cheerfully, his round eyes shining with a golden light. "She flung the door wide apart and sits down on the threshold—sings and sings, the chicken."

Good-hearted Churka asks:

"What was she singing?"

Beating time with his palm lightly against his knee, the Pigeon reproduces his mother's song in a delicate voice:

Softly now
The shepherd taps
The window
With his staff—
I hear his call,
And slip outside:
We laugh
And run away.

The sun goes down
And Borka starts
To play his pipe—
A hollow reed—
And all the town
Is silent now
As evening's light
Recedes.

He knew many amorous songs like this one, and he sang them very skillfully.

"Yes," he continues. "She goes asleep like that in the doorway. The room got so cold I'm shaking all over—I'm nearly frozen! But I didn't have the strength for dragging her inside. This morning I said to her: 'Why are you such a terrible drunkard?' And she says, 'Don't worry—I'll die soon. Hang on just a little longer.'"

Churka affirms this soberly: "She will die soon. She's all swollen."

"Will you be sorry for her?" I ask.

"How couldn't I be?" the Pigeon says, surprised. "She is my good one."

And although we knew that his Mordvinian beat the Pigeon in passing, we all believed that she was good. Sometimes on bad days, Churka would even say:

"Let's all pitch in a kopek to buy some wine for the Pigeon's mother. She'll beat him otherwise!"

Churka and I were the only two in the group who could read. The Pigeon envied us greatly. Pulling on his sharp little mouselike ears, he'd coo:

"I'll lie to resting my Mordvinian and go to school as well! I'll kneel at the teacher's feet until he takes me! I'll finish school and be a gardener for the church archbishops—or for the Tsar himself!"

In the spring a pile of firewood collapsed on the Mordvinian and an old man who'd been collecting money for church construction, crushing them both along with a bottle of vodka. They took the woman to the hospital, and reliable Churka said to the Pigeon:

"Come and live with me now. My mother will teach you how to read. . . ."

And after a little while, the Pigeon would throw back his head and read the street signs out loud:

"Rocger's shop."

"Grocer's shop, you lunatic," Churka corrected him.

"I see them but the tetlers keep on jumping!"

"Letters!"

"They're jumping and jumping! They're glad I read them!"

He surprised us and made us laugh with his love for trees and grass.

Sprawling on the sandy riverbanks, the town was very poor in greenery—only an occasional, sparse white willow or a gnarled elder bush might be found in the courtyards, a few dry, grey blades of grass hiding timidly along the fence lines. If one of us sat on them, the Pigeon would mutter angrily:

"Why can't you leave the grass alone? Sit past it, somewhere on the sand! It makes no difference for you. . . ."

With him nearby it was always awkward to break a willow branch, tear a blooming sprig from an elder bush, or cut a switch from one of the osiers on the Oka's banks. He would always be surprised by such behavior, jerking his shoulders back and spreading out his arms:

"Why do you break everything? There's a bunch of devils!"

His dismay would shame us all.

We invented an entertaining game to play on Saturdays and would spend the week preparing for it by collecting old bast shoes and hiding them in secluded corners. On Saturday evenings, when the band of Tatar stevedores who worked on the Siberian pier was walking home, we would take up a position somewhere at an intersection and begin launching the old shoes at them. At first this irritated the Tatars and they came running after us, cursing. But soon they themselves began to be carried away by the game, and knowing beforehand what awaited them, they began to appear in the field fully armed with their own supply of bast shoes. They often even stole our stock of war materials, having discovered our hiding places during the week.

"That's not part of the game!" we'd complain.

They would divide up the shoes and give us half—and then the battle would begin. They usually formed ranks in an open area while we ran around them, hurling shoes as we shouted and squealed. They howled as well, and burst into deafening laughter when one of us went face down in the sand, his feet knocked out from under him by a skillfully thrown shoe.

The battle would rage a long time, sometimes right until dark. The townspeople would gather and watch us from a corner somewhere, grumbling for the sake of appearances while the dusty, grey shoes sailed through the air like crows. Sometimes one of us would suffer a painful blow, but the pleasure of the game was greater than any injury or offense.

The Tatars would become just as excited as we did during the battle, and afterward, we often went with them to their cooperative, where they fed us sweet horsemeat and a peculiar kind of vegetable soup. After dinner we had sweet dough baked in little balls and tea brewed from briquettes of dried, crushed leaves. We liked those huge men—every one of them was enormously strong, and yet, in each there was something childlike and understandable. I was particularly struck by the careful consideration and the unfaltering, generous goodwill they so consistently demonstrated for one another.

They were all prone to outbursts of glorious laughter that left them teary-eyed and breathless. One of them, a man from Kasimov with a broken nose and fantastic strength, had once picked up a bell that weighed twenty-seven *pood* from a barge and carried it far down the shoreline. As he laughed, he'd howl and shout:

"Vuu, Vuu, words and grass, a silver coin, a piece of brass . . ."

Once he raised the Pigeon high into the air on the palm of his hand and said:

"Here is where you ought to live, sweet bird."

When the weather was bad we gathered at Yaz's, in his father's hut on the graveyard. Yaz's father was all crooked bones, long-armed, and grimy. Dirty hair grew in little patches on his dark face and his small head, which resembled that of a dried-up burdock bloom, his long neck forming the stem. He had a habit of narrowing his strange yellow eyes and putting on a sickly sweet expression as he muttered:

"May God spare you sleeplessness—ukh!"

We'd buy a little sugar and tea, some bread, and for Yaz's father, a few obligatory ounces of vodka. Churka ordered him around severely:

"Put the kettle on, you do-nothing loafer!"

With a little laugh the loafer would put the tin kettle on the stove, then offer us well-meaning advice while we waited for tea and discussed our affairs.

"Day after tomorrow's forty days since they buried Trusov. They'll have a big table there—you watch, that's where you'll find some bones!"

"The cook always collects all the bones at Trusovs," said the all-knowing Churka.

"Soon we'll be going to the woods—just think of it!" the Pigeon would say, daydreaming as he looked out the window at the graveyard.

Yaz remained silent the entire time, watching everyone attentively with his sad eyes. Even when he showed us his toys—wooden soldiers he'd retrieved from a garbage dump, a piece of copper, a horse with no legs, some buttons—he still didn't speak.

Yaz's father would put out various cups and mugs and prepare the samovar, and then Kostroma would sit down at the table to pour tea while he, having drunk his vodka, climbed up onto the stove, from where he craned his neck to watch us with his owlish eyes:

"I wish you'd all drop dead," he'd mutter. "You don't look like boys at all. Bunch of thieves, God spare you sleeplessness!"

"We're not thieves at all!" the Pigeon would tell him.

"Well, you're little thieves."

If we were tired of Yaz's father, Churka would shout at him angrily: "Go away, do-nothing loafer!"

The Pigeon, Churka, and I particularly disliked it when he began to list each household in which someone was ailing, each resident of the town who would soon die. He spoke of this with coldhearted relish, and seeing that his words distressed us, he deliberately tried to disturb and provoke us further:

"Akh, that frightens you, does it, little devils? Well, well. . . . Now, there's a fat one, see, who's going to die soon, and, akh!—he'll just rot forever!"

We'd try to make him stop, but he kept sputtering excitedly:

"You know you're all going to die soon! You can't live long on garbage dumps!"

"Well then, we'll die," the Pigeon said to him. "And they'll take us up with the angels."

"You-uu?" he gasped in amazement. "You? With the angels?"

He burst into laughter and began again to mock us with obscene stories about the dead.

But sometimes, in a hushed and murmuring voice, this man would start to say intriguing things:

"But listen, boys, wait! Look here—three days ago they buried one woman and I found out all about her, my little fellows. Now, just what kind of woman was she?"

He spoke very often about women and always obscenely, but there was something compelling in his stories, something mournful. He seemed to invite us to think with him, and we listened to him closely. He spoke clumsily, incoherently, and he often interrupted his own words with questions. But still his stories always left some kind of shard, some disturbing fragment in one's memory:

"They ask her, 'Who set it on fire?' 'I did!' 'How could you, you fool—you weren't even home that night! You were in the hospital!' 'I set it on fire!' She keeps saying that, but what for? Ukh, God spare you sleeplessness. . . ."

He knew the life story of almost every town resident, each of whom he'd buried in the sand of that sad and desolate cemetery. He seemed to open before us the doors of the houses in town: we entered them, saw how the people lived there, felt something serious and important. It seemed that he could talk all night and into the morning, but as soon as twilight began to cloud the windows of the hut, Churka got up from the table:

"I have to go home or mama will be afraid. Who's coming with me?"

Everyone would leave. Yaz walked us to the fence and locked the gate behind us.

"Goodbye!" he'd say blankly, pressing his dark, bony face to the bars.

We'd also shout, "Goodbye!" to him, but it was always awkward leaving him in the graveyard. Once Kostroma glanced back and said:

"We'll wake up tomorrow and he'll be dead."

"Yaz's life is worse than any of ours," Churka often said.

And the Pigeon would answer him:

"Our lives aren't bad at all."

I also thought we didn't live badly. I liked that independent street existence, and I liked my comrades. They stirred in me some kind of great feeling—a constant, restless urge to do them good.

School again grew difficult. The other children began to ridicule me, calling me "rag dealer" and "tramp," and once, after an argument, they complained to the teacher that I smelled of garbage and therefore, it was impossible to sit next to me. I remember how deeply I was hurt by this complaint and how difficult it was to continue going to school after it had been made. But the complaint itself was completely invented out of spite. I washed diligently every morning and never went to school in the clothes I wore when gathering rags.

But at last I passed the second-year exams and as a prize received a copy of the Gospels, a bound version of Krylov's fables, and another book that lacked a binding and bore the incomprehensible title of *Fata Morgana*. They also gave me a certificate of merit. Grandfather was moved and elated when I brought home these gifts. He announced that all of them should be carefully preserved and that he would lock the books up in his trunk. Grandmother had been lying in bed sick for several days already. She had no money. Grandfather gasped and squealed:

"You're going to drink me dry; the lot of you will gnaw right through my bones. Akh, you-u . . ."

I took the books to a shop, sold them for fifty-five kopeks, and gave the money to grandmother. I defaced the certificate with some sort of inscription and handed it over to grandfather, who carefully hid the paper away without unrolling it, and therefore, never discovered my misdeed.

Finished with school, I began again to live on the street, and it was even better than before. Spring was in full bloom and work was abundant. On early Sunday mornings our entire band went out to the field, to the pine grove, and returned to town only late in the evening, pleasantly tired and still closer to one another.

But that life did not continue long. Dismissed from his job, my stepfather again disappeared somewhere, and my mother and little brother, Nikolai, moved in with grandfather. Grandmother had gone away to town and was living there in the home of a rich merchant, for whom she was sewing a cover for the Shroud of Christ they kept in the family chapel. In her absence, the duties of nursemaid were placed upon me.

Mute and withered, mother barely moved her feet, looking at everything with terrible eyes. My brother had scrofula. There were sores on his ankles, and he was so weak he couldn't even cry loudly; instead, he would let out a disturbing moan if he was hungry. When he was full he dozed, and his breathing was strange somehow—he purred quietly, like a kitten.

Grandfather carefully squeezed the baby's body and said:

"He'll have to be well fed. I don't have enough food for you all!"

Sitting on the bed in the corner, mother sighed hoarsely:

"He only needs a little. . . ."

"A little for this one, a little for that one—and it comes out to be a lot!"

He waved his hand at her and addressed me:

"Nikolai needs to be out in the open, in the sun and the sand. . . ."

I dragged home sacks of clean, dry sand, dumped it in a pile in a sunny place under the window, and covered my brother up to his neck, as ordered by grandfather. Nikolai liked sitting in the sand. He squinted sweetly and aimed at me the light of his extraordinary eyes, which had no whites—each consisted only of a blue center surrounded by a bright ring.

I soon became strongly attached to my brother. It seemed to me that he understood everything I was thinking as we lay together in the sand under the window, from where my grandfather's squeaky voice drifted down to us:

"Dying's no great wisdom! You try being smart enough to live! . . ."

And mother coughed and coughed.

The little boy frees his arms and stretches toward me, his blond head rocking. His hair's sparse, shot with grey, and his face is old and wise.

If a chicken or cat comes close to us, Kolya studies it for a long time, then looks at me and smiles so slightly you can barely notice it. That smile always troubles me. Can my brother tell that I'm bored with him—that I'd like to leave him here and run away into the streets?

Our courtyard's crowded, small, and littered. A line of woodsheds, cellars, and little shacks built from rough planks bends from the gate to the bathhouse. The roofs are heavily laden with pieces of boats, firewood, planks, and wet kindling—anything a local resident could fish from the Oka during the thaws and spring floods. Any open space inside the yard is filled with ugly piles of wood. Heavily saturated with water, it stews in the sun, fills the air with the scent of decay.

There's a slaughterhouse for small livestock next to it. Almost every morning the calves low and the rams bleat. The smell of blood's so strong I sometimes think it's waving in the dusty air like a transparent crimson net.

Stunned by the blow of an axe—its flat side aimed between their horns—the animals bellow, and Kolya narrows his eyes, puffs out his lips as if trying to repeat the sound. But he only blows air:

"Fffooo . . ."

At noon grandfather would stick his head out the window and shout: "Lunch!"

He fed the child himself, holding Nikolai on his lap as he chewed up bits of potato and bread, then stuck it with his crooked finger into the baby's mouth, smearing it on his thin lips and his sharp little chin. After feeding him a little, grandfather would pull up the baby's shirt, poke his swollen belly with his finger, and wonder out loud:

"Is that enough? Give him more?"

My mother's voice would rise from a dark corner near the door:

"Can't you see—he's reaching for the bread!"

"A baby's stupid! He can't know how much he needs to eat!"

And again he'd stick his cud in Kolya's mouth. I found it painfully shameful to watch these feedings. Below my throat something seemed to choke me, make me sick.

"Well, fine!" grandfather would finally say. "Here, give him to his mother."

Kolya would moan and stretch toward the table as I took him away. My mother wheezed as she raised herself up in bed and stretched toward me her emaciated, withered arms. Long and thin, she was like an evergreen with snapped limbs.

She'd grown all but mute, rarely speaking a single word in her rasping voice, and otherwise lying for entire days in the corner, dying silently. That she was dying—this, of course, I knew, sensed, felt. And all too often grandfather spoke importunately of death, especially when it was growing dark in the courtyard and the warm, rich smell of rot hung like sheepskin in the windows.

Grandfather's bed stood in the front corner of the room, almost directly under the icons. He would lie with his head toward them and the window, lie there and mutter in the darkness:

"The time to die is here. And so—with what face shall we stand before God? What will we say? All our lives we fussed. We were hurrying all the time. . . . And where did we get to?"

I slept on the floor between the window and the stove. The space was too short for me, and I had to stick my feet under the stove, where the cockroaches tickled them. That little corner provided me a good share of vicious pleasure, however, for grandfather was constantly breaking the glass in the window with the long handles of the fire poker and the oven fork when he cooked. It was both funny and strange that someone as smart as he didn't think to simply cut the handles down.

Once, something boiled over on the stove, and he jabbed at it so hurriedly with the oven fork that he knocked out the center of the window frame and shattered both panes of glass while simultaneously tipping over the pot and smashing it on the hearth. This so dismayed the old man that he sat down on the floor and began to weep:

"God . . . Oh, God . . ."

One afternoon when he'd left, I took a bread knife and cut the handle of the oven fork down by three quarters, but when he saw my handiwork, grandfather began to curse:

"Damn demon! You should have used a saw to cut it off. A saw! We could have sold the ends as rolling pins, you devil's seed!"

Waving his arms, he ran out to the vestibule, and my mother said:

"Why'd you have to stick your nose in?"

She died in August, on Sunday, around noon. My stepfather had just returned from his trip and was working somewhere again. Grandmother and Kolya were already living with him in a small, clean apartment near the train station. They were supposed to move my mother there any day.

On the morning of her death she said to me quietly, but in a voice clearer and lighter than ever before:

"Go and get Evgeny Vasilevich. Tell him that I'm asking him to come."

She began to lift herself, and with one arm braced against the wall, sat up in bed.

"Run quick," she added.

It seemed to me that she was smiling, that something new was shining in her eyes. My stepfather was at Mass. Grandmother sent me to get tobacco from the Jew who kept the crossing gate at the railroad tracks. But none was ready, and I had to wait while she grated more. Then I took the tobacco back to grandmother.

When I returned to grandfather's house, mother was sitting at the table, dressed in a clean, lilac-colored dress, her hair prettily arranged, all her presence as imposing as it used to be.

"Are you better?" I asked, grown timid for some reason.

Her stare was terrifying.

"Come here!" she said. "Where have you been messing around?"

I didn't have time to answer before she grabbed me by my hair with one hand, picked up with the other a knife made from the long, flexible blade of a saw, and struck me several times with its flat side, swinging her arm as hard as she could with each blow until the knife flew out of her hand.

"Pick it up! Give it to me!"

I picked up the knife and threw it on the table. Mother pushed me away. I sat down on the stove step and watched her fearfully. She rose from the table and slowly moved back into her corner, lay down on the bed, and began to wipe the perspiration from her face. Her hand moved unsteadily. Twice it went past her face and trailed along the pillow.

"Give me some water. . . ."

I ladled some water from the bucket into a cup. She struggled to raise her head to take a few sips. Then she moved my hand away with her cold hand and sighed deeply. She glanced at the icons in the corner, moved her eyes to me. Her lips stirred as if she were starting to smile or laugh very slightly. She slowly lowered the long lashes over her eyes. Her elbows were pressed against her sides while her hands, their fingers moving weakly, crawled over her breast and rose toward her throat. A shadow drifted across her face, then receded into its depths, drawing taut the yellow skin, sharpening the nose. The mouth opened in surprise, but there was no breathing.

I stood there for a time beyond measure, holding the cup in my hand beside my mother's bed, watching her face stiffen, turn grey.

Grandfather came in and I said to him:

"Mother died."

He glanced at the bed.

"What are you lying about!"

He went into the kitchen and began to take a pie out of the oven, rattling the griddle and the screen with deafening force. I watched him, knowing that mother had died, waiting from him to understand.

My stepfather came in a canvas jacket, a white peaked cap. He picked up a chair and carried it soundlessly toward mother's bed, then suddenly struck it against the floor.

"But—she's dead, look . . . ," he bellowed like a bugle.

Grandfather bugged out his eyes and moved quietly away from the stove, stumbling like a blind man, the screen still in his hands.

When they'd covered my mother's coffin with dry sand, my grandmother went wandering among the graves as if blind and stumbled into a cross, smashing her face. Yaz's father brought her to his hut, and while she washed he quietly told me comforting words:

"Akh, you—God spare you sleeplessness, eh? It's just that kind of business. . . . Am I right, grandmother? Richest lord or poorest slave—all are destined for the grave. . . . Isn't that right, grandmother?"

He looked out the window and suddenly rushed outside, then returned with the Pigeon, beaming and happy.

"Take a look at this," he said, handing me a broken spur. "Just look at that! Me and the Pigeon are giving it to you. Look—it's got a little wheel, see? A Cossack must have lost it. I wanted to buy it from the Pigeon—was going to give him two kopeks . . ."

"What are you lying about!" the Pigeon said in a quiet, angry voice. Yaz's father jumped in front of me and winked at him as he said:

"Akh—the Pigeon, eh? He's a strict one! All right, he was going to give it to you. He was, not me. . . ."

Grandmother finished washing, covered her blue, swollen face with a kerchief, and called me home. But I refused, knowing that there, at the wake, they'd drink vodka and probably start to fight. While still at church, Uncle Mikhail had sighed and said to Yakov:

"Let's have a drop or two today, eh? . . ."

The Pigeon started trying to amuse me. He made the spur stick to his chin and reached his tongue toward the star that spun on its little wheel. Yaz's father deliberately burst into loud laughter, squealing:

"Look—just look what he's doing!"

But seeing that none of this made me happy, he said seriously: "Well, enough, then. Come round, now. We all die. Even the birds die. Here's what: I'll cover your mother's grave with turf—want me to? Right now we'll go into the field—you, the Pigeon, me—and my Yaz will come with us too. We'll cut the turf and make the best grave ever!"

I liked this idea, and we went into the field.

Several days after my mother's funeral, grandfather said to me:

"Well, you aren't a medal, Leksey—there's no more room for you around my neck. It's time you made your own way in the world."

So I went out into the world.

ACKNOWLEDGMENTS

I am grateful to David Andrews and Angela Brintlinger for their help with the notes and introduction to this translation.

I wish to thank Ivan Dee for his rare and remarkable commitment to literature and his patient, kind support for translations like this one over the years.

Finally, I would like to express my deepest gratitude to my wife, Mila Medina, without whom this translation would never have been completed, or begun. She meticulously reviewed and corrected several drafts of this manuscript, patiently explained to me the nuances of Gorky's text, conducted extensive research for the notes, and provided unwavering emotional support throughout. In many ways this translation is hers as much as it is mine.

G. H.

Bethesda, Maryland
July 2010

NOTES

CHAPTER I

5 I've been seriously ill until now and only recently left my sickbed. During my illness—I remember this—my father busied himself happily with me. Then he disappeared, was suddenly replaced by my grandmother, a stranger: In 1871, three-year-old Aleksey Peshkov, who would later take the pen name Maksim Gorky, fell ill during a cholera epidemic in Astrakhan. While nursing him, Gorky's father, Maksim Peshkov, was infected with the illness and soon died from it at the age of thirty-one.

6 "It's nothing, Lyosha": The name Aleksey (like all Russian names) has many forms, including: Lyosha, Lyonya, Leksey, and Olyosha.

7 "Thank you, God almighty," says my grandmother. "A boy": Gorky's brother, Maksim, was born on the day of his father's death—July 29, 1871.

12 All this is done in secret because there's a man on board who forbids everyone from eating fruit—takes it away and throws it right into the river: A part of efforts to control the outbreak of cholera, which can be spread through fruit contaminated by water or fertilizer.

CHAPTER II

16 A young, broad-shouldered apprentice from the dye shop called the Gypsy straddled Mikhail's back . . . : The character's nickname in Russian is *Tsyganok*, which might be translated as Little Gypsy. His proper name is Ivan, which takes the forms Vanya, Vanka, Vanyatka, and Vanyushka at various times in the story.

16 Alarmed at the very start of the fight, I'd jumped up onto the stove: Traditional Russian stoves are much larger than those in the west, usually occupying one full corner of a house. They are used to heat the entire living area as well as to cook and bake; a space for lying down is built on top of them. Peasant families often slept in this space during the winter.

17 "That Mishka's a Jesuit! And Yashka's a damn Freemason!": Freemasonry was
    relatively widespread among the Russian nobility until 1822, when it was out-
    lawed, along with all other secret societies, as part of Alexander I's growing
    anxiety about the influence of foreign religion and philosophy in Russia. Among
    the peasantry, Freemasonry was viewed with deep suspicion, and the term "Free-
    mason" came to denote anyone untrustworthy. The Jesuits were expelled from
    St. Petersburg in 1815 and from Russia altogether in 1820. Like the Freemasons,
    Jesuits were widely seen as untrustworthy, dangerous, and foreign enemies of the
    Russian Orthodox Church. See James Billington, *The Icon and the Axe* (New
    York: Vintage Books, 1970).

17 . . . and all their faces resembling those of the dark icons in the corner . . . : Rus-
    sian houses traditionally contained a "beautiful corner"—usually facing east—
    where icons were hung and prayers delivered. Upon entering a house, it was
    considered proper to first bow to this corner.

19 I remember how I ran toward the commotion in the kitchen and saw my grand-
    father jumping comically around the room, grasping his earlobe with his singed
    fingers . . . : Holding one's earlobe was believed to help relieve the pain of a
    burned finger.

21 *Permyak*: One of two branches of the Komi, a Finnic people in northeast Russia.

24 He took from his pocket two carob pods: Pods from carob trees were imported
    to Russia and Central Europe largely from Italy. Carob was a common substitute
    for chocolate and the pods had a sweet taste.

25 *Versts*: A Russian measure of distance equaling 3,500 feet or about two thirds of
    a mile.

25 *Kasha*: A dish of cooked oats or grains, sometimes resembling porridge.

27 Ivan the prince and Ivan the happy fool: Characters from Russian folktales. Ivan
    the fool's sincerity and lack of guile often bring him good fortune. Ivan the
    prince is the resourceful hero of many tales.

CHAPTER III

30 "They scheme and scheme and God just laughs! And your grandfather sees all
    this scheming—he teases Yasha and Misha on purpose, says 'I'll buy Ivan a re-
    cruiter's pass so they don't put him in the army—I need him here with me!'":
    In prerevolutionary Russia, members of more prosperous families could escape
    the draft by buying a "recruiter's pass." Those who lacked the necessary money
    faced military service of twenty-five years. Family members mourned newly
    drafted males as if they were dead, and virtually none returned home.

32 "It's good to share your house with mice. They're smart and tenderhearted, and
    the house spirit loves them. Whoever feeds a mouse will have the house spirit's
    favor": Russian folklore is rich with legends about the origins and habits of the
    house spirit (*domovoi*). Often, he is believed to embody the spirit of a family's
    ancestors, although in some legends house spirits are said to be souls cast down
    from heaven to earth. The house spirit is usually associated with livestock, par-

ticularly horses, which he will protect or harm, depending on whether he likes the particular animal owned by the family whose home he occupies. The house spirit is considered essential to each Russian home and is generally viewed with respect and affection. However, he can also be capricious and vindictive, and therefore, it is important to avoid offending him.

34 Maksim Savvateich: The full name of Aleksey's father is Maksim Savvatievich Peshkov. Grigory and Aleksey's grandmother often refer to him by a shortened form of his patronymic: Savvateich.

42 "I saw him when the business started, and now I'm here watching him as it ends": Toward the turn of the century, industrialization steadily wiped out small artisans like Vasily Kashirin and his sons.

CHAPTER IV

50 The Twelve Great Feasts: A detailed icon depicting twelve major events in Christianity, including the Annunciation and Christ's birth, baptism, crucifixion, and entry into hell. The original was created in the nineteenth century.

50 Fyodorovskaya Holy Mother: One of several Russian icons well known for the tenderness of its portrayal of the Holy Mother and Christ. Accounts of the original icon's history vary, but it is believed to have been created in the twelfth or thirteenth century.

50 Weep Not for Me, O Mother: An icon created in the late eighteenth or early nineteenth century, it depicts the body of Christ, the lower half entombed, the upper half exposed. In many versions the Mother Mary stands to the left of Christ, mourning him.

52 Bandit Princess Engalycheva: Engalychev is a well-known family name dating back to a sixteenth century Tatar prince. Mariya A. Engalycheva was said to have attacked and looted peasant homes and the estates of landholders in the 1740s in the Temnikovksy region, now part of Mordovia. It is not clear if this is the source of the poem recited by Akulina Kashirina.

52 The Holy Man Aleksey: He was said to have been the son of a wealthy senator in fourth century Rome who rejected marriage, left his father's house, and adopted the life of a religious ascetic. After many years in the wilderness, he returned to his father's household, where he lived as a beggar, unrecognized for seventeen years.

52 Ivan the Warrior: According to legend, he served in the army of the Roman emperor Julian the Apostate (303–363) and was dispatched to persecute Christians. While pretending to carry out his orders, he secretly protected and aided the intended victims, for which he was imprisoned until the emperor's death. To some degree, he could be seen as a kind of mirror image to the Ivan of Akulina Ivanovna's poem about the hermit Miron.

52 Wise Vasilisa: A character in Russian fairy tales, she is the daughter of the sea king, well known for her good judgment and her magical ability to change form.

52 The priest who turned into a goat: Probably refers to a folktale in which a priest has his wife attach a goat's hide to him in order to pose as the devil and frighten a peasant out of the gold he's found. When the priest attempts to remove the hide, he discovers it has become part of his flesh and cannot be taken off.

52 The peasant child who sat on God's throne: There are several versions of this story. In one, God agrees to be godfather to a poor peasant's child. God later brings the child to heaven and allows him to sit on His throne, but from his perch the child begins to punish everyday sins with death and destruction, and God returns the child to earth.

52 Marfa of Novgorod: She played a leading role in Novgorod's struggle to gain independence from Moscow in the fifteenth century but was eventually defeated by Ivan the Third. She is referred to as Marfa Posadnitsa in Russian.

52 Baba Usta: The heroine of popular legends in the Volga region about a girl leading a gang of thieves. See comments of I. A. Bocharova in M. Gor'kii, *Sobranie sochinenii v 16-akh tomakh* (Moscow: Pravda, 1979), t. 8.

52 Maria, the sinner of Egypt: She led a dissolute life of sexual dalliance until she traveled to Jerusalem, where an unseen force prevented her from entering the Church of the Holy Sepulcher. She repented and lived as a hermit in the wilderness until her death in 421. She is the patron saint of penitents.

55 It was good the quiet night and the darkness had come back, but I was sorry that the fire was gone: In his wonderful memoir of Gorky, the Russian poet Vladislav Khodasevich includes the following description of the writer when he was living in Sorrento, at the age of fifty-six: "He liked anyone, absolutely anyone who brings an element of rebellion or just of mischief into the world—up to and including compulsive arsonists, about whom he wrote a lot and could talk for hours on end. He himself had a bit of the arsonist in him. Never once after lighting a cigarette did I see him put out the match: he invariably left it burning. It was a favorite and daily habit of his after dinner or at evening tea, when the ashtray was full enough of cigarette butts, matches, and paper to imperceptibly edge a lighted match into it. Then he would try to distract the attention of those present while slyly glancing over his shoulder at the bonfire that was erupting. These little family conflagrations, as I once proposed to call them, seemed to hold some wicked and joyful symbolism for him." See *Gorky's Tolstoy and Other Reminiscences*, translated, edited and introduced by Donald Fanger (New Haven: Yale University Press, 2008).

57 "We have to get the altar doors opened. . . .": It was believed that opening the doors to the altar of a Russian Orthodox church would help a woman struggling in childbirth.

CHAPTER V

60 "I can't answer you, my dear. You'd better go to the monastery at Pechory, to Father Asaf, a *skhimnik* there . . .": *Skhimniks* were monks belonging to the strict-

est order of the Russian Orthodox church. They were believed to be particularly wise, sometimes able to predict the future.

60 "The Virgin's Dream": It was widely believed that by reciting the text of "The Virgin's Dream," in which Mary foresees Christ's suffering, one could prevent illness or other misfortune.

60 ". . . You have to insult *kvas* . . .": A fermented drink made from dried crusts of bread, flour, bran, malt, and water.

61 Akulya: A short form of Akulina.

63 "Come here and sit down, Pickles-for-Brains. You see this letter, *A*? It's *Az*. Say it—*Az*! Now this one, *B*,—it's called Books. This one, *V*, is called Vessel. What's this? . . .": His grandfather teaches Aleksey to read Russian Church Slavonic, the liturgical language of the Russian Orthodox Church, which dates back to roughly 1200 (when it evolved from Old Church Slavonic). Its alphabet is comprised of forty letters, each of which has a specific name. In learning to read, one must first learn the name of each letter in order to refer to it correctly. When spelling out a word, one then cites each letter by its name. With the exception of *Az*, I have not reproduced here the correct names of the Russian Church Slavonic letters; instead, I have invented names that correspond roughly (sometimes very roughly) to the correct name and to the English letter necessary to spell out the words that the child later reads ("Blessed is the man . . ."). The correct names of the Russian Church Slavonic letters in the text are, in order: *az, buki, vedi, glagol', dobro, yest', zemlya, lyudi*.

65 "Yes, of course, when it comes to playing music and singing he's another King David. But when it comes to work—to business—he's as poisonous as Absalom!": David succeeded Saul as king of ancient Israel. His musical skills became legendary, and numerous psalms are attributed to him. Absalom was David's third son; he rebelled against his father and was eventually killed in battle.

65 "To skip and play with joyful feet": A conflation of lines from the Paschal Canon, by St. John of Damascus.

66 ". . . I don't remember it. I started remembering things with the French in 1812 . . .": Napoleon invaded Russia in 1812. Estimates on the size of his army range from 470,000 to 685,000; it is widely believed that only about one-tenth of his troops managed to leave Russia alive.

67 *Pood*: A Russian measurement of weight equal to forty pounds.

68 Stepan Timofeev Razin: A Don Cossack, he led a large uprising of peasants, serfs, and non-Russian groups through the lower Volga region of Russia in 1670. He was eventually captured and executed.

68 Emelyan Ivanov Pugach: Claiming to be Peter III, he led a powerful peasant uprising from 1773 to 1774 when the Russian army was at war with the Ottoman Empire. He was eventually defeated and executed by Catherine the Great. The full form of his last name is Pugachev.

69 "The Olonchans—they were just some peasants that ran away from their duties": Peasants in the Olonetsky region were widely forced into state-owned slavery; many fled and hid in the forests.

70 "That was in '48—the year of the Hungarian campaign": In 1848 Hungary's reformist government rebelled against Hapsburg rule but was put down by a combination of Russian and Austrian forces.

CHAPTER VI

76 Cheremis: A Finnish people inhabiting rural areas of eastern Russia.

CHAPTER VII

81 "Damned Polish plait! I ought to cut you off! Take you out and shoot you!": Polish Plait—*koltun* in Polish and Russian, *Plica Polonica* in Latin—refers to a condition that was found among peasants and, less commonly, members of the higher social classes in Europe from about the sixteenth to the nineteenth century, in which unkempt hair actually began to congeal into a single, damp mass. The condition was often accompanied by lice and severe scalp inflammation. Earlier translations of *Childhood* indicate that Akulina Ivanovna may have suffered from the condition; however, given the narrator's many references to Akulina Ivanovna's long and pleasant hair, it seems far more likely that she is speaking figuratively here—comparing her tangled but evidently healthy hair to this very unpleasant and in some cases quite severe ailment.

82 Chuvash: The Chuvash inhabit primarily the middle Volga region of Russia. A mix of Finnish and Mongolian peoples, they speak a Turkic language and adhere to Russian Orthodox Christianity. They came under Russian rule in the sixteenth century.

85 *Tvorog*: Comparable to cottage cheese.

87 "He's not to sing those songs—and you're not to listen to them! They come from heretics—Old Believers! Apostates!": The Russian church altered several of its rituals in 1650 to correspond more closely to Greek Orthodoxy. The changes triggered a schism within the church; those who refused to accept them came to be known as Old Believers. Many committed suicide or fled to remote areas of Russia.

87 Nikolai: In English he is Nicholas, probably one of the best-known saints in western culture. A Greek born in Asia Minor in the third century, he was famous for acts of kindness and generosity. Because of the many miracles attributed to him, he is often known as "Nikolai the Wonderworker."

87 Yuri: Probably a reference to Yuri II, fourth grand prince of Vladimir, who died in battle against an overwhelming force of Mongols in 1238. He was canonized in 1645. It is also possible the name refers to St. George (Georgy), who is also known as Yuri. He denounced the Roman emperor Diocletian in the early fourth century and publicly proclaimed his Christianity, for which he was tortured and executed.

87 Frol and Lavr: Brothers and Christian martyrs in the second century. According to legend, they were forced to build a pagan temple, during the construction of which a pagan priest was injured. The brothers healed him through Christian prayer, for which they were executed.

87 Joachim and Anna: The parents of Mary, to whom Anna gave birth in old age.

88 Ephrem the Syrian: Considered one of Christianity's great writers, he was born around the year 306 and wrote hymns, poems, and biblical exegeses.

89 "You must fight like Anika the Warrior": A well-known character from Russian folklore, Anika the Warrior boasts about his fighting prowess while attacking weak and defenseless people. When Death confronts him, Anika challenges him to a duel. Death immediately overcomes Anika, who begs for more time, but receives no mercy.

89 Igosha Death in His Pocket: In Slavic mythology an igosha was believed to be the spirit of a child who was stillborn or who died in infancy without being christened. Peasant families often buried such infants near the huts where they'd been born, and many believed that these children continued to live and even grow after their burial.

CHAPTER VIII

94 His entire room was crammed full of boxes, strewn with thick books printed in Russian type, which I couldn't read: While Aleksey has learned to read Russian Church Slavonic from his grandfather, he does not yet know standard Russian.

96 "Well, brother," he exclaimed, winking, "that isn't always so. . . . Do you play knucklebones?": The conversation refers to a Russian children's game called babki or kozny and commonly translated as knucklebones, dibs, or jackstones. These names are somewhat misleading in English, as they usually refer to a game in which a player throws and catches a series of objects. In the Russian game of babki, players arrange a series of knucklebones—typically sheep or cow bones that have been boiled for soup—in a line and try to knock their opponents' bones out of place by hitting them with a weighted object thrown from several yards away. The thrown object was often another knucklebone weighted with lead—hence A Fine Business's offer to the boy.

CHAPTER IX

109 Uncle Pyotr: Pyotr is not actually related to the narrator. "Uncle" and "aunt" are often used by children as a sign of respect or affection for adults.

109 The emancipation: Approximately 23 million people were freed when serfdom was ended in Russia in 1861.

110 "Oh no, Vasily Vasilev, not at all, respected sir," Uncle Pyotr said. "There's a Christian name Tatiana—but there's no such name as Tanka, no sir": The humor in this exchange stems from the fact that Tanka, while not a formal Russian name, is a well-known, familiar form of the name Tatyana or Tanya.

110 *Barin*: A member of the gentry, a landowner.

112 ". . . and Mamont's headed for the churchyard . . .": To the graveyard.

CHAPTER X

131 "Majestic road, so straight and true . . .": Gorky quotes loosely from a poem by Ivan Aksakov that appeared in 1896.

133 Vyazemsky: The lines are probably an inaccurate quote from a poem by Ivan Nikitin (1824–1861) rather than Pyotr Vyazemsky.

136 Kirik and Ulita: According to legend, Ulita was martyred with her son, Kirik in the third century. In Russia she is considered the protector of mothers and those who raise children.

136 Varvara the Great Martyr: The beautiful daughter of a wealthy pagan in the third century, Varvara converted to Christianity, for which she was persecuted and eventually beheaded by her own father, who was then struck down by lightning.

136 Panteleimon (Pantaleon): It is not clear if he actually existed or is legendary. A physician to Emperor Maximian, he is said to have confessed to Christianity and been martyred in the early fourth century. He asked God to forgive his torturers and executioner, for which he received his name, meaning "all compassionate."

139 I climbed into the leather armchair in the corner, which was so big that I could lie down in it, and which, on account of its size, grandfather boastfully called "Prince Gruzinsky's chair": The well-known Gruzinsky line of nobility descended from an eighteenth century Georgian king.

143 Ahab: King of Israel from 874 to 853 BC. He is vilified for converting from the Jewish God to the Phoenician deity Baal under the influence of his wife, Jezebel.

CHAPTER XI

145 *Sarafan:* A sleeveless dress with buttons down the front, worn by peasant women.

146 The Christmas holidays were noisy and festive. People came in costume almost every night to mother's rooms: During Russian Christmastide, which lasted from Christmas to the Epiphany, revelers would often dress up in costume before going out to sing carols.

156 Sunday of Forgiveness: On the Sunday before the Great Fast, which lasts for forty days leading up to Easter, Russians traditionally ask one another for forgiveness.

CHAPTER XII

165 Evgeny Maksimov: The full name of Gorky's stepfather was Evgeny Vasilevich Maksimov; he lived from 1852 to 1881.

167 Zhenya: A short form of the name Evgeny.

170 "So—you're off to the war?": The Russo-Turkish War of 1877–1878 was the last of many fought between the two countries in that century. The Russian victory formally ended Ottoman control of Romania, Serbia, and Montenegro. Roughly 25,000 Russians died in the fighting.

174 When we were moving to the apartment, grandmother took an old bast shoe with a long lace and tossed it into the space under the stove: The house spirit was believed to live in or behind the stove. When moving, a family would enjoin the spirit to come with them to the new location by offering a shoe as a sled. It was common practice to repeat the phrase spoken here as ashes from the old stove were inserted into the new one.

175 "Didn't I say thirty doesn't go with twenty! . . .": The meaning of this sentence is not entirely clear; it evidently refers to the age difference between Gorky's mother and her second husband, who was eight years younger than she.

175 The factory's black smokestacks rose into the air from behind the roofs, each like a thumb thrust between the first two fingers of a fist: Placing one's thumb between the index and the middle finger is a crude gesture of disdain, usually made to indicate refusal to grant a request.

177 He fought more and more with mother, angrily addressing her with formal "you"—a tendency that never failed to plunge me into utter rage: There are two forms of you in Russian—the informal *ty* is used for friends, family members, and children; the formal *vy* is used to address superiors, elders, professional colleagues, and little-known acquaintances. Using it when speaking to a spouse in this context would emphasize one's complete sense of estrangement.

178 . . . on account of the yellow shirt I was dubbed "The Ace of Diamonds": A reference to prison convicts, who were identified by patches of yellow cloth sewn to the backs of their shirts in the shape of diamonds.

178 "God Save the Tsar": The national anthem of Imperial Russia from 1833 to 1917.

178 "Oh You, My Freedom": A popular folksong written in 1861, the year of the serfs' emancipation.

181 *The Notes of a Physician*, by Alexandre Dumas: The second volume of *Joseph Balsamo*, written between 1846 and 1848.

181 I closed it and suddenly realized that for a ruble I could buy not only *The Sacred History* but probably the book about Robinson as well: A reference to Daniel Defoe's *Robinson Crusoe*, published in 1719 and widely translated.

181 . . . two dog-eared collections of stories by Andersen . . . : Hans Christian Andersen (1805–1875), author of children's stories. His works were immensely popular in Russia.

CHAPTER XIII

187 The Falling Sickness: Epilepsy.

211

192 "Day after tomorrow's forty days since they buried Trusov": In Russian Orthodoxy, the traditional mourning period lasts forty days; the soul is believed to
undergo judgment on the final day.

197 She died in August . . . : Gorky's mother died in 1879 at the age of thirty-
five.

199 ". . . and my Yaz will come with us too": The original reads ". . . and my Sanka
will come with us too . . ." Presumably the author confused the names of his
characters here, as there is no earlier indication that the gravedigger's son has
any name other than Yaz, and to this moment the name Sanka has referred only
to the Pigeon. It is, of course, possible that Yaz's real name happens also to be
Sanka, but it seems Gorky would have prepared the reader for this coincidence
earlier. Therefore, with some trepidation, I've changed the name here to Yaz,
believing that this accurately reflects the author's intention.